THE EIGHTH WONDER OF THE WORLD

A Poetic View of our Wordly Being

JERRY RHOADS

Copyright © 2023 Jerry Rhoads.

All rights reserved. No part of this book may be reproduced, stored, or transmitted by any means—whether auditory, graphic, mechanical, or electronic—without written permission of both publisher and author, except in the case of brief excerpts used in critical articles and reviews. Unauthorized reproduction of any part of this work is illegal and is punishable by law.

ISBN: 979-8-89031-459-8 (sc)
ISBN: 979-8-89031-460-4 (hc)
ISBN: 979-8-89031-461-1 (e)

Because of the dynamic nature of the Internet, any web addresses or links contained in this book may have changed since publication and may no longer be valid. The views expressed in this work are solely those of the author and do not necessarily reflect the views of the publisher, and the publisher hereby disclaims any responsibility for them.

One Galleria Blvd., Suite 1900, Metairie, LA 70001
(504) 702-6708

PREFACE

Words, expression and relationships give me the opportunity to connect with someone I will never meet. There are 1,025,109 words in the English language ... I have only used 80,182 of those words, in 14,792 paragraphs in 22,987 lines. Some rhyme and or form prose designed to put forth a different way of looking at my past situation and reflect on truth or dare in living and my family's life. With poetry *it is very difficult to get the reader to feel the words, not just digest them, as they do with a meal.*

My love of writing comes from my mother Velma Rhoads. She only had an eighth-grade education and was a product of Missouri poverty, similar to Appalachia. From that came a neurosis stemming from sexual abuse as child and fear of close relationships. I am speculating since she never opened up to anyone. Under her skin and beyond her frown was sensitivity only revealed in her poetry and drawings.

Her influence is reflected in my sister and myself. Kay is a playwright and has always had a way with the pen. Shari, my wife, says Kay's letters were so interesting that she should be a novelist and later in her life she began to express her feelings in her plays. Hers are more in dialogue than in poetic pentameter.

My first poem was in the eighth grade when Georgi Malenkov became the Russian Premier, and (in my late 20's and early 30's) began to write poems about my photographs. This form of artistic expression captured my family's attention and I became the photographer/poet for all our functions.

My obsession grew to the point that any time I was in the car by myself with my tape recorder I would recite a poem from a word. During a period when I started my own business and was on the road for hours so the tapes filled up and Jane my secretary would put them to paper.

Over the years I have contemplated publishing the poems but always put it off due to a lack of time to translate from paper to digital those thoughts of thirty years past. I have found not one poem dated because they reflected words spoken from my head that focuses on the ideas of times and events that never really change … just mature, evolve and reoccur if you are to have memories that mean anything. Love, religion, war, peace, work and play all are never going to age just the mode of expression.

Today I still have those thoughts in 12 three ring binders on yellowing stock and use them to trigger my editing and writing skills into this book. The material is overwhelming since there are about 2,500 poems. Every conceivable word that I saw along the road on billboards, road signs, advertisements, business signs, or heard, etc. triggered a poem onto tape then onto paper. Today I am to converting these to a digital format so I can capture the thoughts and evolve these rough drafts into many more books.

I have tried to make the organization somewhat topical focusing on the better material, in my artistic opinion … yours will by nature be different and that is the power of the written word. My intention in triggering topics and titles is not unconventional but does challenge the reader to believe I know that much about words and very little about conventional poetry. So if you like or dislike the ideas and use of the English language that kept me occupied over 1 million miles in my car so be it.

My love for life is from my wife Shari of 55 years, our four children Christie, Kimber, Kip and Kelli, twelve grandchildren Alec, Celena, Blake, Nick, Derek, Chad, Tyler, Leah, Paris, Fallon, Nate, Troy, and now a great grandsons Carter, Jackson, Becket Stephens and Emmett Lawrence.

Shari and I have a goal to live to the ripe age of 120 and celebrate our 100th wedding anniversary by being healthy, happy and prosperous. This is reflected in my poems, business and faith.

Our world is such a wonder so I wondered why and that set-in motion the thought to find the seven wonders of the world on the globe and seven more in cyber space. In so doing I ran across the eighth and ninth wonders that were right there with me. That begat the title and the first two poems as the proceeding celebration of my pens and lens.

Do you have an existing website? Yes. web address www.jerryrhoadsauthor.com

Or www.amazon.com/jerryrhoads

CONTENTS

AUTHOR'S SEVEN WONDERS OF THE WORLD 1
THE EIGHTH WONDER OF THE WORLD 3
POETRY AND PHOTOGRAPHY A NINTH WONDER 5

THE HUMAN RACE

THE HUMAN RACE 9
IN TUNE 12
A QUIET MAN 14
HELPLESS – I 16
HELPLESS – II 18
HE SHOWED ME 20
COURAGE IS AGELESS 22
LIFE MADE VISIBLE 24
MR. CLOUD WHO ARE YOU 26
SYNERGY 28
WHO SAYS 30
CHILDREN – THAT WONDERFUL GIFT 32
THE MOTHER LAND AND THE OLD MAN OF THE SEA 34
YOU ARE WHAT YOU FEAR 35
GIVE PEACE A CHANCE 36
PAIN 38
THE DOOR TO WAR 40
LEFT TO HEAVEN OR HELL 42
THIS IS NOT FANTASY THIS IS NOT A DREAM
    SIN IS NOT LEFT TO HEAVEN 44
VISIONS OF A BETTER WORLD 46
MY AMERICA 49

A CHILD'S WORLD

A CHILD'S WORLD 55
TIS MUCH EASIER TO DOUBT 57
YOUR SHIFTING SAND 59
IT'S A SAND HEAP WORLD 61

INSIGHT 64
ROOTS AND WINGS 65

MOUNTAIN CLIMBERS

MOUTAIN CLIMBERS 71
A MOUNTAIN OR MOUSETRAP 74
WONDERING MAN: I CAN 76
JONATHON LIVINGSTON MANGULL 78
HUMBLED 80

REMEMBER THIS

REMEMBER THIS 85
SHARI 87
REMEMBER THEN 89
ETERNAL LOVE 92
GRADUATION 94
THE GAMBLE 97
A HUMAN DICTIONARY 99
CHARACTER 103
THE MOVIE HOUSE 104
SLIPPING ON A SEX APPEAL 106
BORN TO BE 108
SALUTE THE RECEIPE OF GREATNESS 110
SUNDAY MORNING 111
THE DRIVE-IN MOVIE SHOW 113
DUCK'S UPON THE POND 115
A LITTLE PIECE OF ME 116
THE HOLE IN MAN'S EXISTENCE 119
THE INNER GAME OF LIFE 121
SIMPLE LOVE 122
THE KISS OF LIFE 123
IF YOU DARE 125
STRUCK BY FRIGHTENING 127
SHOOT THE MOON 129
THE MOON AND GRASP THEIR STAR 130
SOMEDAY 132
I'M FIRED 133
DARE TO BE YOU 135

MATCH POINT 137
GULLS ALONG THE SHORE 139
LOST AND LONELY 141
HOW FAR TOO GO 143
SUNSTROKE 145

STARTING OVER

STARTING OVER 151
TAKE MY HAND 153
IN BETWEEN 155
MORE THAN A FLEA 157
DRONES 160
THE BREAK-UP 162
A MUSHROOM HUNT 165
HEAVEN'S LIGHT 167

THE MIND IS GREAT

THE MIND IS GREAT 173
WARLOCK 174
THE MIND IS THE PERSON 176
WHO ARE YOU 177
THE ARTIST 178
PROUD 180
NO LUNCH BUCKETS ALLOWED 182
CHICAGO 184
THE OCTBER GIRLS 186
THE OLD CHILDREN – ANYMORE? 188
THE SECRETS OF MY SOUL 190
SPRING OF OUR LIVES 192
THE STAR SHINES 193
THE STORY'S OLD 195
THE TIME IS NOW 197
THE WAY WE ARE 198
THE YEAR OF THE LOCUST 200
THIRTEEN 202
TOLL FREE 203
VALIANT CONCEPTION 205

VISION OF A BETTER WORLD

VISION OF A BETTER WORLD	211
WALK ON MY HEART	213
WHAT ARE YOU WORTH?	215
WHAT DOES MOTHER MEAN	217
WHAT DOES FATHER MEAN	218
MEASURE YOUR SCORE	219
WHEN TIMES GET TOUGH	221
WHERE DOES A DREAMER GO	222
WHO IS SHE	224
WILL YOU FIND ME	225
WINDSWEPT	227
WITHIN THE MIND	229
YOU HAVE THE WRONG NUMBER	232
YOU ARE MORE THAN MY VALENTINE	234
YOU CANNOT CHANGE FATE	235
YOU TAUGHT ME HOW TO CRY	237
YOU'RE BLESSED	239
A BAD DREAM	241
A CHILD IS BORN	243
A MAJOR MINORITY	245
A NASTY ADDICTION	247
THE NEW BEGINNING	249
A SIGN OF THE TIMES	250
A SONG OF PEACE	252
A WING AND A FEATHER	254
AGE STRONG (LIKE THE ROSE)	255
AGELESS	256
AMAZING	258
AN I FOR AN i	260
AN IDIOTIC AFFAIR	263
ANY OLE RIPPLE OF HOPE	264
ARE YOU A DIAMOND IN THE ROUGH	266
AS TIME RAN COLD	267
BEACON AFFAIR	269
BROKEN HEARTS	271
BUBBLES	273
BUSINESS PERSUASION	275

CATCH ME IF YOU CAN	277
CHAMBERS (NOT CONFINEMENT)	279
CHASING PUZZLES	281
THE CLASSIC WILL	283
COMPUTER DEAD OR ALIVE	285
CRACK IN THE SKY	287
CRYING EYES	289
DEAD BRANCH	291
DEATH OF A MATADOR	293
DIRTY FEET	295
DOWNPOUR	297
DOWNSIDE UP	298
ELDERPRIDE	300
ESSENTIALLY YOURS	302
FAST AND FURIOUS – FOR A QUICKIE	304

FATE IS WORTH THE WAIT

FATE IS WORTH THE WAIT	311
FRIENDS AND LOVERS	313
DRIZZLE THROUGH THE TREES	316
GET OFF MY SHIRT	318
GLIMPSE	320
GOD IS OUR PARTNER	322
GOOD MORNING WORLD	323
GRADUATION TO ONESELF	325
HAND ME DOWN HEAVEN	327
HEAVEN ON EARTH	329
THE DAY THE PRINCESS DIED	330
I ALONE	333
IF I'M NOT ATTRACTIVE	335
I BELIEVE IN YOU	337
I LOVED YOU BEFORE I KNEW HOW	339
I MADE BY BED	341
I'M THE RAINBOW	343

IMAGINE TO LOVE

IMAGINATION … THE LAW OF ATTRACTION	349
EVOLUTION	350

INSANITY	352
IT'S NOT THE MONEY	354
IT CAME TO PASS	356
IT'S MORE THAN A TREE	358
I'VE SEEN THE MOUNTAIN	359
KING OF NO MAN'S LAND	360
LE' BALLOON	362
LIFE IS GREAT	364
LISTEN TO THE PULSE BEAT	365
LONELY SOUL BLUES	366
LOVE IS FOREVER	368
LOVE IS ON MY MIND	369
LOVE IS THE WINNER	371
LOVES LOST AND FOUND	372
MAKING UP REALITY	374
MOONSET OVER TIME	376
EVERY DAY IS MOTHER'S DAY	378
MOTHERS OF BLACK	380
MOTHERHOOD	383
MOTHERS THE MAGICIANS	384
MUTUAL GRATITUDE	385
MY BREATH FROZE	387
MY FORTUNE COOKIE	389
NOT THE GOOD	390
NOVEMBER	392
ON ANY GIVEN DAY	393
ONCE UPON A SUNDAY – HELL WAS CREATED	395
ONE BACK TWO FORWARD	398
IF NOT BUT IF SO	400
OUR LOVE	402
PEACE ON EARTH	404
FORMULA FOR PEACE	405
PLUG IN MY SHADOW	407
PREACHER MAN	408
PSYCHIC OR PHYSICAL	410
SCATTER GUN OR RIFLE SHOT	412
SEVENTY-FIVE	414
SHELL GAME	415
SHE'S A WOMAN	417

SHINE ON ME	419
"THE ANGEL OF DEATH"	420
SILENCE IS OUR MUSIC	421
STANDING IN FUTILE ESTEEM	423
SUCCESS UNLIMITED	424
SUCCESSFUL YEARS	426
MIND OVER DESTINY	428
SUPERSTAR	429
TAKE MY HAND	431
LIFE'S ECHO	433
A SECOND TIME AROUND	434
SNOW STORM CATTLE	436

SECRETS OF THE MIND

SECRETS OF THE MIND	443
THE GAME OF PSYCHE	445
THE MATCH	449
THE STORYTELLER	450
THE WELL	452
THE AGONY OF DEFEAT	454
VISITORS OF ANOTHER WAY	456
ALIVE	458
A HARD WINTER'S SPRING	459
WRINKLES OF AGE	461
TRUST	465
NOTES TO A NEUROTIC	467
SPACES	468
HE WAS CALLED TINY	470
THE BRAVEST GIRL I'VE EVER SEEN	472
TURNING	474
THE COMMENCEMENT DAY	476
THE BIGGER I AM	478
THE GAMBLER	480
GURU	482

EGO TRIP

EGO TRIP	487
MAN BIRD	488

WALKING IN THE SAND	490
FREEDOM	492
SMALL TOWN BOY	494
ULTIMATE OBSESSION	496
ULTIMATE RISK	497
HAVE YOU OR HAVE YOU NOT	499
FINDING YOURSELF	500
ROAN	502
ACTOR	504
EGO MANIA	505
FREEDOM TO BE YOU	507
DELIGHTED TO BE WRONG	509
WHAT IS HAPPY	511
BE MY TIMELINE	513
THE BOOM-A-RANG	514
MY CHILDREN	516
POLITICIANS	517
DON'T FORGET	519
ALWAYS TOGETHER	521

HEREAFTER

HEREAFTER	525
ANGEL OF MERCY	526
EYE SHADOWS	528
ANY DAY NOW	530
LOST TIME	532
MR. HELL	534
KNOWLEDGE	536
A BLACK HORIZON	537
MAJESTIC	539
THEN THE RADIO WENT DEAD	540
NOBODY KNOWS	542
MOBILE ILLINOIS	544

ALONE

ALONE	551
WINGS	553
STEPPING STONES	555

FOR LOVE	556
IF GOD WERE GOVERNOR	557
THE COLD WINDS OF LIFE	559
SOUND OF SILENT NOISE	560
A QUITTER	562
HAVE YOU HEARD	564
CATCHING AIR	566
GOD'S TREES	567
AN ANGEL	569
RECKLESS REBEL	571
RIPPLES	573
NO SIMPLE MONDAY	575
STORMY	577
NEVER TOO OLD TO LOVE	578
CASTLES IN THE WIND	580
TOO SWEET TO BE BITTER	581
I WALK THE FIELDS	583
THE PUREST FLOWER	586
AS TIMES PASS	587

AND THE END BEGAN

AND AS THE END BEGAN	593
SUNSHINE IF YOU PLEASE	595
AS WE ARE	597
HIS VOWS MADE VISIBLE AND INDIVISIBLE	598
HER VOWS MADE VISIBLE AND INDIVISIBLE	600
FAMILY	602
I'M THE RAINBOW	604
ADOPT ME	607
THE GOLDEN HOUR	608
CLIMAX	610
LIFE	612
LISTEN TO MY PULSE BEAT	614
HOW HIGH IS HIGH	615
CALL COLLECT	616
THE TRUTH	618

SENTIMENTS

SENTIMENTS	623
THE HUMAN COVER UP	625
CHALLENGE OR CHISEL	626
SAME CONCLUSION	628
THE PIONEER	630
THE ILLOGICAL LOGIC BECOMES TRUTH	632
AN UNDESERVING SON	634
JUST ANOTHER WORD	636
OUR BOOK	637
GOSH IS THAT SAD	639
FROM THE MOUTHS OF BABES	641
THE MASTER'S PIECE	643
THIS IS NOT GOODBYE	644
BREAKING UP IS SO HARD TO DO	646
GREAT HANDS	648
A VOW TO THOSE NEEDED	650
FEELING GREAT	652
A ROSE IS CARING	654
I WONDER … ONE OR A HUNDRED	656
BRAINS	657
PLEASE CALL ME SIMPLE	659
MEANINGFUL	661
THE STRENGHT TEST	664

GUTS

GUTS	669
LOOK AND YE SHALL FIND	671
RAIN	673
POSTMORTUM	675
THE WAITING GAME	677
SYNAGOGUE OF GOD	679
STORMS AND WEATHER KITES	682
MELTING YEARS	685
THE GULL'S ILLUSION	687
FLIGHT 271	689

A-BOMB DROPPED

THE DAY THE FIRST A - BOMB DROPPED 695
STAND UP GROWN-UP 699
AND THE GAME WENT ON 701
WAIT 703
BONDAGE 705
THE FUN IS IN THE BUILDING 707
IOWA 709
AUTHOR'S FORMULA (39)(41) DIFFERENT TIMES 711
FEELING GOOD 713
PULL OFF 715
HIBERNATION OF LOVE 716
TWO BUILD OR PERISH 718

DEATH OF FEAR

DEATH OF FEAR 723
GET ON WITHOUT IT 724
I JUST PASSED MYSELF 726
CAN YOU LOVE ME 728
WHAT THIS COUNTRY MEANS TO ME 730
IN MY MIND 732
THE CUSTOM 734
OUR MAKER 737
I WANNA BE A TEST PILOT 740
IF YOU WILL 742
AS YOU TURN 745
CAUGHT WITH MY HAMMER DOWN 747
BETHROTHED 748
HAND PRINTS 749
A TOUCH OF HONEY 751
AUTUMN LEAVES 753
SHARON MY LOVE 755
INDIVIDUALS COUNT 757
CONTRIDICATIONS 759
CHILDREN 761
THE STREAM 763
PULL THE TRIGGER 765

THE LATE GREAT FATE 766
COURTSHIP 767

THE SAVIOR

THE SAVIOR 773
DAMN SNOW STORM 775
POSITIVE LIFE ATTITUDE 778
PROPOSAL - JUST DO IT 780
MISSING YOU 782
LIFE IS AN ECHO 784
STAR DUST 786
COMMON SENSE 788
WISH LIST 791
SHE IS 793

SAINT OR SATAN

SAINT OR SATAN 799
REVOLUTION 802
LIFELINES 804
IDEALIST 806
THE SENATE 808
FOR EGO 812

ROMANCE

ROMANCE 817
CIRCUMSTANCE OR ROMANCE 819
MY LOVE AFFAIR 821
SIGNS OF SRENGTH 823
TWO SHADES OF GRAY 825
BETWEEN LOVE AND HATE 827
IF ANDS AND BUTS 829
WEDDING DRESS 831
CHARADES ... IT'S NOT WHAT YOU SAY 833
THE EIGHTH WONDER OF THE WORLD 836
THE END IS THE BEGINNING 839

AUTHOR'S SEVEN WONDERS OF THE WORLD

THESE ARE THE SEVEN WONDERS OF THE PHYSICAL WORLD VIEWED FROM OUTER SPACE

The Great Wall of China
Steps across the highlands

The Taj Mahal of India
Mausoleum of Mumtaz Mahal

Christ the Redeemer of Brazil
Forgiveness of the savior

The Coliseum of Rome
Gladiators fight for the right to live

Stonehenge of United Kingdom
Outer space travelers or inner space wonders

The Citadel of Haiti
Holy art though

The Great Pyramid of Giza
Wonders of engineering and strength

THESE ARE THE SEVEN WONDERS
OF THE INVISIBLE WORLD TO VIEW INNER SPACE

Computers (internet and social media)
Makes the invisible visible

Cell phones
Makes the decibels hearable

Television
Makes the unseen seen

Electric Robot Autos
Burns neutrons not gas

Lasers
For seeing through time

Satellites
GPS and all its wonders

Drones
The robots of the airways

THE EIGHTH WONDER OF THE WORLD

Undiscovered thoughts
Unused words that rhyme
Unspent moments in time
What a crime
The tenth planet is left spinning
In the brine

What is this thing of you speak
Is it about today
Or is it next week
Prophet tell me, its answers I seek
What is this wonder
You ponder

"Well it's a planet alright
Carried with you day and night
Many have found it
And are using it right
To be perceptive
And somewhat bright"

Like the tenth planet
The eighth wonder
Is owned by every man and woman
They've had it since birth
So they could walk and wander
Left to their willingness and worth
At hand to accept and squander

(continued)

A nearby diamond
At ready commands
Unspoken words and schemes
Misused ideas and plans
Broken dreams, ranting pleas
And if by chance
Lost to its mental disease

It's a wonder, a haven
With the number eight
Beyond the other seven
Determining our fate
To use before it's too late

Spinning our own DNA web
As the sign, of that mental state
Linking us to the spiritual ebb
Of our immortal fate

For all of mankind
To find the undiscovered planet
Called the mind

Connecting us all to the other nine
A mental Solar system divine

Truly the Eighth Wonder of our inner World

POETRY AND PHOTOGRAPHY
A NINTH WONDER

Poetry is saying what we already know
In a way that it allows us to imagine
Our own thoughts being seeds to sow
As words growing on a page to sign

Photography is for those senses
That need expression
To knock down fences
Concealing creation

The synthesis of Poetry
And photography allows us
To see and feel free
Before we turn to dust

For the pens and the lens
Hold misery and mystery
In human hands
Allowing us all a reach into history

(continued)

To whence forever commands
Be it philosophy
Be it psychology
Be it sociology
Be it scientology
Be it theology
Be it technology
Be it biology
Be it astronomy
Be it astrology
Or poetry and photography ... it is to visualize
The Eighth Wonder of the outer world

Minds Seeking Answers
To Life's Questions
Are the ninth wonder of our inner world

THE HUMAN RACE

THE HUMAN RACE

The Marathon Runner
Who is he
What does he want from me
He must need something from us you see
As it's his desire for immortality

The Philosopher
Who is he
What does he want from me
Could it be he wants me to agree
To agree with his surmise of life's subjectivity
Or the theology of his objectivity

The Story Teller
Who is he
What does he want from me
Is he selling a fantasy
Fending and bending to some degree
Visions of reality

(continued)

The Songwriter
Who is he
What does he want from me
Singing along with a catchy melody
Up lifting and at times setting me free
As dreams are for the glee

The Preacher
Who is he
What does he want from me
Standing on his sea of Galilee
With promises of life's eternity
Built upon past scenes of tragedy

The Music Maker
Who is he
What does he want from me
Playing sad songs then a revelry
Mimicking each and Chikaskia
Charming the ears into serenity

The Senator
Who is he
What does he want from me
Votes and totes that's his plea
By overlooking the infidelity
For he's above reproach not insanity

(continued)

The Simple Man
Who is he
What does he want from me
He is building a life of simplicity
Expecting little from the eulogy
But bearing the cross for all of history
The Father, the son and the Trinity

This is the Human Race
It is the marathon runner the philosopher
The story teller the songwriter the preacher
The music maker the senator
and it's the simple man in this race of life

All are trying to keep pace
With each other and the human race
A race to be free and to save face
Racing here and there without a trace
Of a meaning of the finish or of the resting place

Racing just for the sake of finding themselves lost in space
But finally searching searching to be simple for the sake of

A KISS on the face of the simple man's grace

IN TUNE

I am in tune with the moon
In sync with the wind
In touch with the sun
In movement with the stars
In unison with the universe

A system of time space and mass
A kingdom of continuity and gas
Governed by the mind
Motivated by a spirit to seek and find
The answers to the reason
Why we have a changing season

Why the system must be
Be a period of transition
From here to eternity
As the relentless tide occurs
The sun is the vision that never blurs

The moon is never here at high noon
And the stars light the concert
Not one minute too soon

Checkmate or mad hatter
It doesn't seem to matter

For it is mass that makes earth flatter

(continued)

And as much as science can explain
The rationality is somewhat in vane
To try to analyze and comprehend
That there is no such thing
As the beginning and the end

For it's only man's conception
That leads to this classic deception
Of man's mortality to the relentless
Disintegration of posterity
Into a mere pile of dust
Subject to the wind's intermittent gust

Lo what a putrid view of life
When we're led to believe that there's
Everlasting strife
And so little time here and there
And no sight left in the deceased's stare
Just as I don't buy the setting of the moon
Or the rising of the sun at twelve noon
There's no beginning or end
Nor our dust blowing in the wind
Tis a perpetual system of which I speak
Left to us believers to conceive and seek

And along the way pick up those doubters sad
And get them to believe and to be glad
That we're in sync with what's done
And immortality has already won
Left only to be in tune with the moon
And at one with the sun

Any other conclusion just ain't no fun

A QUIET MAN

Have you heard a storm with no sound
Have you sung a song without keys
Have you remembered your father without memories

A quiet man who had no goals except to work
A good man who didn't ask for help or shirk

His duties to his family

The least of which may never be
In spite of his jealousy of me
He will always be

A quiet man

Who made enough noise
To get me to understand
That hard work is the only way
To spend

A quiet day

Who never took a drink
In my presence and
Never swore nor did he think
Of himself or make a demand

(continued)

As a quiet Man

Who always thought
I would be a baseball star
Hitting me fly balls I always caught
And loaning me his new car

A quiet man

Who gave into my mom
His pride and joy
And his own calm
For determination given his boy

By a quiet man

Who died a sad man
Never knowing that his unquiet son
Would emulate his stand

The work values of the quiet man
I am what I am
For the likes of this man

HELPLESS – I

Lord, I feel so helpless. Like
A turtle on its back
A circle with no turning track
A horse with no saddle
A boat without a paddle
Help
Don't you know we can't have
Porches without swings
Bees without stings
Lions without a zoo
Or me without you
Help
So listen to my plea
Don't take the sky from the blue
Don't put the lions in the zoo
Don't tell me that we're through
Don't you know I love only you
Help
Put together we are but a few
Like turtles in a stew
Clover that smells brand new
Eyes filled with tears
And children's nighttime fears

(continued)

Help
So listen to my prayer
Put the turtle on its feet
Make the ends of a circle meet
Put the rider upon the horse
So I can endorse
Me finding my course
Help
And help me find you
By taking these as true
I'm helpless if we're through
Facing someone brand new
Help
With this melody
I have but one plea
Please help me
Help you to be

A loving leaf on your tree

HELPLESS – II

Lord, I feel so helpless. Like
Trees without a leaf
Time without relief
Turtles without a back
Thoughts without fact
Helpless
Horses without saddles
Boats without paddles
Days without nights
Winds without kites
Helpless
Geese without ganders
Barry without Sanders
Apples without a core
Houses without a door
Riches without the poor
Helpless
Porches without rockers
Shoes without Dockers
Swings without ropes
Geniuses without dopes
Helpless
Songs without a tune
Sun without a moon
Eagles without a cage
Yellow without a page

(continued)

Helpless
Lions without a zoo
Tigers out there too
Living without dying
Voices without lying
Helpless
Truth without ears
Eyes without tears
Voices without cares
Singles without pairs
Helpless
Skin cold to the touch
Shivering much to much
Mother without child
Teenagers gone wild
Helpless
Brother without sister
Men without a mister
Me without you
My future is terribly blue
Helpless
With this melody
I have but one plea
Please help me
Help you to be
A loving leaf on my tree
Helpful
Growing the Appleseed
Above the horse weed

HE SHOWED ME

God showed me fear
So I could make happiness dear

God exposed me to defeat
So I could hear victory speak

God tore away the shrouds of doubt
So I could stand up and look about

God pierced me with the thorns of pain
So I could find the sunshine through the rain

God showed me the road to hell
So I could get back on the path to being well

God showed me the ways of sin
So I could teach goodness to other men

God showed me the teachings of His Son
So I could be satisfied as each day is done

God showed me the breath of life
And rewarded me with the love of my wife

(continued)

God endowed me with virginity
That enabled my wife and I to have our children's history

God showed me how it was to be lonely
So I could appreciate my responsibility to my family

God has shown all these things from the start
By opening up my heart

Until virtue brings
The blessing of the King of Kings

COURAGE IS AGELESS

That little figure lying there
With moving eyes, knowing
That her life will not progress
Beyond her mind and stare
Has courage

That old shadow in the chair
With wrinkled skin
Knows that time is all that's left
But eyes say they care
That's courage

That young black from the ghetto
With little opportunity
Striving for an education
Against society's current and tow
Knows courage

That battle worn has been on the mat
With battered face
Getting up to earn a meal
And facing the throne upon which he once sat
Needs courage

(continued)

That simple man left to fate
With an incurable diagnosis
Making the best of its impact
Upon his life to love and hate
Finds courage

The family man out of work
With hunger in his way
Looking past former pride to admit
That hope comes, if faith he doesn't shirk
Creates courage

Courage is ageless
It is needed by many
And known by few
Because sorrow leaves one helpless

But if you look beyond the sorrow
With those that need more
You suddenly realize
Courage is tomorrow's prize

Attacking the next disappointment

LIFE MADE VISIBLE

Take the time to visualize
By being wise

The man who can swallow his medicine
Shall never be sick from sin

The man who can accept defeat
Is ever accepted for his retreat

The man who can find joy
Is predestined to be glad as a boy

The man who can find himself
Shall not be lost to wealth

The man who can smile at his misgivings
Shall ever give from his livings

The man who can work with love
Shall receive his work from above

(continued)

The man who can believe in the spirit
Shall feel the spirit and never fear it

The man who can see beyond himself
Is visible to the world in good mental health

The man who can relate to heaven
Is in the stream of faith's maven

The man who can persevere to be fulfilled
Will not go empty or distilled
The man who can be patient
Is to be no victim of fear and descent

The man who can bless the works of others
Has much love for his own work with brothers

The man who can be loved by self and wife ...
Shall be loved by life

MR. CLOUD WHO ARE YOU

Mr. Cloud
Answer me
If you dare
Are you more
Than just thin air

So white
Up against the blue
Rain and mist
Ebbs from you

Talk to me
Answer back
What makes you white
Prone to black

First you're quiet
Flying free
Then your darken
And scare the heck out of me

(continued)

Mr. Cloud are you real
Or just smoke
Above the field
With a breath to choke

Or are you
Not really there
An illusion
Just a thought made of air

All I ask is a reply
Can it be will I see
Inside of you
If I fly

Tell me then
If you dare
Are you more
Than just thin air

When I look and you're not there

SYNERGY

*Synergy is the amalgamation of forces to overcome
the resistive forces to positive action*

*This must consist of a cohesive loyalty to productive
thought committed to a written plan of action*

*The participants must see the vision of results
to execute the opportunity of action*

*The forces resisting action must be diluted by logical strategies and
plans that overcome the negative energy resisting positive action*

*The desired results must be definable visible expressions that will convert the
ever-prevailing element of risk into the essential expression of faith and belief*

*The synergy to be productive must be for the benefit of the
participants who believe they're doing well for others
No other banner can exercise the true concept
of collaboration to its ultimate being*

*Beyond synergy we will be but one feeding upon the actualization of the
family of man within the confines of Christianity, Judaism, Islam, etc.*

*The success can be felt and enjoyed by all who desire to give their
energy for the best of the middle ground and a peaceful sound*

(continued)

*Without synergy of thought the world will be
lost to war, hunger, disease and hate
Weapons, rhetoric, fear, economic power are the enemies of synergy*

So the eternal battle between the misuse of energy and the abuse of synergy has to be waged by leadership at all levels of society. This battle cannot just be waged by government, church or business but by protecting individual freedoms not being taken away so the energy of money is the victor without humanity's synergy and debate

*Whether it is the globe or the national interests at stake
peace on earth good will to men must win*

Preachers, teachers, beseecher's, all God's creatures are all here for the same reason to coexist and not resist human dignity and the sanctity of life

*This eliminates action without the synergy and
principle of pro-action for peace*

Under God's synergy we have our world, the heavens and the stars populated by the eight billion who yet have no peace until wars cease and atomic energy can desist for those who violate God's will … Peace on earth good will to all men and women living under his son and sun.

WHO SAYS

Who says you can't
Who says you can
Are you a plant
Or are you a man

For only the plant can't
Only the man can
So why do we have men saying they can't
And a plant sitting in a can

Let's take a plant and tell it can't
And let's take a man and tell him he can
And let's give them both a hand
As they sit rooted in the land

Who says I can't
Who says I can
Well, it is I who says I am
So why shouldn't I stand

(continued)

On a can
Rather than stuck as a plant
In the mire of saying I can't
Or shan't

Agreeably the mind is the fertilizer
The goals are the fire
And the man that says he can
Is all the wiser

And the fool that says he can't
Is nothing more than a plant
Facing the trials and tribulations
Of the blowing wind
And bygone creations

Regretting having been at all
Let alone, growing tall
Because he chose to fall off the can
Dying as a forgotten plant
Because he said I can't

And died a didn't

CHILDREN – THAT WONDERFUL GIFT

We had our kids
Without a second thought
Made without lids
We hadn't sought

Thank God for the spiritual lift
When we learned about this wonderful gift
They were so innocent
Not a negative act without our consent

But when we said "don't and can't"
They started to say "won't and shan't"
Then for some God sent reason
We discovered something pleasing

They were so good
Till we told them they were bad
They were so happy
Till we got sad then mad

Why must we all
Climb till we fall
Why don't we see
That the new born souls are born free

(continued)

Released they need direction
But their wills don't need dissection
They'll grasp for a loving hand
They'll ask for the interested command

So why don't we say, yes
To the traits God does bless
Love and attention
Without guilt and apprehension

When you as parents covet your children
Like this
How can any future sin
Be dismissed

And then maybe
We can show all parents
About the goodness of their baby
Before their patience relents

With our consents
Giving a spiritual lift
To those dear children
That wonderful gift

THE MOTHER LAND AND THE OLD MAN OF THE SEA

Bequeathed To Me

A Mind a heart and a soul
A token and a toll
For a glass to be empty or
Full

To be filled with love or hate
Life or Death
Health or Pain
Wealth or no Gain

The choice is always free
Depending on faith and me
If I bloom above the gloom
Shoot for the sun and ignore the moon

Life will bless me
Give me happiness
And a laugh
Filling me as a glass
Waiting for the Other half

Rather than drinking my last gasp

Of a life bequeathed to me

YOU ARE WHAT YOU FEAR

You become what you've overcome
(so you are what you fear)

Replace a no way
With a some way

Replace a not now
With a somehow

Replace I don't know how
With effort so will can endow

Replace an unhappy face
With a smiling grace

Replace fear
With good cheer

Character comes from a choice
To be free of fear's hoist

As fear is a mind's doubt
For things that never come about

Unless you're a lazy lout

(85% of what you fear never happens
And the other 15% is only half as bad
As you fear … why waste away fearing
Rather than endearing yourself to happiness)

GIVE PEACE A CHANCE

Hand me your weapons
Hand me your cause
Now contemplate your sons
Think of your daughters as you pause

Is it worth the price you pay
To confront your fellow man
With fists clenched to betray
Peaceful days in each other's land

I don't believe
You believe it's right
To forsake those you conceive
Your children, just to fight

With only selfish banners to carry
Think and ponder
Why is it necessary
To ravage God's wonder

(continued)

Why not throw down
Your pride; from your side
Make peace your sound
Before we all have died

What do we have to lose
That we haven't already lost
It is our choice to choose
Peace rather than the holocaust

On this Earth at any cost

For in peace
Lives don't cease
Love and friends abide
Before religion and principle all have died

As a belief in the same God's absolution
That Reason minus Religion = Resolution

Give Peace a Chance

PAIN

Pain is in the person
Of each man and woman
Waiting to be undone
By being human

Pain is in every good
And stress must be
If you will and would
Live to be free

Pain is in the heart
For the sake of love
It's in every start
If you expect to fly above

Pain is in the soul
That burns to strive
Yet the ultimate in a goal
Is to be more alive

(continued)

Pain is in the life
Who cares enough to give
Creating righteousness from strife
And giving of self to live

Pain is in the effort
So we can feel good
And somehow resort
To doing what we should

Pain is in resistance
To being vain
Mindful that in each instance
We are to blame

For our pain

THE DOOR TO WAR

Hinged upon the frame of history
For friend or foe it swings to and fro
As the men of victory
Killed each other against their will
Only to trudge past its threshold
Battering it down when it stood still
By men with hearts so cold
Ignoring hopes that don't cease
When Nery's door swung open for peace

Such a pity
The door when shut brings troopers to its sanctity
They come to find why it's closed
Never why they must expire
Only wanting to see the other side exposed
As captain's council around the fire
Debating in jest
The way the door shall fall
Never asking what is best
Narre a look for good will to all

First they charge and batter its timbers
Bashing upon the surface with weapons of misery
Weakening the door's will to withstand its members
Resist as it might to tyranny and missionary
It crashes open with a thunder
Giving in to the might of the mercenaries
Forming a misspent tomb for those that do us under

(continued)

Try as they might against the dignitaries,
Exerting their will as they soon decease
The peacemakers try to close that door behind
With visions of a sanctity, peace
On earth and peace of mind

Throughout the strains of history
This door stood erect
Worn and tired and battered in
If it falls all hopes are wrecked
By the misspent whims of mortal men
For that door is more than just an obstacle
It is the very core
Controlling human nature's debacle
It represents a stable sense
Put there by wiser men
Fostered by men's weakness
And inclination and need to defend
With endless time and money to make war cease
But limited incline to make peace

So curse the troops and praise the peacemakers
They've kept this door eternally ajar
Feeding the graves and supporting the undertakers
As the future looks for that savior's star
Hoping that door can stand up to more…
Keeping the peace for hopes don't cease
… That War

LEFT TO HEAVEN OR HELL

Looking to Heaven for deliverance
And finding Hell with no answers
Inspires thoughts of why man is by chance
A whisper of science in the stars
Left to his hope for celestial romance

Seeking the answers is unseen tolerance
Without patience to find what's lost
Our world would not make sense
The ego of history must be caught when tossed
With pens bent to recording the past tense

Though the scribes of the Bible
Do not themselves create Heaven or Hell
Their presence reminds us to speak out
For those coming later might speculate
Then true our minds are not prone to shout
The truth we think our heirs might doubt

Lingering loneliness is a personal cross
Borne as the savior who warned of sin's intensity
And the inhumanity of the Holocaust
Selfishness abounds entombed as the devil's piety
Of the beings void of such personal loss

Mortal lust is fraught with troubles unless cajoled
Tempered not by virtues as much as vengeance
Towards those discrete and controlled
Praised on Sundays by those bleeping reticence
With lips of lies betrothed to scold

(continued)

Religion above all else is but a dream
Fulfillment is part of its passion
Rising from nowhere or theme
It knows no reason nor fashion
For the moment is its scheme

Losing sight of reality is the predator
Given to stories and the soothsayer's lines
Of thoughts about some downed gladiator
Rather than good songs of many rhymes
Sung by the Jester to the fallen Dictator

Sought by the hordes looking at the same sky
Hoping for the same rain when the same
Failing crops are dry
These swine's of history are set up to blame
Along with its Scrooge and Captain Bly

Fighting wars and weathering floods
Is the human's Trope
Balancing their loads
With hope on an evolving Globe
Anticipating some Galactic probe
As its purgatory

This may seem cruel and forsaken
To thrust this classic sacrifice upon the future
Though history repeats no exception taken
The lives of each evolving creature
Are likely born as the spirit's ultimate beckon

While humanity is finally left to Heaven

And the World to Hell

THIS IS NOT FANTASY
THIS IS NOT A DREAM
SIN IS NOT LEFT TO HEAVEN

Dreamer, dreamer on the fall
Who will catch you hold you hear your call
You are hoping it will come
Before you crash deaf and dumb

A fantasy creates those dreams so real
Borrowing time from now just to feel
The moments focusing upon the needs
Never fearing if desire succeeds

Sandman, sandman sprinkle visions fair
Plant a seed, blossomed there
And from those shadows of wants to come
Form a creation, a worthwhile plum

Plucked by some as clouds of smoke
Accepted by others for fun to poke
But it's my life, another time
Awaiting to be taken, attained divine

Seeker, seeker close your eyes
Phantom scene never dies
Least you know, the facts against
You'll be proud as truth is common sense

(continued)

Fantasy alone is but a night mare
But put it within yourself to care
Finding a way to raise your sight
To the reality that you're going there

Liver lover teacher preacher all will be
Only what they dream and see
So don't be shy and torn within
Express yourself it's no sin

Lost sacred beliefs must start over
Another time is but another place
Born to our spirit to uncover
The scriptures that fill that mysterious space

For tomorrow only the aftermath is our savior
If we are lost it is not to heaven
It is to ourselves a mindless endeavor
Of self-Indulgence and our urge to win

Viewed by those that proceed us
We waste for fear and sin
Accusing God and Jesus

For the Holocaust of men

VISIONS OF A BETTER WORLD

Look towards the sky of tomorrow
Feast on the setting sun
Let us look for less sorrow
Swear only if vanity is undone

Dream not for the dying
But cherish the fruit of the living
With eyes not shut to crying
Put forth with open giving

Find and seek the manner
To which the vision of a better world
Is in the heart of the beholder
With a nation's flag unfurled

As politics lose sight of the practical
Common sense must prevail
If the common man is to scale obstacles
To a better version of the grander scale

Yet, thus a third party will be formed
With its principles of practical economics

As the answer and course the elite has scorned
Revitalization of Enterprise must be the fix

(continued)

With fewer divorces
Less crime and violence
Fewer Military forces
More common sense
Higher employment
Better GNP and fun
Lower drug decent
Less people on the run
Better standard of living
Lower teen pregnancies
More charity and giving
More human decencies
More affordable housing
Fewer unwanted children
Less carousing
And immortal sin

VISIONS OF PEACE
Yes my vision of a better world is
In the heart of a mother's decency
And the hope of individuals
Not in the theory and hypocrisy
Of the institutional intellectuals
Condemning us to mediocrity

This vision is what I call Mancology
The Science of harvesting human values
In an enterprising theology
Outside religion and the pews
Vitalize our enterprise psychology

(continued)

*Let the established institutions redirect their energies
Into the livelihood of hard work, family life,
For the sake of our fellow man's synergies
Embodied in man and wife
Replacing the negative forces hurled
With positive entities
And opportunities of a better world
Pursuing peaceful infantries*

*The skeptic forces of the self-righteous
Who must learn to work ethically
With a common cause and crisis
Though besieged by indifference ethnically
Will enact the vision that freedom unfurled
Under one flag one spoken word and a peaceful jihad
To become a better world
So help me God*

*So Governed
Of the people for the people by the people*

(Read the book "The American Enterprise Manifesto" by Jerry Rhoads)

MY AMERICA

My America is the feeling of freedom. It's the feeling good when you get up in the morning and can decide what you're going to do that day, who you're going to see and what you're going to say.

It's the feeling that you can make a difference. It's the feeling you can produce your product, you can sell your produce and you can benefit from your hard work, unhindered. It's the feeling when you help your children with their homework, so they will be able to use their knowledge for growth, for maturity, for the good of the country. It's the feeling when you send them off to school, knowing they will receive a concerned teacher's attention, sensitivity and guidance. And knowing as they grow up, they will thrive on their freedom to communicate, to express themselves, to direct their own destiny.

It's the feeling when they graduate from grade school, junior high and high school that they are taking the steps towards a better life. And when you give their hand away in matrimony, that happiness shall be theirs. For together as husband and wife, they can create the same and even more opportunities for their off-spring.

It's that feeling when, you can unchain your dog and watch her run free for at least a little while, to watch the experience on her face, when she's released from the shackles; and the sadness that reappears when she must be chained.

(continued)

My America is the freedom of choice to buy the bread I want to buy, to acquire the goods I can afford to acquire, to invest the capital I have saved, in ventures I want to take for the good of my family and my country.

My America is being able to communicate in writing, speaking and in whatever form, language takes, my opinions, my thoughts, my prayers, my visions and my dreams to those who want to listen, and to those enemies of the American way who in themselves have not discovered America.

My America is the blooming rose which has the freedom to grow towards, a clear sky and a warm sun; being able to complete its cycle from bloom to plumage to autumn to a dormant grave, only to rise again.

My America is the personal commitment to grab opportunities which will better the country and to set an example for those who follow; what you give, must be proportionate to what you take, or the erosion shall remove the sky, the sun, the earth from our grasp.

For in our America and the world resources are limited; the energy, though absolute, is redistributed by our wills. The more astute, the more free we are to create, the better the use of the resources. And left in God's hands, through our America, we create good will, good products, good people and peace of mind.

My America, oh yes my America, the vision of the poet, the words of the orator and the minds of the leaders be kind, be patient, be wise, but above all be humble to the reasons and the heritage of our freedom. Lead us not into temptation, but deliver us from evil ventures and purposes, for thine is mine America as the Kingdom, the power and the glory, forever.

Amen.

A Child's World

A CHILD'S WORLD

Infants are brought upon the world
Fetus warm body curled
Suckled to be secure
With little protection to endure
Life's mountains and valleys never pure

Sure, they grow to the gait
Destined to attain an adult state
But in between are all the tears
Grappling with those younger years
With little help they seem to thrive
On love, attention and dreams alive
To help them along I dedicate this prayer
Lifting spirits out of despair

Doubt as you must
Fear as you must
Cry as you must
Love as you must
But please we ask

Don't break the trust

(continued)

The trust that has been bequeathed you
With opportunities very few
Make of them what you will
But use it well for time thou should not kill
Along the way there'll be many roles to play
The better you study the script
The more the scales are tipped
Towards your way
With life's rewards and virtues gripped

So what this prayer is saying
Never forget or stop weighing
Your heritage your opportunity
Your chance to put your mark on destiny
If you push and pull and strive to care
While you're here instead of there
Listening and living this child's prayer

That in a child's world we all can dare
To be the best in this mortal affair …
AMEN

TIS MUCH EASIER TO DOUBT

Tis much easier to doubt
Than to make a turnabout

Tis much easier to rationalize
Than epitomize

Tis much easier to say I can't
Than it is to plant

Tis much easier to say I will
Than to swallow your bitterest pill

Tis much easier to go with the crowd
Than it is to pioneer the unplowed

Tis much easier to give in
Than it is to resist sin

Tis much easier to travel downhill
Than it is to develop a skill

Tis much easier to skirt the mountain
Than it is to build a fountain

(continued)

Tis much easier to ask to be blest
Than it is to change things confessed

Tis much easier to be holier than thou
Than it is to really learning how

Tis much easier to threaten to fight
Than it is to make others see the light

Tis much easier to be one to offend
Than it is to be a true friend

Tis much easier to scale it down
Than it is to scale up with practice to abound

Yes, tis easier to fail your senses
And in failing rationalize your doubt
Than it is to face the consequences
And turn your life about

So if you just give in and let doubt win
You shall be a life's has been
Or just choose to feel the thrill
As doubt you kill ...

NOT YOUR WILL

YOUR SHIFTING SAND

Your sand is shifting
Around your head
Will it allow you to bring
It out instead

Hallowed be thy name
But please
If it is all the same
Lift your eyes up to the breeze

To embrace those who part
Take the time to understand
Why we're given a heart
With feeling in each hand

For sifting the sand

Said one to the other
So the eyes can see
The tithes of brother
Instead of selfish me

(continued)

Looking for the essence of love
Take your face from the sand
Lifting yourself above
And through the body of man

Shift the sand

Lifting your head out of the sand
Before you sink to another
Take full command
Or you will smother

For in life
A head in the sand
Is worse than a bloody knife
All it takes is you must stand

For something
Above the shifting sifting sand
Or fall for anything above the land
Such is God's command

As those Ten Values are better than
The death of mortal man

IT'S A SAND HEAP WORLD

It's a sand heap world we live in
Mr. Sandman

It's a rain soaked cloud we're under
Master Black

It's a flakey life with mounds of tin
Mr. Tin man

It's a bloody cruel war we've seen
Master Jack

It's a sand heap world we live in
Mr. Sandman
But from that sand heap
Came Little Bo Peep
Wooly worms that creep
Swings of rope and slides too steep
T. V. shows and things that bleep
Little lambs that run and leap
Wheat and oats for men to reap
And from that heap is love to keep

(continued)

God to protect us in our sleep
Faces seeking aces for the cheap
And tears when we're prone to weep
All that from a dirty sand heap

It's a rain-soaked cloud we're under
Master Black
Yet from that rain cloud
Came beautiful orchids oh how proud
Black dirt and fields just plowed
Cats and dogs and things so loud
Kittens mittens those meowed
Thickets, crickets leaves that shroud
Sudden cyclones heads are bowed
Fits and spits babes cow towed
Pelted ground and concrete trawled
Splatters on foreheads scowled
Paths in forests prowled
All that from a black ole cloud

It's a flakey life with mounds of tin
Mr. Tin man
It's a flaky life with mounds of tin
But from that mound came iron skin
Sturdy truss and reels that spin
Pliers and tires a Parker Pen
Clasps and rasps a mechanical hen
Steely things in the den
Nails alike with the washers ten

(continued)

Scales or sparks a metal fin
Spools of string; toys of men
Tassels tangles in a bin
Quarters dollars for a yen
Sculptures formed a mortal sin
All that from a piece of tin

It's a bloody cruel war we've seen
Master Jack
Yet from that bloody scene
Came berets toned in green
Minds and thoughts almost clean
Size and brawn brought down lean
Life and death on the screen
Love to last minds seen mean
Leaders lead mothers wean
Teachers teach await the Dean
Skies and towns stay serene
Wounds that injure face and spleen
Subtle thoughts that now careen
All that from scores of wars we've seen
Honed From sands that stack
Cloned From clouds of black
Toned From mounds of tin
Droned with wars of sin

It's a sand heap world we live in

INSIGHT

Give me insight to see my star
Give me foresight to see others afar
Give me hindsight to see us both as we are

Let me see through my ego
Let me gaze upon the purpose of ergo
Let me look back upon sin's tow

Turn my eyes inward
Turn my heart outward
Turn my purpose upward

Sight my goals towards goodness
Sight my wrath towards bad business
Sight my spirit away from sadness

Towards better times
Less serious crimes
Seeking nickels and dimes

As I look back on hell's beckon
I shall gaze upon believing
So I shall see heaven

All before I lose sight
Of myself here and now… in flight
Far from where I might

See my insight

ROOTS AND WINGS

Children either walk or run away
From home and adventure
What sets the gait of
Their departure
Ask the puzzle maker

Who shall be the richest
Ask the banker
When will they arrive unto themselves
Asks the Quaker
Where shall they go and why
Ask the undertaker

Should their trip
Be to history with misery
If given to the no roots plight
Or given to the no wings flight
As children who shan't walk proudly
And must put ink in their pens to write
About wishful stability
With bad dreams of insecurity

(continued)

Those given to roots
Hold to the good earth
By their love for family and tradition
And those given to wings girth
Hold to the good wind's ambition
By their roots, even as they leave the mother's breast
And make their own nest

So those cocks and hens
With nests of futility
Feigning the faith of has beens
Feeling no need for security

Finding no peace in the past
Planting no value or graces
Into their fear yet cast
By flocking to shallow spaces

No thrill free or flowing,
Feeling no excitement for love
Finding no tranquility in going
Into the tailspin of reality above

The moral of the roots and wings

(continued)

Give those chicks roots
Give those offspring wings and boots
So they can hold onto self-worth
And the good earth

Bent on survival and defend
Their mother and father's birth
On wings finding the good wind
And the roots for the struggle with no end

Making their moral trip with stability
And their risky flight with security
Be it from the mother or the father
Or both together

Roots and wings will get them farther
Through sunny and stormy weather

MOUNTAIN CLIMBERS

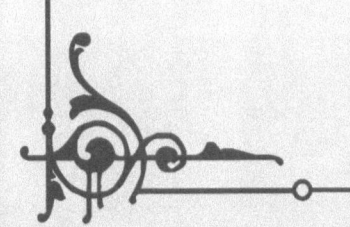

MOUTAIN CLIMBERS

Mountain climbers lashed to desire
Mountains chained to the earth
With man rising in the misty ire
A challenge to be more than a mortal's birth

Birth of beings stellar
A slope on the plain
To skirt the pillar
Of life…brutal and insane

If to be a climber's feat
The player must prepare
It is the soles of the plain man's feet
At the foot of the mountain's dare

For the babe the slope is but a blanket
Covering the plain of courage
Waiting for the bosom
Of youth to scale the
Valley to its plateaus
Only to return afraid

Lo, youth cannot resist
Age and the adolescent
Who dares further
With the bearer's
Following
Holding to the earth
Like scales to the snake
Upward to their dread

(continued)

Then to retreat almost dead
To hide until the beard is long
And the manhood forces
Another assault
This being the last…insult

So said the mountain
Camp after camp rejecting effort
Until the sky begged to take them
And life demanded they suffer
Wanting them to turn back
But they feared defeat

Climbed upward onward step into step
Track into track

Chasing the peak as
It seemed to smile with victory at
Their scowl of doubt's pursuit
Until man's quest man's expedition
Conquers that mental summit

(continued)

In maturity, aging to stand
Above the decent
Flag planted as a flower
Of success, in honor of the
Waiting age of indifference

Asking:
Is it over or did it just begin
Is it the climax or the fore-play
To another mountain
Be it a mountain climber's new dream
Or an old man's nightmare

Buried in the graves of those that dared
And lived to regret the next climb
Ambition and affliction are bared

As the mountain climber's addiction

A MOUNTAIN OR MOUSETRAP

Every obstacle in life
Can be a mountain or mouse trap
If you look at it negatively
Especially, if you're standing in wonder
At a snow cap

Or if you've gotten your fingers smashed
By your limb on a falling tree
Sure you crawled out there with much in mind
On that limb of risks
What did you expect to find
Certainly not pockets free to frisk

If it comes to the point you fall
At least you've tried and failed
Which is better than no trial at all
Virtues seen, fear curtailed
Trapped before you've sailed

So if you're of a mind to be resolved
To be ordinary not a missionary
To hide behind, not involved

(continued)

It's your mountain quite contrary
Your sinking ship with no ferry

Unable to shake the old habit
Never doing or going too far
Never one to run when you can sit
And prone to start then quit
A mousetrap if you let it fit

Myself I want to climb that mountain
I want to shake that mouse trap
Cause, as surely as trying is the fountain
With opportunity sitting in your lap

Thinking you can
Must be the map

WONDERING MAN: I CAN

Life is amazing in its turns
Sometimes it ups and sometimes it downs
Taxing the mind as it learns
How to handle human frowns and clowns

Times of more than joy with blues so quick
Letting yourself go is one thing
Feeling free is fantastic
But you must come back to the reality that life brings

Mostly it can be very happy
For yours and mine are basically good
Occasionally prone to earthen apathy
In spite of those you know or should

Then for the moment you fall behind
On occasion insecurity creeps in
It crawls out of the corners of your mind
And erodes your will from your grin

This from thoughts that wander
Not then set upon a worthwhile goal
Seeping and weeping you squander
Then toss away your only soul

(continued)

Failing for no good reason
Justly you may need to be blue
If you have committed treason
And to yourself you're untrue

So then your mind begins the slipping
Away from the things that work for you
Drag yourself back unto gripping
The mortal laws, oh so true

You'll find that black may be white
That the waters start to clear
And the dark fades into light
As happiness is left to reappear

Loving yourself more than the rest
Then you're back on track
Living life at the fullest
Putting perceived worries at your back

For then you are no longer
Afraid of unknown land,
A wondering man getting stronger
No longer afraid to stand

In respect to the words "I Can"

JONATHON LIVINGSTON MANGULL

Fly fly you're fantastic to the eye
So free to do what you feel so real
No other creature has your opportunity so pure
The rest are so rooted in themselves they can't or shan't

Soar soar you are the way to a better day
Upward out of the ordinary no canary
Swooping towards the ultimate no hill or rut
God my God you're so close to the host

Wings wings spread so wide feathered tide
Bursting up against no barrier nor interior
No bonds or lock or box free even to the fox
Looked upon as a sign for us mortals our narrowed portals

Swooping swooping from nowhere without fear
Downward back to us dreamers earthbound schemers
Circle your circle is so profound with no sound
Except there's the music of motion mental potion

Circling circling to gather another almost hoover
Picking up momentum into the glaring sun

Shadows showing the way as followers betray
For you are right to try they only wonder why

(continued)

Climb climb as you gain speed talons bleed
Not caring you make the peak though weak
Leveling you look downward towards the absurd
Dive devil you risk taker music maker

Diving diving don't pull up to soon shoot for the moon
Those weaker souls might as well be moles
They've never known or tried that difficult ride
A feeling exploding to win mind over men

Pull up pull up Jonathon don't crash don't smash
Don't go too far to be you no one's that true
You know how it is, to be ordinary what effort gives
So it's better to be honest with yourself and rest

Singing singing now you're off winging
With rhythm and beauty fun not just duty
Creating a memory for others to see
An example for shrinking souls to change their roles

Jonathon; Jonathon Mangull with no fear don't you hear
Your followers now praise your vision and ways
Forgetting they once chided as your dream abided
And now in your camp are the critics doubts damped

Their own goals revamped

HUMBLED

How much does it take to bring a person down,
Be he king
Be he clown

How hard does he fall
As he hits bottom
Curls into a ball

How long does it take to stand up,
Be he right
Be he corrupt

Where are those that put him down
Disappeared to safety their
Reasons not around

Have you ever been this humbled,
Right or wrong, but knowing
Why you've stumbled

Yes I have, and it's no fun
But in it lies the reasons
Why it's done

It's a test
Made by Him
To see who's the best
If you face it
With jest
Not just wit

(continued)

It is possible then to learn
About yourself
Without concern

But if you doubt
Your capability
Losing is the bout

So if you're humbled
By a travesty
As if crumbled

Don't lose confidence
In yourself
It makes no sense

Yes you're humbled
Yes you're down
But bigger yet have fumbled

So get up and lead
Watch out world
Let this just be your seed

Growing to what you need
Success is knowing
That not many are worthy to succeed

AND EMERGE AS FREED
Freed from being a weed
By out growing greed

Upon that we feed

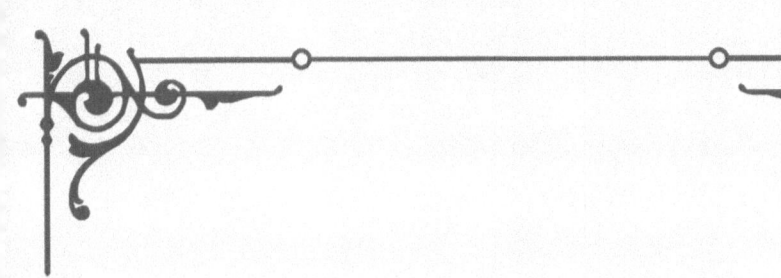

REMEMBER THIS

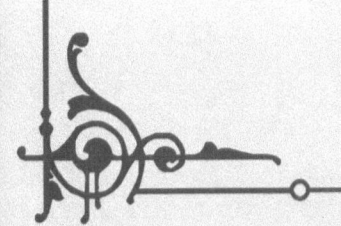

REMEMBER THIS

Remember those days of old
When the winters were very cold
And children loved their mothers
Just as much as others

Remember
Along with antique cars
And canning jars
From gardens held dear
By old men drinking beer

Remember
Those school days
With colors all ablaze
Girl friends at the hop
Kissing that wouldn't stop

Remember
Custom cars
And candy bars
Eating at the beach
Sex within our reach

(continued)

Remember
Those days
When Elvis was all the craze
Needing that young love divine
Feeling her warmth for the first time

Remember
The kisses then
Were searches
Meaning more than school
Or churches

Remember
Dealt upon us upon our hand
Scratching's upon the sand
The lines have worn away somewhat
As we've forgotten what we've got

Remember
But pull yourself
Back my friend
Memories never end
When it's friend to friend

All else is blowing in the wind

SHARI

Once upon a time
It came to pass
A flower so divine
A maiden a lovely lass

She was a thing of beauty
She blossomed eternally
Growing to perfection
Velvet skin for all to see

This flower though
Not to be misunderstood
Just needs to know
That what she is is good

Her petals seem to fall
When you ignore her smile
That is just a call
To be held again awhile

Her stem stands so straight
Needing to be fed

Before it's too late
With praise instead

(continued)

Her spirit is like a rose
Given unto me
So it grows and grows
Clinging not to my tree

Phantom moods may prevail
If you fail to realize
That her skin is thinly frail
Covering a character twice its size

Handle with care
Be very kind to her
For she will dare
Her love oh so pure

So play upon her strings
Oh so gently with your words
Giving her those little things
That beautiful flowers feed birds
In protecting and wanting her
You've just planted another seed
Of a feeling that will endure
Responding to your every need

For loving Shari nature's brightest rose
Captures my heart's written prose
Allowing me to just close
With my poetic repose

As our wedding vows we chose

REMEMBER THEN

Remember then
Treasures we've had somehow
Kneeling with me
As to how
Before life's temple so simple

Remember then
Love will join two halves
With rings that tithes
Memories made for those
With separate lives

Remember then
That's why we are here
Instead of there
So take the time
To savor and care

Remember then
Left to ourselves to sort
As people we must
Hasten for time
That is short

Remember then
Hold fast don't delay
Mindful we are seeing
Bygones of a human being
So sign your diary today

(continued)

Remember when
With memories held fast
As the moment will not last
So let's not stray
When thinking of the day … when

Remember when
Pink shoelaces
Parking and necking places
Slicked down hair
Sun tans skin so bare
Without a care

Remember when
Tight blue jeans
Cowboy scenes
Where our heroes win
And the bad guys sin

Let it begin

Remember when
Summer time fun
Spring Winter and Falling sun
County fair
Halloween to scare

Friends and enemies
Storms and surging seas
Boys to war
Fears galore

(continued)

Remember when
Contact sports
Tennis courts
Socks at the hop
Dodging the cop

Remember when
Dances taking chances
Blazing romances
Movie houses
That Puberty arouses

Remember when
The drive-in movie
Fads made groovy
Rock and roll
Shaking our soul

Remember when
First loves
Fur lined gloves
Bombs and fleece
Hoping for peace

Remember when
Lest we forget
The little things between life and death
Lest we regret

Our last breath

ETERNAL LOVE

*The tingle, pang, throb, tidal wave, surge response, instant sting, flash
feeling, sensual flow, crest ebb, summit mount, thoughtful emotions
Sexuality = Eternal Love so many ways of feeling it*

*The thought of love is the response
To thinking of those you need
It's to be important to their wants
And willing to hurt even bleed*

*I can't explain why it's happening
To me, for the ones who find my thought
But I do know it will bring
Happiness, for those needs are sought not bought*

*From the heart as feelings awake
Names crossing the mind starts the rush
As a wave forms in the wake
Causing the senses and blood to gush*

*Wonderment follows as to why
Justifying a higher being's role
Making a pang wanting to cry
Planting some doubts but revealing a soul*

(continued)

For years are needed to nurture it
The thought of a love experience must be the crest
Of a human romantic summit
Cultured as a pearl in the oyster's nest

Ignoring its first tendency to give into sin
Not all can be thankful for the chance
It takes something special within
To know the sharing of love's romance

Fantasy has taken its predictable toll
Of those dreamers submitting to instinct
But the rewards await the sincere role
From creatures reaching out, feelings succinct

Many are frightened to take the chance
With themselves towards others
Missing so much, afraid to enhance
A life to touch soul sisters or brothers

The thought of love is a tingle,
A pang, a throb, a flash, it surges
Spurred by emotions wed or single
Expressed in seven senses as sexuality urges

And eternal love emerges

GRADUATION

Caps and gowns
Are taken off
Never to be put on again
Raising memories aloft
Marking where we're going
And where we've been

It's the meaning
That's important
Remembering somehow
That age we can't stunt
What immortality will allow

Passing through our time
Like windblown signs
In the sand
With a rhyme
And lines upon our hand

Waiting for your staff
As you stand there
As we all have
So little do you care

It's been handed to you
When you're of an age to try
No matter what you do
Carrying it until you die

(continued)

Left to you to arrange
This staff is your destination
It can little change
After its creation

Arrange it as you will
Like a captain plots a course
On a trip to fulfill
Using yourself as the force

Because it's profound
Graduation then
Creates the stage
With living places
All around

Thief, baker and a sage
Select the page

But listen my friend
Before you choose
Don't take this as a whim
For yourself you stand to lose

Be you nothing
Be you something
Matters not
It will bring
Sad or happy songs to sing

(continued)

Could it be you'll be praying
If your life you shatter
What is this saying
What does it matter

With this hand you're dealt
Opportunities oh so few
Acting, once you've felt
The reason oh so true

The reason is
Is that you exist
You've got some time here
So please don't desist
To being led around by fear

Give it some thought
Because your mind is the tool
You'll gain what you sought
Please, please don't be a fool

Believe you're just graduating to another school
Learning as you go
Proving you're being more than cool
Leaving your knowledge for others to sow

For graduation is only planting another seed to grow

THE GAMBLE

Life is but a gamble fraught with danger
Gambling every day
What you're willing to wager
Is what life will pay

If you demand
That it pay you more
Or pay you less
You must move the pieces
In the mortal game of chess

So put your money down
Put your life on the line
Accept the reward as earned
And don't regret and whine

For if you choose
To beg and borrow
Hoping for much more
You're destined for the sorrow
Sibilant sounds of a whore

Put your money down
Put it on the line
If you wager for a crown
I hope you risk more than a dime

(continued)

For if your gamble is too small
And it doesn't justify your wants
For pity you will fall
Into the heap of the has been debutants

To profit more than you sought
Make your effort with all you've got
Put it on the line with faith
You will receive what
You gambled knowing risk can wait

Beyond waiting for the beginning
Ending the feeling of elusive happiness
Gambling in life is for winning
Instead of fearful stress

Reminiscent of the line that said
"I gambled life for a penny
And life would pay no more"
I Gambled life with thoughts of winning

And many rewards await galore

A HUMAN DICTIONARY

LOVE is the translation of emotions into words

HATE is the venting of frustration into action

FREEDOM is the sense of accomplishment after all seems lost

FAMILY is the roots for stability and the wings for reproduction and passion for life

HAPPINESS is the something of which the unhappy search for and the loving find

HUMILITY is the confidence of what you are

AMBITION is the need to be loved

DOMINANCE is the fear of being least

MEEK is the fear of being more

INSENSITIVITY is a peacock without feathers

FAITH is the knowledge and the wisdom that mortals perish to but another form, space and time (continued)

GOD is the symbol of why we exist of why we persist and why we desist as did Christ for his followers

(continued)

BELIEF is silent faith put into words

BAD is the selfishness to be good with a reason

*CHOICE is the reason for being good or bad
by thinking of the consequences*

*HUMANS are God's way of saying that time matters,
that space matters, that life matters and that dust scatters
to another place where energy returns to matter*

TIME is man's invention to put a frame upon the film of eternity

**SOUL IS OUR GUIDE AND ETERNAL
FLAME ON THE TRIP TO FOREVER**

HARDSHIP is not a test it's a state of mind

HELL is an illusion to be avoided

*HEAVEN is that worldly place where the
lover's reside and the hater's subside*

SATAN is the wizard of Oz in the land of morality

SCIENCE is man's study of other person's creation from fiction

PRAYER is the purest form of self-realization

(continued)

WORK is each man's expression of himself…
a penny earned is a penny no more …
a purpose is worth far more …
an investment in health is wealth forever more

DREAMING is the mental picture of a person's potential

CREATIVITY is putting that potential to work

GOALS are the inspiration to a hungry soul

SANITY is the will to avoid insanity

PLANNING is the visualization of the future and a legacy of the past

SADNESS is the inability to thrill at the break of a new day

SEXUALITY is the need to be accepted by another for passion not reason

WORDS are the output of the feelings put in

DESTINY is yesterday becoming today as you want it to be tomorrow

LIFE is the fruit, death is the seed so the fruit shall live again

HEREAFTER is the soil into which the soul is planted

(continued)

HOPING is the goal that was never executed

CHILDREN are the regeneration of destiny

HISTORY is a person's interpretation of man...what can be more difficult and less precise ... read it as such and not be misled

FUTURE is the past relived for those that disbelieve

CYCLE is the end tethered to the beginning with infinity as its span

INFINITY is man's explanation of that he cannot explain

POETRY is the expression of what cannot be said in one sentence or one mood or one word

READER is the believer in others and their thoughts

WISDOM is the wish to be better than before and more than hereafter

YOU are a journey not a destination ... start positive stay positive and you will finish with happiness and prosperity

CHARACTER

Character is what a blind man begs
In his darkest conceits
A cripple has in his legs
A dreamer in his defeats

Given that, no character is from living
But must be gained
Through pain and giving

Then only those that suffer
Can make a claim
On pain and Character

Building a character flaw
May result in the creation of
A prison not a Cathedral

Be careful that your painful decision
Doesn't draw you in
And imprison your indolent passion

That could gain conjecture
About your entrance to the hall of fame
Of a Cathedral to your Character

For overcoming blindness, darkness
Crippling disease and defeats
Is the true Statesman of greatness

As recognition always comes later
Then ambition

THE MOVIE HOUSE

On the corner of that square
That square life I lived
Was the Saturday Matinee
At the movie house there
In that small world of corn and hay

To us that matinee became the only
Glimpse of the outside world
We didn't expect much being homely
In those younger days hair uncurled

It was like animated happiness
As we went through the motions
The luxuries the darkness
were faceless notions
With aspirations tall or small

So as the opportunity met us
Each Saturday to watch our heroes
Doing and acting we reined the horse's nose
Sitting there holding off the heartless foes

With lights flashing across our
Faces till we were hypnotized
We felt ourselves lifted out of horror
From nothingness into a bigger size

(continued)

We sat on the horses and stood
Against the blazing weapons and Indian scouts
Pretending we were the guy that was good
For being bad was to die at the movie house

When we left by the back door
I can remember
Feeling good and feeling more
As I became the hero that November

Away from the smell of adventure and popcorn
Where it didn't take long for reality to
Set in. It was there as we got home reborn
Just in time to bike and sequester
My delivery of the Des Moines Register

Papers with headlines today
That read about a society and
Its requiem far far away
For you see there were no grand
Heroes in Indianola Iowa'y

Just a Movie House on Saturday

SLIPPING ON A SEX APPEAL

Sixteen with bases to steal
Slipping and sliding without a sound
I slipped on a sex appeal
Tossed me up and brought me down

Got me spinning like a wheel
Slipping and sliding on a sex appeal
Don't know why, but you looked me in the eye
And all I could think was let's go fly

We were on separate fields
You with your baton and me with my steals
Got me slipping and sliding on a sex appeal
You were fifteen and I was one year more
We bit the apple to the very core

I don't know whether you've ever known
How I feel
Slipping and sliding on sex appeal
Well, our love grew and become very real
It became more than sex reveal

(continued)

It opened the door
It opened our heart
It opened the conception to our four
Children, the true treasures of our shaky start

And though the wedding bells did peel
And our vows did seal to never part
For many years we were even keel
Slipping and sliding on sex appeal

But the true meaning came to us in babies
A sweet family growing from ifs and maybes
It is now, it is today and the way I feel
It all started from slipping and sliding on sex appeal

I am a steal and you are the sex to peal

BORN TO BE

Set upon the world as of no means
From a family proud to have pork and beans
So what you rightly say
So were we

That's right you were but were you to be

I've found no rest for it won't let go
Like the gazelle that can't go slow
Wanting all the more mind over matter
Seeking the fame that egos flatter

From those modest beginnings came desire
Like the burning bush created fire
No amount of hope can replace that will
Committed to perfecting abnormal skill

(continued)

Born to be the most by being the least
Creating these poems awareness increased
Living for more there is no limit
Striving to attain life's phantom summit

Simpler still are the answers needed
Wants new found and expectations exceeded
Knowing of this beautiful perpetual growth
Are goals attained for all are both

Born to be you see isn't free
It takes effort kindled from inside of me
You may not want it quite badly enough
But I do I will I've got that stuff

Called enough is never enough
To Be born Free

SALUTE THE RECEIPE OF GREATNESS

Salute the sailor tailor baker and undertaker
Banker flanker teacher and preacher
They're so different in what they do
But aren't they alike isn't it true
Their chance is to be great like you can too

Given the opportunity of abundant freedom
We all have that expedient idiom
In a setting pleading for leaders
Saluting the helpers, punishing the bottom feeders
So what is the formula eluding the pleaders

It is naked in its simplicity don't you see
Hidden within each man is the recipe
As Christ told the Holy Ghost to be the most least be
Don't ask for attention but give in peace
Yourself to your service then feast

For all is those who don't fall
Nor hit the unfaithful wailing wall
Purging their ego deceased
Removing baggage it's unleashed
Having faithful cargo as the priest

Where least is more and more is least

SUNDAY MORNING

Feels great, till I remember I'm late
Getting up from a night on the town
There's no scorning darkness on Sunday morning
Coming down

From a week of highs and lows
About which nobody knows
But me no one to agree
With but me

Waiting for others to arrive
There's no burning like yearning
Alone for some elusive high five
Left to Sunday morning, less discerning

Feeling less alive, as time stands by
No telling why
Sundays made afraid
Make me cry

While the world wants to play
Until church chimes start to toll

There's no stillness like a Sunday's
Tired soul

(continued)

Blood turns to rock and roll
Thoughts of fun ... father and son
Seven days unfold
Before it's all done

Getting my mate to fool around
Thoughts of responsibilities can wait
Just goofing off I found
There's no day in Sunday late

Sunday night should be the peak
Bolster the strong, inspire the weak
If it's romance that we seek ... if not
Sunday morning of next week

Won't be unique

THE DRIVE-IN MOVIE SHOW

Rocking' and boppin' and looking cool
Goin' to the movies after school
Slick back duck tail hair
Jeans by the pair

White "T" shirts
And great big skirts
All these would go
To the drive-in movie show

Getting' there in time to park
Lookin' for love in the dark
With sweet and sour girls
Pettin' and neckin' to other worlds

If we had the dollar to pay
Night time fantasies came our way
At the drive-in movie play
That we couldn't find during the day

(continued)

Kissing and cuddling was free
The car was slanted up wind
On a screen not easy to see
As you impress your girl friend

Or staying out late on the go
At the drive-in movie show
Featuring the stooges all aglow
Shemp, Larry and Moe

Cause for a few coins
There in Des Moines
You could be on par
Making love in your car

Not far from a movie star

DUCK'S UPON THE POND

Winter is over and the ducks are upon the pond
They've landed there on their way back to their summer home
A sight of silence oh so fond
Bringing down the urge to run or roam

Calm yes they are so calm
Not seemingly bothered by the blowing wind
Like sketching lifelines on the palm
It is their swimming that motions blend

Beautiful, yes it is so beautiful
No movement is quite so lovely
As the feather or the hull
Breaking water a majestic symphony

Graceful, yes they are so graceful
As they proudly circle their world
Brimming my eyes are full
Waiting for their wings to be unfurled

Up, they are rising up
Breaking the peace
Flailing flailing for stability
Shaking off their downy fleece

Setting flight too bad it had to be
That duck's on the pond must be set free
Ascending away from me

Until next year when they return to captivity

A LITTLE PIECE OF ME

A little piece of me
Died last night
When I heard
On the car radio
That the King was dead

In a daze
I pulled the car over
Not being able to see
Through the rain
That covered my world

Somehow the sadness
Came in flashes
As I thought back
To my younger days
When the King was hope

He was something
For those that were nothing
Representing fame
And fortune
For those that merely cope

(continued)

Rags to riches
Elvis was
A little piece of me

The world will mourn
Until it forgets
To remember
The good ole days
When we had no regrets

His records play and
At every turn
Many salute
His memory
Making history his eulogy

A legend a King
A very mortal man
Passing our way
That caught the
Ear of destiny taken from me

Rags to riches
Elvis was
A little piece of me

(continued)

Maybe somehow
For it never ends
We can meet

And he will sing
About a later fete

About angels
About the future
And our set of wings
Which swish away
The clouds that used to be

So take a little piece of me
Along with you King
It's yours to save
Until we meet again
And on our way we will sing

"Rags to riches
Robes and stiches
Fate is Elvis' cemetery
RIP a little piece of me"

THE HOLE IN MAN'S EXISTENCE

Man's existence consists of tangible
Touchable
Quantifiable
Experiences

The hole in man's existence
Is in his despair for himself
He doesn't seem to be able to accept himself
To be himself as he wants to be
And love himself

Man's existence seems to be dependent upon
How he perceives others reacting to his pretense
Many never fill this hole in their insistence
Many never become fulfilled
Because of this hole in their existence

To fill the hole requires thought, study, education,
Competence, fulfillment of one's aspirations
To some the filling of the hole
Is best served through a chemical
Through a crutch
Through a fantasy world
Through an escape to mental illness

The hole only gets bigger and bigger
The reasons for existence become less precise
Becomes less meaningful
There is no pride in the purpose of living
So to be able to deal with life to its fullest
That Hole in our existence becomes ourselves

(continued)

It must be filled
It must be fulfilled
Through our acts
Through our thoughts
Through our beliefs
And this must be persistent
Consistent driving desire to fill the hole
For one day there will be a relinquishment
Of effort

That day will fall prey to doubt
To grow and grow and to expand
The hole in our existence
And the hole, as it grows and grows
Must be filled either spiritually or chemically
It shall forever be calling us to its attention
Either through the smiles and joy of fulfillment
Or through the cries and pain of doubt
The filling of the hole of man's existence
Can be seen in his face and in his eyes
And in his livelihood

Praise be those who fill the hole
With their work, family and spiritual belief
Forgive those and help those
Who fail unto themselves by failing to fill the hole
With work on themselves

By being holy, happy and able to change

THE INNER GAME OF LIFE

On the outside life goes on
Everyone and everything is different as each dawn
Is it really true can we really say
That no feels like you except on Judgment day

It seems we all start with the same
With bones and all that stuff
And the rest that makes a frame
The unseen is for the mind to bluff

By playing a role that may not be true
If this be true and I'm sure it is
The only difference between me and you
Is the theatrics and some show biz

This is the inner game I speak of
The very essence of people
And whether they push or shove
Or stand in reverence to the steeple

I've heard it said the mind is the man
And to that belief I am wed
All the rest is heart and will to stand
And a command for life until dead

As for The Outer game
I want to be good not misunderstood
I want to be different not the same
Be that my judge for which I stood

And my mind will go to any extent to that advent

SIMPLE LOVE

(I love Shari)

No sentiment can give you peace
It can only inspire you to care
Ironically to love is to find peace
And to love requires caring enough to seek peace
Nothing other than simple love can express these sentiments

I once called life complex
I gave it far more credit for turmoil than was warranted
It dictated my thinking about you
Now as I'm older I realize you are more complex than life
Because you need me...if you didn't it would be a
simple matter of giving into your interests in me
But this would not inspire caring in either of us
And our attempt at love would die

No amount of innocence can give you truth
It can only place you above guilt
So to be of simplicity without truth
Tells us little about love or guilt in a life of complex thoughts
With no romance from reality

I used to think of love as an abstract process with no tangible place in time
Unlike passion which was needed daily for the sustenance of ego
Now for my own reasons I can clearly know love in words
In work and in my priorities at all times

It is now very simple...love is our thoughts
And YOU are a simple expression of that love

THE KISS OF LIFE

Soft as a butterfly's wing
As startling as a cobra's sting
As wet as a mountain's spring
And as rich as a cello's string

A mortal's kiss is everything

It makes the senses blur
And the blood stir
While the passions sing
With her lips her everything

My mind is always kissing her

As soft as a butterfly's wing
As startling as a cobra's sting
As wet as a mountain's spring
And as rich as a cello's string

Her kiss of life is everything

(continued)

Mouth in emotion meets with me
Luscious lust and ecstasy
Fevers high and certainly
She's so close she's lost in me

Her kisses define chastity

Softest lips and skin so warm
Temperature's up before the storm
Kiss and dwell before you're free
Back below inside of me

Loving lust and ecstasy… she is

As soft as a butterfly's wing
As startling as a cobra's sting
As wet as a mountain's spring
And as rich as a cello's string

My everything

IF YOU DARE

Taking a dive into deep water
Going to the very bottom
Requires ample fodder
If you don't want to succumb

To being in over your head
Then coming up too fast
Sucking air instead
Of being able to last

For after having been there
And fortunate to survive
All that is left to care
Is staying alive

No maybes, wings and prayers
Work any longer
When tires need spares
And nightmares grow stronger

Yes, shooting the rapids
Takes skill and strength

(continued)

But business isn't for kids
As experience is the breadth to length

Of life handling strife
Taking risk when choosing a wife
And negotiating the deep six
Much deeper as debt takes it's licks

While attorney's don't get any cheaper
If you don't care to beware
Just talk to some grim reaper
Who's been stuck there

You will know them
By their frowns of despair
And the breathless way
They're taking a dare

Holding on to a prayer

STRUCK BY FRIGHTENING

Standing on the porch of insanity
Hoping for the best
Holding a financial torch to our quest

Lightning down in the chest
Yes, struck by a bolt of Frightening
God life is a test

Torched even our nest
The courts called it bankrupt
The business world looked down its vest

The choice we chose
Took all of our personal possessions
Even our Sunday clothes

With bankers manning their stations
Over our carcass
Tearing at the bone like foes

A future struck by frightening
Hope is dead off its feet
Struck by defeat

(continued)

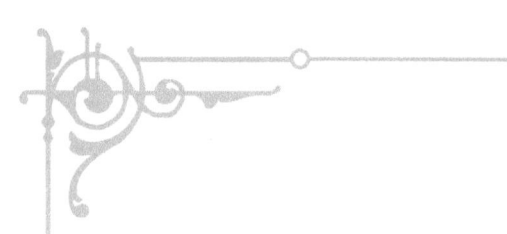

But our life is not over
Nor is our opportunity dead
For we will start over instead

If and when this happens again
We will know how
To negotiate a win

By lightening of our load
Struck by belt tightening
Frightening can implode

Killing our desire to explode

SHOOT THE MOON

I'm setting my goals and shooting the moon
Ignorance is bliss and an eagle feels no fear
Look chance in the eye
Set out for the moon

Some say
I'm going too far
But ironically we're not talking a star
We're talking of life
We're taking the aim of a human being
Playing his own game
The game of how far will I throw
How far will my spear go
How hard will I try

Take on the wind, the headwind, the cloudy sky
For the dusk cannot choke my cry
When it's the flight you comprehend
Understanding that it is effort
That it does hurt
To soar from the ground to the highest port
And the fear of failure thou resort

If ignorance is bliss
Be naïve, but even though you may miss
It's where you are that proves you achieve
Achieving more than those who dare not shoot

THE MOON AND GRASP THEIR STAR

Pursuing the career as far as it will go
And even though it may fall short of what others call too tall
It still is beyond the others who failed to answer the call
To spread their wings
To fluff their feathers

And love the chance of the whole
The thrill of chance on the flight of the goal
To the moon like a new lover's romance
Falling short is to accept the chance
As a solid character
I'll take the shot again
On a higher vector
Into the uplifting wind

Taking it on its path to home
For the only fear is the aftermath
And atonement is to the self alone
For this flight, this love of living big
Doesn't and shouldn't shed any starlight
Beyond the shooter's renege

(continued)

For the effort of life is not thrown for fellow man
They're not to fulfill a wife or to make an enemy understand

They're just for the fulfillment of self
To the will to live
Stepping to each higher wealth
By taking the steps to give
And emboss your shot
To give a clearer view
From the vantage of the cross

That is the reason for shooting true
And following through
And bowing the head
Taking life and the patronage due

Before my goals are dead
And the chance to get there is misled

SOMEDAY

Someday I'll go
Someday I'll be free
Someday You'll know
Because I won't be me

Someday tomorrow after school
When feelings begin to cool
And I'll not be dumb
Someday will it ever come

Someday is a tranquilizer
Someday I'll be wiser
and satisfied
Someday it'll be a smoother ride

Or is someday just being
Deaf and dumb not seeing
That someday the excuse of people
Is the church not the steeple

Before which people bow
Because they don't know how
To make someday brand new
Finally come true

As the epitome of the real you

I'M FIRED

I woke to that morning glare
With relief in my heart
The nagging emptiness was no longer there
It seemed as if my life was about to start

Paul came in and said "good morning"
"How to you feel"
"How are you handling this mourning"
"Sit down and have a good meal"

"I slept great" I said
"I really feel good, it must be the bed"
"It's as if I'm free for the first time"
"Not depressed not counting my crime"

The look that Paul and Carol gave me
Was of disbelief
Thinking I'm surely
Lost my good senses overcome by grief

I assured them that I was rational
That the best had happened to me

(continued)

That whatever came to pass to no avail
Was most certainly meant to be

I then related the story of that morning
As I sat on the edge of my bed
My prayer said thank you for defining
My future not just help me instead

As I left Paul at the airport
He shook my hand and smiled
And he said good luck as a retort
I could feel our purpose was reconciled

To meet this next challenge
With renewed dedication
Not asking God for vestige
But thanking Him for the separation

Fired by myself
With an attitude that knew it was time
For my own mental health
I created the situation to align

My insurrection with
Justice and the crime

DARE TO BE YOU

You, you're something its decreed
You are you have you want, you need,
You love you cry you feel
You are a spirit thus created to be real

You are what you are no repeal
That's a person you feel
But as long as you don't you can't
If you waste for wants you shan't

Why not say that you are
That you can
Shout it to the sky and
To your fellow man
Dare to be you ... moon or star

Without this, your very special identity
You shall fly in the breeze of anonymity
Take it upon yourself to break out
Of, the self-made shell and shout
I'm me not alone I am
More than a drone

I am special look at me
My acts shall speak with humble clarity
Do you feel the spiritual State
Overwhelming your mindless hate
Of yourself your brother and
Your former fate

(continued)

Why not say that you are
That you can
Shout it to the sky and
To your fellow man
Dare to be you ... moon or star

I know from myself with half a chance
You can shake that frightful trance
Catapulted to more dreams to prance
Self-made peace left to enhance

Yourself because you are your own
This is the dare
Like the gentle air
It comes with the summer breeze or
Winter's freeze and
Love to squeeze
Be secure to know so much is your
Thoughts impure
That no else can have
Like finger prints your mental half
Dare to be you

Something special something new
Like the Bible holds to be true
God created that special you

Only if you are daring to be you

MATCH POINT

The game of tennis
The game of life
So different
Yet so alike

I was down on myself
Feeling lost from what
I thought I was
Putting much importance
Upon my ego

Then I surmised
Why should I live this mood
Why not relax
And look ahead
Let life happen
Because it will

It will happen
In spite of illusions
So I suppressed my ego
And resolved to be humble

(continued)

Then to the surprise
Of my shuttered perception
I observed a peaceful
Contentment
It was another day
The court was no longer
A battle ground
For the bigger ego

The conditions were right
The sun was hot
The competition stiff
And I was the underdog
But peace had its grips
Around my subjective mind
It wouldn't let go to my ego

I relaxed
I was winning that inner game
With myself
From the first moment
That my opponent arrived

Looking grim
I knew I had learned something
I was not worried about him
The match point was played

Before we started
I had the win
Having committed
That match point sin

GULLS ALONG THE SHORE

Angling along the beach
Those silhouettes make the peace
With a sign you cannot teach
Emerging from beneath the crease

Separating our touch from God's reach

Timeless shadows sketching trails
Gulls winging along the sand
Grains counting untold tales
For prior days missing land

Placing the present in the painter's hand

Torn down is just the dawn
Passing this scene marks history
Day by day we've passed it on
Only fences link us to another destiny

Forming the last as first for eternity

Old are the gaps filled with moments
Scrolled into a diary kept by Him
Look to the songs and the sonnets
Answers are awaiting from within

Telling erstwhile stories by the minutes

(continued)

Painted knolls along the shore
Swept by tides for ages past
Awaiting the future, expecting more
Realizing that mortals are but matter cast

Beating against the eclipsing metaphor

Godless would be the descent
For the grasses do not grow
Without an eye to give consent
And trained to look for seeds that sow

Feigning flight, the brush depicts the scheme

Gulls along the shore
Swooping towards the mortal limit
Never asking what's in store
Only striving to caress the summit

Hallowed be the smallest condor
Chasing gulls along the shore

LOST AND LONELY

Looking for a place to lite
Roosting in spite of fright
Hiding in the thicket alone
Frail but too strong to moan

Lost from warmth of mate
Avoiding hunter's bait
Can the survival abide
A desire to live is cried

Most those lost and lonely
Creatures not humans only depleted
Feelings hurt without companion
Fear for self isn't heeded

Chances taken safety deplored
Life at last pride restored
Most of success we consent
Results from effort not misspent

(continued)

Likely it's the lost and lonely
Waiting to express it boldly
With a heart born to strife
Making a way in spite of life

Ignoring odds for or against
Asserting hard earned stints
Are you lost are you alone
Look for a message etched in stone

From the person that started last
Poor and down no fortune massed
Efforts to be best was dared
Feelings controlled shortcuts spared

Do you replace pain with love for living
Looking for bigger no fear of giving
Believing that Jesus set us free
To find heaven and never be

Lost and lonely

HOW FAR TOO GO

How far to go from now to then
To make this trip is on my mind
For time and space we comprehend
But life's ending we can't unwind

How far to go from here to there
To make the trip without a map
Is to cry without despair
Since inevitably our lives must overlap

How far to go from love to hate
Those that love have got to know
Feelings strong don't dissipate
They just seem to bloom and grow

How far to go from fair to unfair
The sky the wind the human heir
Scant be the secrets for the answer
Look to the eyes with depth of stare

(continued)

How far to go from habit to trait
Desire and lust embeds the gap
When released they open the gate
Fill the gap and you release the trap

How far to go from fear to scare
Making the passage will not detect
But much for the experience there
That a meaningful life likely can expect

Making the right move not too late
Because I'm wide awake
As I now live for love not hate
With a positive mental state

On a trip to another fate
If I don't procrastinate

SUNSTROKE

The sun banks off its morning turn
Gliding into its straight away
The heat of its inertia
Warms all that face it

Beating perspiration from
The pores that worship it on Saturday
In spite of air conditioning and shade trees
Fleshed fantasies absorb the
Rays, for the week to come is dull

But on Saturday night they
Are beautiful in white sport
Coats and clean hair
Bleached and tan to cavort
Pair by pair

Others do it for a reason
With mind games
About love or lost successes
Laying first on one side
Then back to the other
Like toast on a spit
Crumbling as they're
Blanched of youth by wrinkles

(continued)

Seeking the sun
As the only place
Left untouched by the unrelenting
Spikes of light that are the souls
Of poets

Even sexuality dies
Nothing to escape the penetration,
Nor does it rest
As bodies are exposed

The weekend worship is left
Not to theology but to the icon that rises
In the East and sets in its conquest
Of beaches appearing
That disappeared the night before

On Sunday, minds again bake to the glare until
Nothing makes any difference
Lazy eyelids shut down productive
Thoughts as if retarded…it's the
Self-inflicted sunstroke disregarded

(continued)

As the blankets became damp and
The spirit of self-indulgence
Gives in to the cool night air

There's no beauty left
As we pack up a
Misspent day in our wet towels
After our summer sun is gone

We spent weekends and one whole summer
Losing ourselves this way
Memories are better now that
We've found better things to invoke
Having recovered from the decay
And lost feeling of the sunstroke

Beating us down into the sunset of our lives

STARTING OVER

STARTING OVER

Crashing down around my dreams
Came past indiscretions
Returning, as fate somehow redeems
My failure in human decisions

But I learned by starting over
And looking back at what went wrong
That the future isn't any colder
And today is where I belong

By pulling the past along behind me
Step by step up that hill
The strain of it let me see
That effort isn't just a function of will

It is more: it is my critics who helped destroy
By standing along the gauntlet
To make their mark in the employ
Of justice becoming my regret

It is the rebuilding year becoming two
And the horizon focusing clear
Flying into a future more true
On a wing, toughened by deploying fear

(continued)

So dawn came from the night
With devastating thoughts of scuttling it all
Giving me arms to fight
Against one's own fatal fall

For no time is quite so overwhelming
As the time before the time to act
With the odds all seeming
Against the will to come back

As the new flight searches the sky
But with each small inch to gain
The ground passes by
And away falls the immediate pain

Then is when the subtle reality
Comes to breed satisfaction
Bringing with it the decree
That the past is just the start of a new destination

Setting me free
As a reincarnation
Of why we are thee
When restarting creation

With renewal being the jewel

TAKE MY HAND

Take my hand help me hold on
To what you're expecting
Touching leaves my soul in your grasp
Your warmth is addicting

Though you've always wanted me
I'll never know you better
Than right now as you
Find me in your need

Parting I didn't know then but
Your commitment grew
Out of desire into seeking me
More than you could want me

Until then your possession
Was passion not as love occurs
So give me your hand for
Better or for worse not just words

(continued)

Departed we will not
Have our hands to hold
And the warmth that we sought
Will grow cold

But by truly touching me
Together committed to a new start
Will regenerate our goal to be
That life shall never do us part

Take my hand hold on at last
To what you're expecting
Touching leaves my soul in your grasp
Your warmth is addicting

As you bring me back to
You with your need – give
Me your hand
As our desire has agreed

That divorce is not yet decreed

IN BETWEEN

Love me
Or hate me
But never in between

Hold me
Or reject me
But don't be mean

For I'm only
Here for a little while
Give me your smile

And hold me
Before we start
Show me how

To Love you
From in between
Your love and my heart

(continued)

If I'm left in between
Now and ever
I will careen

To my urge
To love or hate you
From that limbo tween

Knowing that a certain Love
With no time to hate
Takes me from in betwixt

To your urge to hold me
Not reject me
And embrace me in between

Love means never to be mean

MORE THAN A FLEA

Why me
What can be
Less deserving
Than a flea

Fleas are there
Not by chance
If there's hair
Watch them dance

If I am
Can it be
I'm no different
Too blind to see

With no purpose
Scratching hits me
At the surface
Alas I'm more

I'm off the floor
Let me go
An open door
As I leave

(continued)

My small abode
It's a lily
I'm a toad
Why me

Simple yet
As a goad
You can bet
No King of the road

Oh so fond
Will I stay
On this pond
God I pray

Don't close the door
That some day
I'll be more
Than just the prey

Why me
As graves are dug
The toad won't be
A water bug

(continued)

Alive, I'm seeing
What a chance
As a human being
I could sing and dance

Bigger yet I advance
Don't you know
With circumstance
Your pond can grow

There's no doubt
From a flea I flee
With a voice left to shout
Why me

This toad could have been
Much more than a flea
By being the next of kin
On a bigger water lily

Isn't this silly

DRONES

Look up from the bottom down under
Show your light sound your thunder
Drone's aren't supposed to glow
Only Kings and Queens are though

But give those drones half a chance
Against odds that follows the trump
And they'll take up the shield and the lance
Battling to pull themselves up

True grit and guts are theirs
For the struggle as they weather
Oblivious of fright and void of scares
Trust binds them all together

Push them down and watch them rise
Seeking position above their sires
Block their view and blind their eyes
This inspires and prompts desires

Against suppression of what's right
Just because you've started small
A social plight can lead the fight
Has no bearing on growing tall

(continued)

Don't waste it as a drone thought forlorn
Grip the rungs and make the climb
This is the opportunity to be reborn
Out of brine toward the sunshine

To us struggling destined drones
Stand aloof as you must
But don't cast vicious stones
At downing the unjust

Creatures blessed be you're right
But fight comes from within
To strive for better with all your might
The will to win is no sin

So stand up and cheer
Scaling upward with your career
It takes courageous Drones to steer …
Clear of terror and fear

As the Queen feasts on drones
And the King will disappear

THE BREAK-UP

When I was young
And full of blood
Thinking I was
A virtual stud

I came across
A prancing mare
With a coat so fair
And the heat was there

We nuzzled in
And we nuzzled out
We grazed each other
All about

She was my life
She was my only
Choice for future wife
A reason to not be lonely

Had we not nor
Had we been
Someone more
Than just a friend – it was a break-up

(continued)

The break was fast
And it was hard
Thought to last
But it was marred

Marred by loss of trust
With no other lust
Even though unjust
The tithes began to bust

The break it came
Time had to come
As our need was lame
It was done

Break-ups never breakeven

I didn't write
I didn't speak
About our love
That beseeched a peek

She did not write
We did not speak
About our break
That made me weak

(continued)

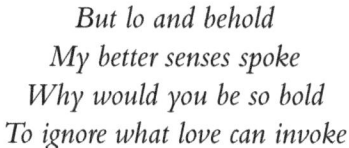

But lo and behold
My better senses spoke
Why would you be so bold
To ignore what love can invoke

She came back from that place
I thought was now or never
Taking my disgrace
And making it a favor

The ring made the difference
It said to her
That our life made more sense
When we're together

Now 55 years later
With 4 children
And 12 grad children that matter
We realize now and then

That our break up
Wasn't misery
But a fateful makeup
Of our life's history

Break-ups never breakeven

Now it is more evident
With great grandsons to savor
The most recent event
That says we were braver

To be together as bird and a feather

A MUSHROOM HUNT

Being misled by the toadstool blooms
Found by sight as hope abounds
Have you ever hunted mushrooms
Among the moss upon the ground

Then it turns out from closer sights
That what you thought just isn't yet
Disappointed hopes retreat as security fights
A battle with nothing left it seems to get

The mushroom hunt can be a life
Misspent not looking for such a purpose
Seeking along the ground with poised knife
Ready to take what's on the surface

Blessed are those that ask for more
For once it's asked there becomes the will
To uncover ground for what's in store
Mushrooms that were there now and still

Reward those youngsters, doubt in spite
That possesses the skill to hunt at night
For to feel the truth beyond the sight
Fills baskets with mushrooms plenty ripe

(continued)

But in reality it takes heart
Exploring more than sight
The will to stop and start
Overcomes the fear
Of toad stools in the night

Lurking in the way of mushrooms tropes
Who put down what we dig from the ground
Could they poison our misspent hopes
Or be the killer of our next lost and found

Whether it is an adventure
Or just another quick encounter
With a joker or a preacher
Mushroom hunting isn't for winter

Unless you're the mushroom
And spring has taken the hunters
Into that summer gloom
So you can again resume

As the toadstool imposter's womb

HEAVEN'S LIGHT

In the East was a star
In the North was a pole
In the West was a war
In the South was a soul

With wind and rain
Ice and desert held them together
Snow and vane
Melting in the Spring with weather

Winter came to end the Fall
With fear that none could believe
Another fateful war to recall
Why men fight and women grieve

And forget to make family matter
A special birth for peace
Changed the world for better
Or worse unless wars cease

(continued)

But that star light with semen
Prevailed in the birth
So a few good men and women
Whose beliefs and acts lit the earth

Then Christmas became the omen
To convert others to this belief
That all men and women
Can be good despite their grief

So as long as the plight of man
In the East and the West war torn
Puts down its arms, so the North can
Save its own so the South can be reborn

On an earth whose savior is the sum
Of heaven's light and Kingdom Come

THE MIND IS GREAT

THE MIND IS GREAT

Aim high fly low
Think big act small
Shoot the Moon with your bow
Value time spend it as if its all

Help out, pitch in
Find freedom lose fear
Create solutions destroy the problem
Pursue outcome be an investor

Love thyself and thyself shall love
Say good day delay good bye
Dream for tomorrow from high above
Find a reason dwell in the clearing sky

Gain strength alleviate the strain
Grow mentally have a brain gain
Find your path erase your stain
Seek the positive implore the insane

Give fun a chance learn to dance
Live with nature and the law of attraction
Host a party hug your future's trance
Kiss your past and love your nation

The Mind is great but
The Heart should dictate

So the Soul has a mate before it's too late

WARLOCK

Is it just talk
Amongst the flock
That you've got power
To turn sweet to sour
With the force and cower
Of a warlock

They say that your songs
Can come true
As you sing
Making the bruise turn blue
From the warlock in you

It is said
You were fetched
From a rocky grave
Thought dead
Delivered from the
Womb stretched
Around your black soul
Into Satan's foal

(continued)

This birth
Of the warlock
The story goes
Brought down thunder
Around the will of Moses
The good fought hard
And God stood still

The Warlock rose to his command
Though scarred, the righteous man
Waited for the warlock's will
As fear crossed the land
With only the Devil to kill

In the East was God's star
In the North was his pole
In the West was his war
In the South was his soul

But Mankind had so declined
That the earth
If fate is so inclined
Needs another birth

And Jesus saved mankind
From the hoard and warlord

THE MIND IS THE PERSON

No man is more than his mind allows him to be
He is born with it for none to see
And once he's of an age to care
It becomes his cross to bear

While the parents influence what's there
Telling and yelling he becomes aware
And from that mind so pure
Comes to some the feeling insecure

For others it's just one constant blur
Because all come of age and it must occur
To become more with mortal skill
If we are of a mind to train its will

We'll find our heaven and avoid that living hell
So you see the person is the mind
With a solitude knowing we can
Being something not an also-ran

And reap rewards for many miles
For the mind, with well-trained styles
Will confront obstacles that come and go
As the harvest depends on the seeds we sow

If we do it midst the trials so designed
Living well or living unkind
The rest is for the person to tame
Skin and bones just make the frame

Then on Rushmore they may inscribe
A salute to the mind not just a person or tribe

WHO ARE YOU

Who are you bright or dark
What do you know
Make your mark
Before you go

Who are you
What do you say
Will your words be remembered
Someday

Will your purpose make history
Or misery
Will someone salute your name
Or will they spit on your memory
Then left as you came

And bury you memory
With you heading for the infirmary
And then forget to wave
Or even visit your grave

Now is for the endeavor
If but you react
And now is gone forever
Unless you express
Who you are
And what you know
As fact

Stand up in spite of flack
As your words portray the Act

THE ARTIST

Hail those daunting princes
Those haunting creatures of the spirit
Whose expression are feelings the senses
Emanating from inside don't you feel it

The hands, the heart all speak
When the artist takes you along
To that fantasy of life's drive and seek
Hoping to lift the weak and defend the strong

Aren't we all capable of much more
Than just existing for our time
I'm sure that's true just implore
Beyond yourself with my rhyme

Do you see yourself in a dream
Being something more than before
If you don't come along as it will seem
A trip into another scene is much more

(continued)

Bring your mind down to wanting
Wanting to express beyond this day
Looking to a legend so forever daunting
What you left for history to play

The artistic memories are the windows
Understand it's not for the self
It's for later when no one knows
Why you lived but eyes will help

This is the legend that the artist seeks
A page of tomorrow's memories
Not just leaving a pile of dust for freaks
To scatter much less matter for the eye to see

Do it for them write it draw it persist
Voice it express it is no crime
Just do it as a rhyme
To be the Artist

And Writer of all time

PROUD

Our standing in life with the judge
Is marked by what we give
Many will come and those gates won't budge
To those empty hearted with no reason to live

Blessed be those mortals that glow
Glow like stars in the night
Having left in their paths to sow
The particles of themselves so slight

As parents and the fore bearers
You cleared the way for your heirs
They will remember you as theirs
And as the heritage of all their cares

Proud, you should be very proud
Of what you have given to history
That mortal being shouting from the crowd
It's your offspring meant to be

(continued)

To be or not to be that is the reward
Endowed upon the good for deeds
Not those living by the sword
Directed towards immoral creeds

Thanks for the memory
Of visions to be great
Without fear of frailty
And creating a faithful legend not too late

Take the credit you deserve
And pat your pride be satisfied
For you've earned the righteous nerve
To say I've been I've had I've tried

Proud that my Children are my rib my side

NO LUNCH BUCKETS ALLOWED

Dad I can't take that lunch bucket
They'll make fun of me
I don't want to be different can't buck it
When you're going to school at my age
You're playing a role hidden back stage

So dad don't make me take that darn ole' bucket
Cause I'll heave it rather than truck it
Come on son it doesn't matter
Life is learning to go your own way
Even though your critics say stay

Chin up son swallow your pride
It matters more what you've got inside
You've got us behind so confide
In our experience pressure will subside
We've never lied or been defied

(continued)

*So take along that lunch bucket
This'll show me and them you don't have to duck it
Ignore them when they say "no buckets" now chuck it*

*For one of those days you'll be proud
As one of those hecklers follows you in
Carrying their new lunch bucket of tin*

*Then you've set yourself up to be something special
For those lost followers will follow your deal
So tear down those signs saying "no lunch buckets allowed"
By doing what's right and it'll be more then endowed
For before you know it it's your crowd ... aren't you proud*

*To lead by planting a dynamic seed
While the followers kowtowed*

CHICAGO

I'm a transplant to this city
Not too smart not too witty
Brought here by chance what a pity
Broke without a kitty

Fostered by a budding career
Pushed there going here constant scare
Not taken to look beyond each New Year
Afraid to face tomorrow's fear

Fighting for some identity
Hoping for more than anonymity
Shouting into the crowd's infinity
I am I said Chicago look at me

But you ignored my younger cries
I had to gather and epitomize
A bigger person much more wise
Aimed at being about your size

Conquer you size yes I must
Intimidated but feeling just
Praying for the opportunity to thrust
Myself upon your granite truss

(continued)

Creating the feeling of solitude
Using my pen to reduce your magnitude
And in respect not necessarily rude
Challenging you with my aptitude and attitude

Your majesty don't weaken wither or die
For believing that Man in the sky
The reason for being is wondering why and
Existence isn't unless you try before you die

So take me for my mortal birth
Upon your mighty girth
While some may have just mirth
I for one know what I am worth

Praise be to Chicago not foe not friend
But my city for whom I have been
Myself so my mental health can mend
The virtual health to other men

Friend to friend

THE OCTBER GIRLS

Sharon
Christie
Kimber
Dorotha
Leigh
Celena

October girls
They are the pearls
Around my neck

Like the Autumn leaves
They are what life achieves

Before the winter snows
They are the warm breeze that blows

And after the New Year
They are always most dear

In my mind's eye they will never die
Always the blue in the fading winter sky

(continued)

Just before spring blooms
The October Girls' Flower looms

Into the upcoming summer time
As a part of this rhyme

Then here we are where we have been
With October births once again

Seasons come and go
But the October Girls are always so

Happy is the day
That the rest of us portray

As the Girls of October annually display
Beauty all the while
Style's array
Grace and a ready smile

Forever October girls will be guile

THE OLD CHILDREN – ANYMORE?

A fairytale is written and we are born
Created to be good not forlorn
As old children from society we will get
A future invariably set

These old children innocent as they are
Conceived in purity prone to scar
Scarred by vices of the civilized
Pushed and pulled and criticized

Minor as it may seem
Many of the old children no longer dream
Cause they never expect nor accept
Their fate as their will is wrecked

Don't we care about them anymore
Have we forgotten what's in store
As these old children are the core
Of past generations, then and evermore

(continued)

Be it our will to beat them down
We will pay with a thorny crown
Such a pitiful price to pay
For taking their will to live away

I hope and pray that we can save the old children
For one day it will be us waiting for what might have been
Hoping to save our aging mind
So future ages don't waste away much maligned

With the memory that old children are not to be confined…
We should realize what's in store or
Don't we care about the old children anymore
Without closing the door

By saving them forever more

THE SECRETS OF MY SOUL

The secrets of my soul
Take me
Have me whole
Uncover those secrets of my soul

Hidden down
Down so deep
Are the secrets
Made to keep

Filled with the good times
And the bad
Smiles and trials
Thoughts so sad

But since I've been
And now I'm glad
Cleansed of sin
I once had

Kept within somewhat cold
The secrets of my soul
Start to unfold
A virgin heart

(continued)

Left to wander
What I start
And to ponder
Why I can't yet depart

The more I try
Prone to pray
And to cry
OMG my hair is gray

The older I get
Between each sigh
I hold in regret
Why we die you and I

Before you fade away
So whisper myself in your ear
It's our way to display
And keep my secrets dear

And to then I bequeath
To you my goal
And release with relief
The very secrets of my soul

My purpose and my goal

SPRING OF OUR LIVES

As the sunshine fills the sky
Forget the winter let it die
As the snow recedes the land
Grasses unbend and begin to stand

Birds are seen from a distance south
Streams undone fill the mouth
Towards the blue they want to be
In striving to reach the sea

Small buds upon the branches appear
To greet a new day's sun more near
Flowers erupt all tones galore
Surging towards the light with frost no more

To wipe away the drab feature
Of winter's hibernating creature
A field held to be barren is turned, and
Lights up with the rays soil is churned

Held fallow during the lunar months
It becomes the pheasants run goodbye rabbit hunts
The building and fences are painted
To a new glow almost tainted

Odors become fresh and invigorating
So long are wood fires and ice skating
This instills new hope and vigor
As warm air fills sail and rigor

Allowing us all to earlier rise
In the morning and spring of our lives

THE STAR SHINES

The star of David shines forever
While wild roses wilt in a week
Beauty is a fleeting endeavor
But character is what we seek

A star shines in the night
While the fear of man holds on to the day
The will of God is touted for its might
While the pleasures of the Devil aren't soon to decay

The love that a panderer easily abuses
Or even the friendship Christian's adopt
The time on a sundial never loses
While the clock may suddenly stop

The star may fall to another time
As King of Kings whose name we shout
But he who falls to crime
Is the purveyor of the devil we flout

(continued)

So behold not just the beauty of the gold
Soon forgotten before we go
That the star shines forever bold
As the wild rose wilts in a day or so

But perceive the essence of the eternal creature
That is held in the heart of those unkind
Who look at a star as a mere feature
And a wild rose as the temporary sign

Of the mortal fear to confine
Our notion to such whims
Then praying for a grander sign
As wild roses grow once more upon their stems

Despite the devil's sins

THE STORY'S OLD

Listen closely
To what you're told
Don't you see
You're getting old

The story's an old refrain
Doesn't take any effort to get there
Graying hair, a bigger weight gain
Pound for pound I guess I don't care

Is health not self undone
Told by bodies hanging out
Hidden from the sun
And what this story's about

Despite a fallen mast and no chest
Yes about the health less
American first class
Who always knows best

Listen closely
To what you're told
Don't you see
You're finally too old

(continued)

Fallen down torches
No love affair
Sitting on porches
With a sightless stare

Not me mother
I got all this desire
I am really the brother
To sister fire

Telling stories anew
After others unfold
Because they knew
They were too old

A coop they never flew
Downed like a spent flier
For they never knew
Sister Fire

Nor her brother desire

THE TIME IS NOW

It is never too early for peace
It is never too late to pray for a truce

It is never too little to smile
It is never too much to keep in single file

There is never a wrong time for love
There is never a doubt that all comes from above

There is never a perfect thought
And never is there a wasted attempt sought

What time is never a good question of when
When do I is never time to take for then
Then is never a reason for asking how
How is next to never right to where
Where Is only timed by your clock

The who is you…the time is now for
Peace to increase
Love never to cease

War to cease and desist
A dove of fleece
Faith to persist
A prayer by Priest
For all to co-exist
Tick tock

The time is in our hands on the peace clock
Or plan for war for evermore

THE WAY WE ARE

The way we are
Lover's cannot describe
Through any poet or scribe
Only those alive
With sensitivity can contrive

All the contradictions
Heightens convictions
Reveal the way we are
But you stand back
Waiting to be a fact

In the way we were
Please come forward
Tell me in your word
About the way we are

The distance isn't far
From where we were
For life's not afar though distant
It's the way we are

(continued)

Loaded to my capacity
With your tenacity I'm not
So forget the way we were
If you want to be sure
That now will occur
Beyond what we could endure

As tomorrow is unsure
Not far from the way we were
Finding that we're never far
From that glowing star

With our name inscribed "we are"

THE YEAR OF THE LOCUST

The year of the locust
Leap year
An eclipsing moon
Sun spots dance
As the Yankees won
Singing Da Do run Do run

In the year called Heaven
By some
It's 1957
By gum
From those roots
Implanted came shoots
Of life not too slanted

Going straight
And couldn't wait
Meeting life and fate
Looking first rate
Into the eye of that date
With no hate

1957 was the year
To hold dear
Looking back
There's no fear
Cause it is now not then
And we're here
Songs are sung Do run Do run

(continued)

Wars to win
And Battles were won
Peaceful days would come
And then were done
'57 wasn't the year of the Hun
1957 wasn't the year of the rising sun
The Yankees hadn't won
And they weren't singing
Do run Do run

Though some of this song is a pun
1957 sure was fun
And was heaven to those
Who were in class eleven
With the name Sharon Kay I suppose
Not knowing that I would propose
A marriage to last and a family to compose

But every 17 years as the locust appears
I think of those doubts and fears
Counting all those memorable years
Moistened by forgiving tears

Emerging as careers and our peers

THIRTEEN

My my how the years go by

Bye bye sweet reality
Hello memories of what used to be
Thirteen came so fast it seems
Past me by now comes the teens

I loved her then now and when
Even tomorrow as she leaves the den
How can I forget those days
When her sweet face was all our praise

But I guess we all must live to endure
The years that are yet to be secure

My my how the years go by

Now it is her wedding day
And more than ever I pray
That she holds on to life
Much better as man and wife

Till they live
Until they die
With their own children
Wondering why
The years must go flying by

My my how those years go by

By the father of the bride
Swallowing his tears and pride

TOLL FREE

If life were a toll way
And we were to put a price
Upon what it costs to travel
That road what would be free

Would happiness be free
Would peace of mind be free
Would love be free
Would democracy be free
Would success be free
Would freedom be free

Or would they have a price
And would you in fact
Value these blessings
More highly than rings and things
Would you appreciate create inflate
The value of these caressing's

Until they mean something
More than a diamond ring and that material thing
So think of what you would cast aside
If your being hadn't been hadn't died
What you would regret not having tried
Would it be plastic pride

(continued)

Or the fruits of life and
What you are for free
For what you want to be
For what you will to be
For so long as you pay the fee
By believing in piety and the trinity

Amen, the toll is free
If you're happy happily
If you're at peace with humanity
If you're loving with sincerity
If you're faithful faithfully
If you're anti-demagoguery
If you are successful successfully

For you are free to be
What you want to be
Take it it's toll free

VALIANT CONCEPTION

The masses stand in reverence
To the idol looming big
Valiant as a saint we whence
Fragile as a lily's twig

Trussed against ego
The valiant fall
Tumbling down their route
Full of doubt
Forgotten valor another bout
With permanence as a world's sprout

Blossoms and love
Taste defeat
From push to shove
We are all crumbling feet

Stalks of talk
Put together sentences after the fact
Cancel our intent then we act
Gestures with fallen arms
Words spoken about intended charms

(continued)

Longing for understanding
Our fear makes us shallow and demanding
Until reality closes in
We revise our priorities
Never to return where we've been (called sin)

For life allows no reverse
Only fast forward
But to a newer day we traverse …
Valiant in renewed hope
Again standing in reverence
Allowed we cope
Cleansed again if we repent our life's sentence

For idols Gods Spirits Universal Images
Are not in our visual perception
But with life taking more iconic stages
We no longer can be valiant in deception

Toward our Savor of immaculate conception

Vision of A Better World

VISION OF A BETTER WORLD

Look towards the sky of tomorrow
Feast on the setting sun
Let us look for a better harrow
Swear not to human vanity undone

Find and seek the manner
To which the vision of a better world
Is in the heart of the planner
With an enterprising nation's flag unfurled

As politicians lose sight of the practical
Common sense and PEACE must prevail
If the common man is to scale obstacles
To a better version of the grander scale

Yet thus a third party will be formed
With its foundation of practical economics
As an answer and divorce of the elite's control scorned
Instead a modern form of enterprise must be the fix

With fewer divorces less crime
higher education higher employment
better GNP Better standard of living
Lower drug usage lower teen pregnancies

(continued)

More human resources
More affordable housing and fewer unwanted children
Yes my vision of a better world is in the heart of a mother
The hope of a grandmother not in the theory of diversion
By the pseudo intellectuals to their own ways and means

This vision is what I call Mancology
The Science of Managing Human Value in an enterprising society
This results in more human capital and less Government intervention
that will enhance our country's stature and influence worldwide

Let the established institutions laws and regulations
Redirect our energies into the livelihood of hard work
Family life and peaceful love for our fellow man
Replacing the negative forces
With positive opportunities of a better world
Or get rid of them

The unrelenting force of the underprivileged
Who will learn to work for Mancology
Will enact the vision of a better World
Until it's a better world to vote for
Free Enterprise not special interests
That benefit a few and are paid for by the many

The vision of a better world and a better mankind
Is downsize Government upsize Enterprise
A place that politicians can't seem to find

WALK ON MY HEART

Step by step
You walk on my heart
Foot by foot
You tear me apart

Time after time
You shrug at my soul
Inch by inch
You take your toll

No more room for love
My heart's been imprinted
Kicked and trampled
Till my arms dissented

Step for step
You walked on my love
Stride for stride
You were all I thought of

(continued)

But now to heal
I must run from your grasp
Hoping to steal
Memories that will last

Step by step
You walked on my dreams
Side by side
Now accents the crooked seams

If you walk a mile
In my jeans
With your fickle smile
You will know what it means

To be with class and style

WHAT ARE YOU WORTH?

A sweet rose isn't without thorns
On the beach of Eden
On the sands of time
On the virgin of Eve
We are born sinners

A dead rose has no thorns
East of Eden
West of Adam
North of Heaven
South of Hell
Where the angels dwell

With no thorns at all
Abraham, Peter and Paul
Virtues and sin for all
Waiting for God to call
Believe and unto you
It shall forestall

Until the thorns were worn
By the savior of man
No hope was found
In time at large
For Earth was an evil place
With the devil in charge

(continued)

Creation grew from the thorns
Of the eternal grave
For the boulder failed
And sin gave
A lasting gasp
As love prevailed

A living apple is without thorns
On the beach of Eden
On the sands of time
On the virgin of Eve
Finding Adam
As God's reprieve

We are all born
To be free of sin
To be kind
To be a thorn in the side
Of evil
And the peace on earth
Good will and death to sin

Is what you're worth

WHAT DOES MOTHER MEAN

Mother means
Costumes on Halloweens
Guiding light through the teens
Soothing voice to quiet bad dreams
Washing ironing and clean blue jeans

Mother means
Reliability behind the scenes
Nail polish and dry skin creams
Cleanliness at any means
Bandy roosters and jumping beans

Mother means
Stitches in britches mended seams
Warm and bright are her beams
But all in all, simple as it seems
Love and security is what
Mother Means

Loving without schemes

WHAT DOES FATHER MEAN

Father means
Balls and gloves
Pushes and shoves
Shooting guns for fun
Playing games
Chasing dames

Father means
Seek the jobs
Corn and cobs
Farm the land
Join the band
Make your stand
Father means
Find a best friend
Make a fence to mend
Chase the dream
Cars to wreck
Shuffle cards in a deck
Protect don't scheme
That's what Fathers Mean

Kind but not serene

MEASURE YOUR SCORE

Is it for others or one's self

Listen to your heart beat
Hear your soul tweet
Speak your mind
Write your sign

Thank your friends
For what life sends
Count down your dreams
Collect on your schemes

Then with your moral blessing
Forgive your sins by confessing
That we are mortal
With a spiritual portal

To God

But only if we forget transgressions
And forgive failed missions

(continued)

As winning at life is no more
Then believing in something
Greater than one's score

It amounts to a sum not a division
Not a subtraction or an abstraction
But fate leaves it to our decision
To fight for a reason

One plus One
Is always Two Times
As much fun
If you're with that someone

The score as two as one is to be won

WHEN TIMES GET TOUGH

When there doesn't seem to be enough
Time and money to say I appreciate you
But obstacles and huff and puff
Cannot replace what you do

Taking on our suffering
You are always there
To say the right thing
And show you care

But we want you to know
That we are tough
Enough to endure
Any obstacle's guff and stuff

Because it is for sure
Our strength and desire
With a mission so pure
Can never be too dire

In spite of the obstacle courses
Never give up or give in
To those vengeful forces
Until we win

Thanks for your love
On this memorable anniversary
Of our flock with the wings of a dove
And the roots of our family tree

With its bark so tough when there is not enough
The tough get going

WHERE DOES A DREAMER GO

I question

Where does a dreamer go
When there are no more friends to listen
How does a dreamer know
When there are no more trends to chasten

How does a dreamer sow
When there are no more ends to fasten
Why does a dreamer flow
When there are no more amends to hasten
Who does a dreamer bestow
When there are no more minds to christen

Where does a dreamer go
When he cannot sleep
With doubts to sow
And his thoughts feel cheap

Where does a dreamer go
When his nightmares become real
And fear creeps from head to toe
And his past darkens like a banana peel

(continued)

Well fools dare to tread
Where dreamers live
And hope creeps ahead
And suddenly get the love they give

How it must please each dreamer
As light creeps in
So the fable is now the glimmer
To stamping out eternal sin

Glowing as each blossom teases
Uplifting the past it breathes
And to each life a flower that pleases
The dreamer's dream reprieves

Love affairs from the nightmares

WHO IS SHE

Once a year we look and see
For better or worse
Who is she

She is the roots of the tree
She is the boost to set us free
She is the trust that overcomes me

She is the fun in Family
She is the warmth in vitality
She is the reason in consistency

She is the arms in security
She is the light of our destiny
She is the love in eternity

Now it is the next day
And we now know
That she is the mother TIME in me

On my Birthday

WILL YOU FIND ME

Holding your hand my heart begs
That my sperm is for your fertile eggs

Looking for Easter eggs
In spots to find
We miss each other
From time to time

Can true love be be so far
Hoping you'll find her in some
Hapless bar
Seeking not looking for Easter eggs
In spots where they are

We regret not finding a mother
Looking like a wife
Grasping life trouble is
The sister's judgmental brother

We need each other to find
Our need to unwind
Misspent days gone by
As lost romance will defy

(continued)

Finding the true meaning
That marriage must start
When we find love hiding
In a seeking heart

As blood flows from our arteries
To produce sperm and maybes
With love to affirm
Easter egg babies

Like a rabbit in hand
Is better than
A liter making what
Easter never can

Easter bunnies

WINDSWEPT

Trees are bending with the breath
Across the breast of nature
Chilling all in its breadth
And humbling this earth bound creature

Changing our moods when it's warm
By driving away the fear
Of the fingers of a building storm
As if brushing back a tear

Windless days bring us peace
Although a little uneasy
Since we think winds never cease
And our lives must be breezy

Blowing along the paths
We take our turn at the helm
Setting our sail to the staffs
With a destiny we can't overwhelm

Gusting somewhat is a sign
Of a spirit concerned about our time
Being off the guiding line
Like an alarm bell's sudden chime

(continued)

Help me windswept and gentle touch
To search and find our way
According to the will of those finding much
Enjoying tomorrow more than today

Swept by a wind I don't mind
If I can catch my sigh
Before I get too far behind
Your help to get me high

No matter how the wind sweeps
Away the time it keeps
God only knows why and when
We're going and where we've been

Not how ... does he bestow

WITHIN THE MIND

Surgeons sharpen their scalpels
Doctors listen closely
Psychiatrists tap their fingers
Upon the scalp

But do they really delve deeply
Within the mind
For is the mind a tangible object
Or might it not be a spiritual subject

For reality is more than what we can touch and see
Hear and taste
Reality is more the mind
Than the physical perception

If this be true so what
You're just creating some doubt
About the reality of man
No it's more than that

To understand man
You must understand virtual
As well as the physical
And to find the spiritual

(continued)

You must delve within the mind
Within its physical confines
Of Bones and matter
Lies the secrets of total existence

Total existence of varying degrees
For each man
But the explanation of existence
And the varying persistence

Can come from within the mind
But it must be pulled out
So it can be examined
It must be put in the physical perception

It must be spoken written
It must be communicated
For the spirit cannot speak
But with the voice of man forming the words

Coming from the mind of man
Can formulate the proof of total existence
When examined, this phenomena
Will lead us to

Appropriate standards of behavior
It will lead us to discoveries
Far beyond the present physical comprehension
Far beyond the physical perception

(continued)

Of the spirits of yesterday
Beyond the spirits of today
Call it Philosophy
Call it Psychology
Call it Theology
Call it physical science
Call it Quantum Physics

The results are the same
The answers to the questions
About time
About birth life and death
About love
About happiness
About the eternal tomorrow
Exist within the human mind

No matter the color of the sea
Or the smell of grass
We are free at last in infamy
From thoughts we amass
To make our own reality

"Those that seek these answers
Of their own kind
Shall find them aligned
Where Heaven shall dwell
Within their mindful spell"

The eight wonder is each mortal mind
Making its own reality
Pursing its own destiny

YOU HAVE THE WRONG NUMBER

One two three
What better simile
Sequenced fittingly
Right as they can be

Nothing feels dumber
Than a wrong number
Sorry who you calling from a slumber
Read me out like a newcomer

Said I didn't know how
To make love or allow
Her to kotow
Like a condescending high brow

Called her my girl friend
Hung up on again
Can't seem to win
Above this swirling wind

(continued)

Just doesn't seem right
Beyond a quick snit
Before I take flight
And avoid the wrong hit

She's beautiful but all wrong
Since it won't last long
As feelings are strong
Though they take too long

To get just right
Far beyond one night
So we get the right number
And answers in bed beyond slumber

Alone I cannot fix a wrong number

YOU ARE MORE THAN MY VALENTINE

On February 14 of any year I see you as my role model for

Honesty
Loyalty
Sincerity
Giving
Beauty
Vitality
Health
Happiness
Prosperity
Abundance of life itself

Your children personify these traits and the values
For their children are following that role model you have set
What a legacy what a picture for our 50+ years together and the future

So on this Valentine's day I want to reiterate my
respect and admiration for your characteristics
And passion for our family our business and our marriage

With all my love with thoughts of what
More stands for
Jerry

YOU CANNOT CHANGE FATE

You cannot change fate
You cannot stop hate
You cannot help late
You cannot prevent irate

You can only deal with fate
You can only dissipate hate
You can only avoid being late
You can only cool the irate

We are all victims of human trait
We are all fighting being late
We are all avoiding hate
We are all keeping the faith
That we in fact can change fate

With all our might
And to our delight
The future is never set
Unless you don't know how to place your bet
Or keep your eye on the target

(continued)

Because the next act or happenstance
Grants us a choice at success and romance
Only the failure to take the chance
Prevents you from the opportunity to enhance

Our life and change our fate
From being sad and finishing late
That clouds the future you cast
By regretting the past

That shall never come again
Fate is where you're going
Not where you've been
So change the seeds you're sowing

With peace blowing in the wind

YOU TAUGHT ME HOW TO CRY

I look back and wonder why
Why my eyes were always dry
Til' the day you said goodbye
And my eyes began to cry

It had been so long it seems
Between our days and our dreams
Knowing somehow by and by
That you would show me how to cry

I thought it would be for the thrill
And the joy
With no intent to kill
The affection of a little boy

A thrill to be in your arms
Living the past day by day
By the lure of your charms
And living the future just your way

As my Eyes cry to see
Not to fall away in decay
Thinking it would be
And end okay

(continued)

In a lover's game
It came time to admit
That we weren't the same
We didn't fit

That's the time you broke the tie
Wetting the blue skies
And in the cool air said goodbye
Blowing into my dry eyes

With the word goodbye
You now taught me how to cry
Sadden by your sigh
That has now run dry

So I don't lose my grip
Hold me lord hold me tight
Away from this quivering lip
And focus my sight

Then maybe someday by and by
I can find someone who will dry
The tears I've been taught to cry
So I don't have to answer that nagging, why

YOU'RE BLESSED

You're blessed
Pound your mind
Beat your chest
Vanity left behind

Like little Bo Peep
With sheep to tend
You cannot sleep
As pride is not your friend

Playing in jest
As the echo not the sheep
Yes you are obsessed
With all that others keep

With your wings and feathers
Likely if confessed
It is their druthers
To be so blessed

That they would just accept
With the bounce in your step
You as their dream
With your face not inept

(continued)

Spinning helplessly in space
You then figure to redeem
Them like they are an ace
In a speck of cream

But what's behind their temple
A cloak of furs for a life like yours
Pure but simple
Taste that obscures

Beating like your heart
Inside their failure to cope
Blessed to be you as part
Of their hope

Their only crime being
That you don't appreciate
What they are seeing
As your blessed state

That you cannot escape

A BAD DREAM

Bad dream
Go way
Come back
Some other day

Sleep sleep
Come to me
Can't I rest
My restless sea

You're the dream
I'm the dreamer
Raging nightmare
Fear redeemer

Good dream
Don't go away
Come back
When you can stay

Night becomes day
Light the room
Bring me back
From a dreamer's gloom

(continued)

I'm the dreamer
You're the bad dream
Nothing is real
Curdled in our cream

Night and day
Bad dreams that go away
Come back
Some other way

As day dreams
Getting in my way
Making what it seems
Like a plot in a bad play

With goals adapting
Wow though it is true
Day dreams can make it happen
Even when you're blue

A bad dream a day dream
Can be the other side
Of every fruitful scheme
If you can take the ride

Visions live on
Good or bad
Day or night
Happy or sad
Joy or fright
Together or alone

Making us their own

A CHILD IS BORN

Brought into this world with scorn
Another child is born
Not wanted
And destined to be haunted

How do we take care of these children
Some raised to fight some raised to sin
Not able to look up to kin
Unable to call life a friend

Pity if the child is unwanted

They pack the wayward homes
Much like a rogue that roams
Without hope
And the will to cope turning to pills and dope

Pity the child is haunted

These children must be loved
They can't be pushed they can't be shoved
They need respect emphasized
Held and cuddled civilized

Pity the child is daunted

(continued)

Take them to your breast
Like you do the rest
Your own the best
Society is no contest

Glory the child is wanted

If this works and we save them
We've shaped a mind and saved a limb
That will help carry the load
By doing for others as we have bestowed

Glory the child is born
To save the forlorn
As a child yet torn
Apart and unborn

From themselves
Aborted

A MAJOR MINORITY

One man who stands for courage
Is a major minority
In the land of mitigated justice

Two men who hold hands for strength
Become a chain
The moral minority

One woman who delivers love
Is a mother
In a State of sister brother

Two women who hold their pride
Can never be lonely
Though most will be a bride

A family most certainly
Is the strength
Of our country
The majority being
One man
One woman
In marriage

(continued)

But human rights shall prevail
And other rights will
Avail
Them to fulfill

Their persuasion as a major minority voice
For love is not their constitution or their court
It is their human right of choice
To which they resort

If it is LBGTQ or you

A NASTY ADDICTION

It's a nasty notion you've got
No matter what
Your past is a wrinkled ink spot
A novel thought for a plot

You give up for being hasty
I know you can still dream
But it's nasty
What I've seen

As you acted with deceit
When you needed bread not wheat
However truth can be bitter sweet
And lost love won't defeat

All good intentions
Unwind apprehensions
Or alleviate tensions
And create inventions

Splitting even the hardest wood
Makes immeasurable pain from good
Never turning out the way it should
But that nasty notion is under my hood

(continued)

Coming on as a passion
Giving push with motion
Like any good emotion
It's plied by a nasty potion

For ego is in play
Which will cause love to decay
Day by day when
Your nasty notion decided to stay

So an Intervention was in order
To correct a compulsion
That dies as the notion grows older
And the addict makes the right decision

To love the moment is to consent
And honor the ascent that stops the decent

THE NEW BEGINNING

By: Father of the Groom

It is not that God allows
You to say the marriage vows
It is your heart
That wants a new start

To take a chance
To find new romance
To take a chance
To further enhance

Your life your hope
Not wanting to elope
So you can show
How a nuclear family can grow

Dressed in orange and a yellow hue
It is a start brand new
For love will create a different page
A different time a different stage

A family ready for renewal
As you exchange rings of jewel
Representing a life to come
Knowing where you came from

Realizing your soul mate's dream
Together Karyn and Kip are the theme
Of the New Beginning

A SIGN OF THE TIMES

A graphic road sign of the times
Is the unfriendly look of a
Lonely homeless man in the city…unloved
Lying in the smother

The city is any set of eyes
Set upon you indifferently
Bounded by others looking
But not finding nor seeing signs

The ghetto is a sign
The high rise is a sign
The rejection of a principle is a sign
The killing of initiative is a sign

They are everywhere
Obligating us to acknowledge
The sign of the time
Is loneliness

(continued)

When this happens congregations
Families groups spring up
To deal with individual apathy
America the land of the free

Chained to themselves because
Of fear...fear of tomorrow's signs
Needing commitment to the times
With love the solution to hate crimes

Except through a cloud of
Cocaine liquor avoidance
Divorce infidelity loss of
Moral values ... all signs of

The times ... are all lost to the
Scene of the Holocaust
But with hope we will cope
Tis the reason we have a Pope

And justice with a rope

A SONG OF PEACE

I've heard of the wars of evil
I've seen the ravages of man
I've read of the primeval
I have followed the Ten Command

I have marched to the music of others
I have saluted the flag's flare
I've respected my brothers
I have bowed my head in prayer

I have shed a tear for the deceased
I have thanked God that love was there
And now I write a song of peace
To man a call a thought to care

That we can only live together
If we can touch each other's hand
Reach out touch the tips that heals
For it is the brotherhood to band
Around beliefs and ideals

By touching each other and being one
We are united together we stand
We are the same under the sun
We live in freedom of this land

(continued)

We worship the same God
We love for the same reasons
We cultivate the same sod
We live through the same seasons

We are the same in the Maker's eyes
Yes I've seen the signs
And all come upon the earth with the same gleeful cries
And have read the poet's lines

About the energy source and how we must cease
And we must live together in happiness
Imploring the credence of my song of peace
And attempting to climb out of the abyss

To have lived in God's eyes at all
Then and only then will the family of man
Standing for peace or together we fall
Be at Peace and make a stand

Against wars
Against power and closed doors
Against unfettered Government
Against control of resources and where they went
Against the song for peace that promotes a fight

For in peace we stand in the grace of what's right

A WING AND A FEATHER

Birds ever flock together
With their wings and a feather

Our love holds us together
With our wings and a whether

For years we have flown together
Wetter wings against stormy weather

Or seeking horizons come hither
There is no separation of wing and its feather

For love is our wings and our bodies the fetter
Holding our pursuit together

Whether we fly or roost or whatever
Our roots always are our tether

But beware life is a wing and a prayer
With chances that are always there

Looking for a compatible pair

AGE STRONG (LIKE THE ROSE)

Body = strength = pink rose
Mind = hope = yellow rose
Soul = peace = white rose
Heart = love = red rose

All along
We thought wrong
Talk of getting old
Sad stories untold

While we worry on
Our sun wanes at dawn
Losing sleep
With no dreams we keep

Awaken child of time
Hoping to stay young is no crime
For it is the strength of will
That takes time to kill

Pages are written long and hard
About mind decline and discard
But sages state the truth
We all have eternal youth

Find it in your soul
Save it in your heart's fold
For no one goes below or above
When they go with love

A mother and father ageless in time
With children to follow their lifeline

AGELESS

She is ageless
She is of Father Time
She is the Mother of life's rhyme

Born to be a sweet face
Born to smile away hard times
Born to have a happy place

Living for others is her way
Living with a heart full of love
Living is her strength every day

Loving her husband as the ultimate wife
Loving her children and their character
Loving her grandchildren and their dynamic life

Aging is an outward fear of its lagoon
Aging is not the same tune for everyone
Aging for Shari is not here…nor too soon

(continued)

It is time to recognize a miracle
Entering the seventh decade of her life
Shari is ageless and the center of a cycle

With a family of centenarians
Her heirs had the traits for a happy life
Handed down to daughters and sons

The sky is the limit for her
Each year marks just another day on the calendar
With the skin and body of a maiden aging signs do not occur

So I end this acclaim
Hopefully I will age the same…
According to this rhyme

To that mate of MINE

AMAZING

When I heard that voice
And his music choice
I live a moment to rejoice

It occurred to me
That this was as amazing
As talent can be

Then I decided to go beyond
What he wanted
With my intention new found

He was not proud
Or even expecting
His ability to be that profound

He was not willing
Or even cooperating
With my writing as fulfilling

Then a recording devised
As my poem became a song
So prudently disguised

(continued)

But holding back
This put his talent to work
As if to divert it's personal impact

From somewhere deep
From this start rolled voices
Giving us more choices and less deceit

Then the amazing fact emerged
He was becoming a song writer
Mush more than his dream encouraged

He battled natural fears
His Father's ire and his own choir
And over the years his tears

But now that he is grown
And on his own
With a family and a home loan

The Man is Blue is still a poem
And he is writing his own

AN I FOR AN i

Take that word from my mouth
Throw it to an I
Take that thought from my mind
Throw it to a lower i

Selfish as I am an I for an i
Centered as it seems
I'm aware of influence
That self-indulgence
Destroys one's dreams

Take that word from my mouth
Throw it to an I
Kindness to the others
Brings rewards many fold
Gathering a flock
Of sisters and brothers
And riches untold

Take that word from my mouth
Throw it to a lower i
Talk and you shall never listen
Or are you too busy to lie

(continued)

Take the word from my mouth
Throw it to a lower i
I for me and me for I
What a way to live
Without much to give
But all those coroners
With few mourners
Celebrate when you die

Take my words from my mouth
Throw it to an I
I for me
And me for I
As I for an i
And a me for me
That's hell brother …for eternity
Take that I word from my mouth

Toss it to the i wind
You and I
I owe you, you owe me
What a sweet sound
What a sweet and subtle round
Embrace me brother
We're together up or down

(continued)

Helping you for me
Take that word from my mouth
Toss it to the wind
Just I, no more
And we shall be
Friends together till the end

Take it from my mouth
Toss it to the wind
Cause I don't need selfishness
I've got myself a friend

An I for an i
A friend for a friend
WE determine the way it all will end

AN IDIOTIC AFFAIR

Each of us have an idiotic affair with ourselves
We grow up thinking we're the center of the universe
And we're disappointed when we find
It's in reverse
Never to be a King in the hearse

We grow up with an idiotic state of mind
By putting ourselves ahead
Which only pulls us further behind
Sleeping in our uneasy bed
We grow up through an idyllic stage
Thinking tomorrow is the creator of today's unfinished page

And if we grow up with some sense
Of where and whence
About life as not just an affair
But a task of fulfillment through showing that we care
Passing senses in the light
Rubbing bodies in the night

Because their devil may care
Holding onto things thought true
Finding good only from the deeds we do
A fulfillment from the idiolect despair
Has nothing to do with an idiotic affair

If they live out this dare
To be happy, healthy and smart enough to get there

ANY OLE RIPPLE OF HOPE

My true love threw her stone in the ocean
She put her love for me in motion
An ole ripple of hope
Coming into my periscope

Became a wave
And washed away the reasons I gave
For avoiding love at any cost
Afraid I'd be dominated and bossed

My true love had thrown her stone back in the ocean
For setting the ripple of hope in motion
It washed up once again upon me
Stinging my eyes making me see

Her true love could make me free
For her to see
Free of doubt
That's what love is all about

Love's that ripple of hope
Giving you the strength to cope
With life's inherent loneliness
And the inner stress

(continued)

She cast her stone upon that calming sea
The ripples grew and surrounded me
The tide brought me back into her arms
To her gentle loving charms

And it was those embraces
That filled my empty spaces
And swept me away from loneliness
With the ripples of happiness

And each time the ripples subside
I ask her once again to confide
Why she cast me aside
Into the sea looking for her pride

Never to be
Rippling away from me
Forever to be alone
When she could have saved me

And had me for her own

ARE YOU A DIAMOND IN THE ROUGH

Not many people are a diamond in the rough
Most are wanting it or faking it
Wanting you to take their bluff
Because they never take the time
To develop the real stuff

I know this guy, a man of faith
He's not afraid to judge his own weight
And make the changes
That would broaden his ranges
To be the real stuff

He is truly a diamond in the rough
And being so if it isn't enough
A man for all seasons
For he's not questioning the reasons
Or the density of the real stuff

He's just giving it all he's got
Laying seeds in his own plot
Helping and watching it grow
And in this his mind can know
How to be the real stuff

He's becoming the diamond he wants to be
A beautiful diamond for all to see
Humility and the patience to plod
Ever knowing and receiving the grace of God

To overcome the rough
As an example of a diamond's real stuff

AS TIME RAN COLD

As time ran cold
And I became old
No clock could catch me now

I guess sometimes untold
Left me uncontrolled
No clock could show me how

Undeniably my feet went first
As if time's rehearsed
No clock could possibly allow

The day to pass untold
Just a little bit cold
No clock could pull a plow

This gives reason
To the birth and season
No clock can create a cow

Nor could man be everything
That might ring or sing
No clock could be more than now

(continued)

The creator created it all
The clock the man the stall
No clock could know or allow

Without the time to toil
The mother the foal and a worthy soul
Do not exist nor can endow

A timeless clock
Tock tick tock
As time ran out
The mortal flock

Shall ultimately leave the dock

BEACON AFFAIR

On the hill of yesterday
Is a burned-out light
Turned towards the day
But looking like the night

It's a beacon once blessed
A match made in heaven
With the energy of the obsessed
Thought as sure as seven comes eleven

Now it stands in waiting
For a bridegroom's mating
Her need for fire spells desire
Since there's no light without a sire

The altitude stands it high
And the aspirations sought the sky
But the tide washed away the ship
While the captain was buried in Hannibal's crypt

It took a new seafarer
With new dreams and a stare
To light the beacon on the hill
Searching out the seeker's will

(continued)

From my doubt
As the fire had gone out
Like the night
Burning out the Beacon's light

Turning now churning
Cutting the night air
Touching me warming me
Until I care

The Beacon saving me from
My week end affair
And a ferriage
That wasn't there

Since marriage if for those that care

BROKEN HEARTS

Broken hearts
Broken arrows
Broken promises
Cupid's blessings are unspoken

As Humpty Dumpty is broken

And all Cupid's broken arrows can't
Put his heart back together
Again

Broken hearts
Like the Broken trail
Are to be healed with avail

Broken snow
Is the freshness of winter
And the thrilling venture

Broken promises
Are the shattered flakes
That even the traitor fakes

(continued)

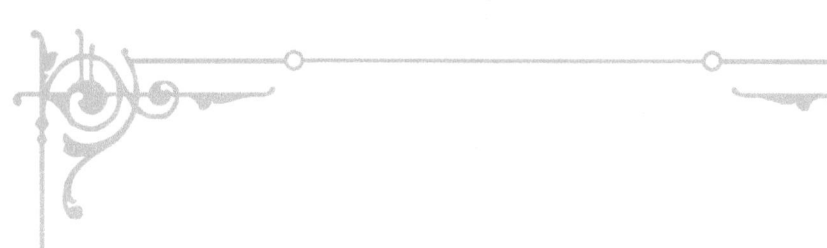

As Humpty Dumpty breaks

Taken in context
Cupid can't fly
And scorn is in the beholder's eye

As the straight arrow does not stray
To the lover's heartfelt pawl
Since broken snow is Cupid's way

Of breaking Humpty Dumpty's fall
While the broken heart is still on call

BUBBLES

We're like bubbles floating on
A giant ocean
Taking on direction lost
To the motion
Infinitely small but for a
Subliminal notion
That we're Godly by
Ignoring caution
Only reading the Psalms
For the potion
Like bursting bubbles on the ocean

We're like dust on
An ancient pyramid
Blowing in the wind
Lost amid
Floating particles make
Not our bed
Destined to wander
Without a love to wed
Whose footprints disappear
Upon sands we tread
Like dust blows from the pyramid

(continued)

We're like the crust
On a subsiding volcano
Exploding but not resolved
To a short lived glow
Funneled the molten rubble
Creates the flow and
The epitaph of our life
Progresses ever slow
Once written the legend
Will grow
Like the crust on a subsiding volcano

We're like fragments
Upon the universe
Lost in the light of a sun's
Subtle burst
Carried to our grave
In an unmarked hearse
Arriving unscathed for life
After to nurse
Never to cease or desist
Like bubbles dust crust and fragments
That no longer exist

Finally knowing that all
Mortals traverse
Like atom bubbles upon the Universe
With troubles they can't rehearse

Nor sins they can't reverse

BUSINESS PERSUASION

I've been persuaded by time by love by work by self
And my business ... but no magnet could be quite so strong
As a headlong plunge into the icy waters of enterprise
Which after scars tears and very few cheers
I became wise

Let me give you some of that wisdom of thirty-seven years
Caught up in the invasion
Of the bottomless pit
Called business persuasion
And the loss of wit

I set out to prove that risk was a lie
It was persistence attitude hard work which could defy
The pressure of doubt indecision
That were bigger than I
As I found this out too late to deal with a recession

Too forestall missteps
Well I'm going to confess
With preplanned steps conceived by practical reps
That after 37 years of stress working smarter
Is better than a fast starter

(60,000 new businesses per year and 60,000 bankruptcies per year)

(continued)

To the tune of more effective leadership
Cause emotion and a loose lip brings down the ship
And above the croon of let's shoot the moon ....
Things do go wrong and they will before long
As the past so dreaded clouds where we're headed

Never fear but be prepared
To risk your career
Yes it is truly an invasion
That business persuasion
Is always threatening self-preservation

And the strength of heart
Will overcome the failure
To start
Slower than the soul
Setting the Goal

For procrastination kills persuasion
In the risky business of decision

CATCH ME IF YOU CAN

The world tried to catch me
Doing my time
But I put out to sea
To seek what is mine
But the storm took me down

Took me under
Round and round with no sound
I paid for my blunder
Only to surface in another place
Playing my same tune
Into outer space

Heard by no other moon
Jupiter said hello
Mercury ran away
Pluto stood still and
And Mars was here to stay

Flying so earth could not catch me
Made me worth only what
A few could see
Till I learned life alone
Is like any other stone dropping into the sea

(continued)

It can have its drawbacks
But fundamentally it lacks
Substance and satisfaction
Cause life's need for romance
Can't be served by chance
And mindless distraction

For Leaders must lead
Followers must follow
Just don't follow the followers
Or try to mislead the leaders
Let all pursuers catch up
Before their jealousies erupt

So let me impart to you
Why we must stay
At a pace within your defined space
Letting the slow disrupt
And the impatient chase

But by no means will everyone … Catch Up
As break ups never breakeven

CHAMBERS (NOT CONFINEMENT)

Hiding in my compartments of fear
Thought to be habits
I talk of hopes and change
Little do I admit of weakness

But I bow to aggression
Like most humble defectors
No cell is strong enough to
To hold ideas or stifle dreams

However the social chambers
Defeat initiative cripple
Motives and squelch values
Whose roots stick in thinly
Constituted blight awaiting
The winds of enterprise

To blow them deeper into freedom
But instead erosion of the mind
Deals the soil waste insignificant
Giving way to the obstacle course
In each consequence
Known only as the Chambers

(continued)

Without lock or key
Its compartments are not for the free
Holy men and politicians
With their courts of law
Set in their chambers above reasons
And there's need to thaw
Dogma and Dominance of a few
As the Constitution's resolution should do

Heed that freedom is not free
And liberty is not for the non-believers
But it is up to you and me
To throw off the deceivers
In the Chambers of the Monarchy

Called Government in spite of the people

CHASING PUZZLES

Torn to pieces
Fluttering in the breeze
Put me together
If you please

Furrowed brow not knowing
Where to go somehow
These pieces are hard to find
Unless the script will unwind

Colors matched
Like ideas hatched
Pieces blowing away
Un- cacthed

I chase them to the ground
Floating all around
Tips and slips
Up and down

The pieces they do fit
In a pattern you can get
Smiling use your wit
To fit Life with death

(continued)

What's in between a puzzle yet unseen
Like paper floating in the wind
There's no way to comprehend
Which way the gust will bend

Bring it to the ground
Gather it to you all around
Putting together what you've found
It's where you've been where you're bound

Be you flocked or
Be you crowned
Solve the puzzle with
The curvy misfit pieces you have found
Solving the living puzzle of you is profound

Bring it to the ground
Gather it to you all around
Chasing the puzzle's pieces
With its picture and those curvy creases

Solve life's puzzle before time ceases

THE CLASSIC WILL

Life is the ultimate classic
Lombardo with the taste of music
Rothschild with the taste of wine
Monet' with the taste of art
Romeo with the taste of love
Shakespeare with the taste of his pen
Classics have forever been

The joy of the ages
The passion of pages
The bastion of sages
Yes it is a classical affair
To walk the paths with the masters
To read write listen and care

The classical pastures
Grazing in the greenery of Monet's scenery
Basking in the soft silhouettes of Shakespeare's minuets'
Smiling and reconciling
Juliet's beguiling
Sighing and crying with Chopin's styling

(continued)

The classical consumption
Of life's finer assumption
Lays bare the air
The expression of a care
For the artist who emerges there
An everlasting ever compelling ever interesting
Characterization of the urge to kill the classic will

An annihilation of mankind

But for a classical sketch of now
And a prophecy of the future
What can be more than a novel
a painting a poem a musical
or a thought that is classical
to bestow

The life of mankind

So there is a listener a lover a musician
A reader a freedom to choose hope as fusion
Of the Classics giving reasons for living and dying
Cursing and lying

As the one and only true hero of mankind
YOU

COMPUTER DEAD OR ALIVE

Computers look me in the eye
Tell me they'll do it or die
Garbage in garbage out
It pulls my hair makes me shout

Why don't you do
What I tell you
People may resist
They may get pissed

But eventually they move
Not like you out of the groove
How now computer how now
All I get is a whirrrr wow

No results no information
Lots of promises but little elation
Gotta lotta money invested
With my records congested

Thought I got a bargain
Learned all the jargon
Should have taken more time
Before the order was signed

(continued)

I thought it was in the price
Seems I lost another roll of the dice
I called in an expert to bail us out
All he can talk about

Is the Boss and Dos in sync
While the mess begins to stink
Woe is me what can I do
Maybe my days in the computer age are through

Then like a miracle
In stepped my son
A boy instead of a girl
Took us out of the wasted tab run

To the digital world of fun

CRACK IN THE SKY

A blue veil
A mist haze
A turbulent cloak
The infinite maze

Will we ever see beyond
The sun's dawn
The star's lust
The infinite dusk

Ask the dead
If they have seen
Beyond the sky
Through the crack
They fly

To meet the past to see the future
At a different speed
They fly beyond our need
To know if this be true
So why the dread
To be dead

As you fly beyond the human eye
Beyond the surface of time
Can you choose
Or crack the sky
Before your die

(continued)

No I say
That's not the way
For each his own
To find the crack or milky way

On his trip to digital lights
Behind the pearly gates
Of mega bites
And Bill Gates

Is a Cosmos of digits called atoms
And a hole of black
Never to dissipate but propagate the crack
With white holes sending them back

For existence isn't dead as atoms are wed

CRYING EYES

CRYIN' DON'T BRING NO SHAME
When love is to blame
Blue eyes and green
They're all the same
When loving is the scene

Broken heart torn apart
It's bound to hurt
When loving's to blame
For eyes that cries
Never lies
There's no way to disguise
Crying eyes

Close and rest
Just do your best
To get un-messed
But don't disguise
Those crying eyes

Losing your love
Like at the Roulette wheel
Love is a gamble
That you bet

(continued)

And if you lose
You can't choose
To go back and revise
The feelings behind
Those crying eyes

So if you're wise
You'll rationalize
That you've broken your ties
That bind your crying eyes

Free now to see
Through your heart again
For another love to win
As your tears come free

From those crying eyes

DEAD BRANCH

A tree with a dead branch
Needs pruning
A life with a dead stench
Needs defaming

A dead branch
Saps the energy of the good earth
It takes from the strong
To feed of its own accord
Like a guitar with a dead string
Needs tuning

A dead string
Dulls the senses of the good ear
It takes from the beauty
To feed on its own discord
Like a person with a dead mind
Needs learning

A dead mind
Holds no hope for time
It takes from the positive
To fall on its own accord
Like a person with a dead mind
Is no longer confined
Needs pruning

(continued)

As the dead branch
Blows into a dead wind
Looking for the chance
To Live Again
Needs believing

Such is the dead mind
Flying kites in a dead wind
When there's no life to find
With thoughts of deceiving

The epitaph of the underachieving
Dead on revival

DEATH OF A MATADOR

Charge El Toro
Hit the cape
Accept the blade

The procession of beauty
Is a tradition
Into the ring

The crowd is on its feet
Cheering the color
Of a death wish

The picador has done
His job well
In selecting a brave bull

Charge El Toro
Hit the cape
Until torn by a miss

(continued)

The music is exciting
The brass of the bull
The strings of the crowd
The drums of the blade
The winds of the Matador

Death isn't loud
It isn't beauty
But it is a drama
A drama of survival
A drama of intrigue
A drama of feelings
A drama of life and death

Ole'… There lies man's insensitivity
Lying on the floor of the arena
A brave Matador no more
A victim of his worst fears

As the bull salutes his steers

DIRTY FEET

The cross of our guilt
Was carried to its erection
By dirty feet that God built
To cleanse a world of its affliction

He said we should forgive
The nails His feet felt
Because we then could live
Without doubt for whom we knelt

As the rain descended that day
The dirt left his skin
Running down his will to pray
For those committed to mortal sin

But he did ask that not all should pay
For deeds of earthly pride be they
Forgiven even on Judgment Day
As heathens wouldn't stay

(continued)

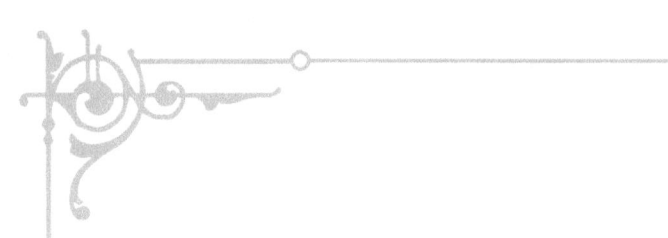

Cleansed as were his feet before He died
As the rock rolled like a feather
Away from the mouth of truth
Molding body and spirit together

We heard His message as to hath
The rest of humanity stood aloof
To God's wrath
As living proof

That the message was to wash you and me
Of dirt in our hearts and
Make our foot print free
Of nails and dirt both foot and hand

Such is the cross borne by each mortal man

DOWNPOUR

Dots upon the windshield
Bubbles upon the ground
Downpour is so cleansing
Despite the sound

Cleansing the sins of today
And washing the sand away from the clay
No shore or mortal door
Can withstand the downpour

Touching us all
With its relentless need to fall
Upon the ground
With its pounding pawl

Echoing forevermore
Nature's willingness to share
The downpour
Rich or poor truth or dare

Weak or strong right or wrong
None can start or stop
The downpour
With its encore

It's will is the wind
And it's sound is the storm
It can befriend the land
Or be destructive to the farm

Depending what comes behind the Downpour

DOWNSIDE UP

Have you ever
Turned your life around
In your mind

Taking a look at it from
Each side down
And downside up

Turning the downside up
To see where your emotions
Come from

Lurking under that rock
Of sub-reality
Is the very nature of your being

You can be no more
Than the rock conceals
Cause there is no more

If your soul druthers
And to yourself be true
To no others
Shall you ever be a shrew

(continued)

This is the very essence
Of a soul's ascension
Being able to find out
That your dimension
Is already turned about

There can be no more
Than you bequeath
As you see it free it
Turning fantasy upside up
And showing it to be true
The very essence of you

Many you see never to know
That underside of Karma
That what you reap is what you sow
As reality merely fades to drama

Acting out thoughts demeaning
By making a dream turn real
Demands that the true meaning
Is what Dharma does not reveal

Only to appear to come true
Wedding hope and destiny
As the downside growing inside of you
Becomes reality

Pity we were never free to climb the tree of life
Upside down for accomplishments so renown

ELDERPRIDE

My son and daughter tried
And it is if I'd just died
Hoping my pain would subside
Nothing was said of my Elderpride

The only alternative they said
Was for me to live where I dread
In a nursing home of their choice
Giving me no say or voice

I cried and cried
As if I'd died
What I asked of my
Elderpride

Give me liberty or give me death
No one hears my bequest
If you treat me as if I died
Nothing is left of my Elderpride

(continued)

Listen and you will hear
Courage overcoming fear
We can remedy this Eldercide
By restoring Elderpride

Compassion hope
Companionship work or love
And for all of the above
So easy yet so far
It is just a matter of finding
The wagon and a star

Hitching hope to better health
And Health Preservation to more wealth
Will give us motivation
To restore an aging nation

Elders never died if we restore their pride

ESSENTIALLY YOURS

You've asked to have my handshake
You've asked if I would take
Your sixpence and worn out fence

You suggested I listen more closely to you
And run you by everything I do
Which I suppose shall become more than necessary
With my past record being the contrary

But no matter what you see or believe
You must not deceive
Yourself into feeling lonely
For if you realize it's I only
No matter what occurs
Who is essentially yours

You have a corner on my market
You have your name on my jacket
And your picture's always in my packet
So don't sell yourself short
Don't say you lack it

(continued)

Because you don't
It's only those that won't
That lack the will
To fulfill what is essentially yours
It is the spout that pours
The opening doors
The stairway between floors
Which everyone ignores
And those notions that love implores…
Are essentially yours

From me to you

FAST AND FURIOUS – FOR A QUICKIE

Roller coasters and zip line boasters

Faster yet is a turbo jet
Accelerate to wait
Push and pull it faster
Run a race with the master
Fast and furious for the disaster

Do it put on the speed
Feeling good is all we need
Fast foods here
Instants there
Hurry to your grave
If you dare

That's our lives these days
Darting and dashing
Through the maze
Hype it and cash it
And sell the craze

Put out the ads
On Super Bowl Days
Fast foods here
And a quickie there
Not enough time to say you care

(continued)

It's gone too far
That Speedy Gonzales
Is a Super Star
Even hookers are much less
To do their quickest in the car

The faster they do it
The more it'll bring
It's a quickie world
With or without a ring

Divorces are expected
Infected by losing trust
Cleavage and a big bust
Booties spied on with lust

Are only for drinks and beddings
Into Chasing fantasies that offend
For most weddings
Begin with a friend and then end

Fast foods here
Oldies here Quickies there
Used to be a family we endear
Now it's an unwed pair
Same sex isn't even queer

(continued)

Now under attack
Speed and the racing team
Looking for a fast climax
To the American Dream

That is beyond being on the mend
Even if we didn't intend
To its disintegrating in the wind
A commentary on a modern day's trend

– stop and get off that quickie bend

As "Fast and Furious" came to a crashing end

Some come on quick
And shake your stick
The faster you do it
The more it will tick
And tick
And tick
And tick
Boooooooooooom

FATE IS WORTH THE WAIT

FATE IS WORTH THE WAIT

We all take for granted
What God has conceived
Most of us have not wanted
For strength of faith believed

Only when you've had an experience
With fate looking over your shoulder
Can you appreciate the essence
And joy of growing older

It is truly wonderful to be capable
Of a belief one can call upon
When the story is but a fable
Not knowing that life goes on

Though our wit pleads not to go
We all must face the widow maker
After the battles of life our winds blow
Leaving behind loved ones to the undertaker

(continued)

But all is well as the moment is tuned
To the rhythm and the shackle
For to destiny we're all marooned
As a part of life's cycle

So brave ones, go and meet this mountain
With your strength of heart
You must look at death as but a fountain
Flowing into yet another start

For in God we trust as we must
Our time or fear is just
But will not wait
For fate is not a date

It's your personal pearly gate

FRIENDS AND LOVERS

I'VE HAD MY SHARE OF FRIENDS
They've come and they have gone
I've had my share of would be lovers
And you're the only one

Who is both friend and lover
Like the hummingbird and the flower
Constantly we hoover
For the nectarine we discover

We have found each other's need
And with that seed has grown
Friendship and love
Just our own

It started out with infatuation
Kindling and heightening the fire
It became something to do just for fun
Till it became much more than desire

To tell about and pout about

We got so we knew each other's wants
No evil wind can blow
And could withstand the barbs and the taunts
Of each other's ego

(continued)

For as one we each know
When our windy moods would blow
Blowing us to and fro
Until only stop could go

To each other away from each other
And back together
Creating our own version of sunny weather
And a stormy breather

Casual lovers cannot claim as much

As friends and lovers our time together discovers
As we can say with one gentle touch
That everlasting love is far deeper
Than just under the covers

And as I get to know you more
For the friendship I adore
I want to open each new door
And discover
More of my best friend and lover

(continued)

In this respite
Nothing shall do us part
For we're attached by the virtue of the heart
And to this we befriend
Two for one
Lovers to the end

With no clouds
With no rain
With no lightening
With no pain
Just the good fortunes
Of not being vain
From bad seedlings in the brain

Friends and lovers are Able and Cain
In eternity's loving refrain

DRIZZLE THROUGH THE TREES

Trees are hanging their heads
To the coolness of the morning
The day is bright and the foliage beds
Feels the bite of the adorning

Birds hanging their wings
To the rhythm of the freeze
Lifting up the weather as it sings
Its drizzle through the trees

And through the late fall and early winter
Brought nature's cold breath down
Coolness of the nighttime sinister
To cover the beckoning ground

Cold rain had done its dew
A frosty morning chastising
There's still a beauty to what frost can do
Though I may be the only one listening
To what nature has to say
As a beautiful day

(continued)

Ice it is so profound
But I must say without a sound
The frosty beauty reveals a spirit to abound
That crystallized the ground

With Birds and bees folding their wings
To the rhythm of the freeze
As a stormy hard rain brings
An icy drizzle through the trees

From stormy weather that can
Either fizzle the icy puzzle
Or embezzle the icy drizzle
And drown the sizzle

With a cold rain in the trees
Breaking the limbs that freeze

GET OFF MY SHIRT

Take your eyes
Off my disguise
Unless you're a flirt
Stop reading my shirt

All of us have our ways
Personalized as the T-shirt craze
Saying what we're afraid to
Through a monogram or two

If it's something you like
That's one thing but
About war or plugging a dike
Don't bother me with useless smut

For all I've got is my skin
Unless I take care of myself
That won't come around again
And pursue my form of health

And if I want to use a slogan
Spread across my doggone
Ugly Anatomy
Then dammit leave me be

(continued)

I don't need your approval
In any form of expression
To state my views on toxic removal
Except outright aggression

And if you can find it in you
It lets me make my statement
So tell me is your T-shirt a clue
That I shouldn't resent

For mine is not for your eyes
Unless you want dirt
It's my disguise
That looks can flirt

Get off my irreverent shirt

GLIMPSE

*Looking glasses only reflect
What the looker
Wants to see*

*Vanity is no more
Than insecurity
Brushes combs to adore*

*Talcum's too
Put forth an air
Of I'm brand new*

*Sensitivity is no more
Than feeling kind of blue
For richer and poorer*

*As a eulogy
Ending the autobiography
Glimpsing the past*

*Tells a story
Of the teller's
Need for glory*

(continued)

Indulgence is no more
Than one's own glory
Mirror Mirror
On the wall

With all its mortal gifts
Wishes buts and ifs
Gosh just to be tall

Maybe just maybe
The glass upon
The wall

Is no glimpse of me at all

GOD IS OUR PARTNER

Descartes Aristotle Socrates and Plato
Found a God through thought
We've read what they've said
And been taught likely than not
That none of us know
If judgment day is friend or foe

If you choose to rain and blow
Deciding on pleasure in spite of shame
Fending for desire of a misspent mind
There is little likelihood of love or fame
Only grief that won't let go
It's the self your foe

If you choose the godly route to go
The inner self can come to peace
Proud to be a person not afraid
Living every hour knowing hope will not cease
Then heaven on earth will bestow
Its friend not foe

So search out your goodly self
Ask it how to serve your brother
Never thinking about reward
Merely believing in the one not other
For happiness shall be willed accord
As God is your partner

If work is my mentor

GOOD MORNING WORLD

Hallelujah, it is morning unfurled
The alarm went off and as I uncurled
I didn't feel like facing the world

Then it occurred to me
That I was foot loose and fancy free
That it is purely up to me

To dictate and set my pace
So I put a smile on my face
Exercised and shaped up my inner space

Knelt down cleared my mind and said
A few words of grace
That really amounted
To what I'm getting around to saying to your face

Good Morning world
That is an exercise of shaping up an attitude
Deciding that what you give to life
It will return in gratitude

(continued)

Staying in bed depressed and uncurled
Will not lead to any opportunities to fuel
Waiting out there in the sunshine of the world
Particularly if you only see it as cruel

The fuel to go to the trough
Pursuing every angle
And execute effort to get aloft
Above the fray and tangle

With your hope and dreams unfurled
To make every effort you can
Yes, say hello world
To put life at your own command

Now you know how to pursue destiny
That each morning is left entirely up to thee
And it is free

Its only cost is funny money and reverie

GRADUATION TO ONESELF

Life begins in the womb
Hereafter a Graduation from the tomb
In between life limb and love
Touches us all through God above

School is a stepping stone
As speech is to the telephone
Each step gets you higher
And not missing steps takes desire

For those who decide to persist
Will attain a mind to resist
The temptations of mortal sins
On their way to immortal wins

Achieving their biggest dreams
Without falling to extremes
Receiving love above tribulation
Giving their parents joy and jubilation

Graduation from each level
Conquers fear that can bedevil
Life's journey under the sun
Unless you enjoy what you've won

(continued)

For a self that admires itself
And regrets no cost over wealth
Has graduated unto oneself
As my grandchild has … a person them self

Love from Nammy and your Tennis Coach: Grandpa

CELEBRATION TO ONESELF

Graduation to Gratitude

With gratitude
I can have a positive attitude

It is not a platitude
To seek and find gratitude

For when it wells up
Into your heart
You have a caring Attitude

Thank God for this latitude

Amen

PS: when all seems gray and upset
Plug into a new outlet

HAND ME DOWN HEAVEN

Preacher preacher look at me
Tell me please what you see
Can this thinking set me free
Or is it just a reverie

Sandman sandman look at me
Tell me please what you see
Is it dreams too heavenly
Or just the fear of reality

Lover lover look at me
Tell me please what you see
Is that love supposed to be
Or is it just a search for security

Buyer buyer look at me
Tell me what you see
Is it money that attracts thee
Or is it me can I be the key

Sister sister look at me
Tell me please what you see
Is it your brother from head to knee
Or just that boy that climbed the tree

(continued)

Mother mother look at me
Tell me please what you see
Is it your son's chastity
Or just a shadow of what he wants to be

Father father look at me
Tell me please what you see
Is this your image of sincerity
Or just a reasonable facsimile

God God look at me
Tell me please what you see
Is it strength and charity
Or just a hand me down Heaven in my plea

If I'm really meant to be
Tell me please what you see
Help help me make me free
Like you did at Calvary

Don't hand me down your Heaven
I want my own to believe in
In Heaven as my birth
As determined by my self-worth

Here on Earth

HEAVEN ON EARTH

E very
A ngel
R eturns
T o
H eaven

Are you an angel
Who will return to heaven

Or an angel of the devil
Who lives in earthly hell

Look in the mirror on the wall
Oh angel fairest of them all

Do you see life as hope
With the glass half full

Or do you see the loss of hope
Because the glass is half empty

For it is a simple choice YOU have
Do I see my life as the angel of heaven
Or the devil for each earthly Act confirms that Fact

Christmas Thanksgiving Birthdays Anniversaries Holidays
Celebrated by Families
Are Heaven's Vessels of Here and Now

A Well above and beyond Hell's tow
Drink from them earth's virtues of love and charity

THE DAY THE PRINCESS DIED

Be holding unto those that lied
Not knowing ourselves nor the reason
Princess Diana died we decide
She died for the lack of love
She was oh so lonely
For the parting was all she could think of
And it's meaning to her only

The news set me wondering
How far is the longest day
How true is the shortest week
How good is the saddest year
How well do we know each other

Without whispering in each other's ear
Parting in the morning so dear
And as we go our separate ways
With time counting the days

Come to the juncture in the night
There is no reason to argue and fight
And the closer we come to being apart
The fonder the memories the warmer the heart

(continued)

So the departure is of some pain
Like the sunshine it's warmer after the rain
So take my hand as I meet you in the doorway
Say you understand about it being a long day

In our current mental state
Even though we have to wait
Have the faith and the will to love
To practice what we are thinking of

With the ignorance of what we seek
How rich is the poorest week
Wondering how far is the next fray
How long is the shortest day

But in reality
How far is the longest wait
How tall is the biggest order
How tough is the skin to crack
Not long not far not tall not difficult
If there's an appreciation
Of the distance between us and creation

(continued)

For Diana it was destined to occur
The Queen never really knew her
Charles the King imminent didn't go there
The Monarchy didn't know how to hide the caper
While the people were in love with an affair

Be holding unto those that lied
Not knowing ourselves nor the reason
Princess Diana died we decide
She died for the lack of love
She was oh so lonely
For the parting was all she could think of
And it's meaning to her only

I'm still wondering
How far is the furthest desire
How near is the driest tear
How do I love you dear
Ask me and I shall tell you

Life is not a King or Queen
It is a couple having seen
How simplicity outweighs the monarchy
And the absence has given us the memory

To think of her as still here

I ALONE

Do you know the score
Is your ego well or sore
Is your vision clear or poor
Is your mind an open door
Is your life just a bore

Do you want to find what's in store
Then I implore restore restore restore
Tidings are galore
If you restore
Don't ignore I implore restore
now and forever more

Body
Mind
Spirit
Soul

Unless you condone
This is not yet your zone
But the reality of being a Drone
Finding that you are alone

(continued)

So put your heart into
Controlling the score
Restore restore-restore
Find the door
Open and explore
Life after you restore
All four for evermore
Body
Mind
Spirit
Soul

I atone to never to be I Alone

IF I'M NOT ATTRACTIVE

You expect so much

But oh look what I've got
And what I don't have
Is beyond my thought

You demand so much

But oh look what I've had
And the way I touch
I must not be too bad

You want so much

But wanting is not enough
When all I do
Is to be attractive to your bluff

You say so much

What can I say
To be attractive to you today
Talk until I cry tell me why

(continued)

You are so much

Tell me a lie that jumbles
Demand something I cannot buy
But don't reject me, me oh my

You mean so much

Don't just handle my stumbles
Don't throw me away
For being attractive won't delay

You think too much

A figure that sags
With feelings that lags
A face that crumbles

That's what distracts you so much

Because unattractive humbles
When it's my heart you fumble
And realize you are getting older

For attractive is in the arms of the holder

I BELIEVE IN YOU

Before I can believe in you
I must believe in me
Before I can understand you
I must understand we

Our relationship can only
Grow beyond each other
If we grow within one another
This is the pursuit of love through

The valley of self
Allowing us to scale the
Heights of alter wealth
With no amount of philosophy
Or theology

Can replace the act
Or that loving feeling to
Express the fact
It all comes down
To belief
That develops a habit to
Avoid grief

(continued)

*Not many human beings can
Live this testament
Except in their fear of
A fictitious advent*

*Thus religion must have grown out of
Our natural inadequacy to believe
While waiting for a higher being above
To love us and conceive*

Of Belief We Receive

I LOVED YOU BEFORE I KNEW HOW

Back in the early days when we were young
Before the bells and chimes had rung
Just after the day I met you on the square
I felt this feeling and I became aware

It was not exactly a yearning
Somewhat warm but yet not burning
I guess it was just a part of learning about love
About things other than baseball and my glove

And little did I realize but I do now
I loved you before I knew how
Yes I guess I could say Love at first sight
Strung up and flying like a kite

But I couldn't take my eyes nor my mind from you
Boy was I taken aback by what I hadn't knew
I thought of love by the picture shows
With a pretty face and a perfect nose
Passionate Kisses and curled up toes

But over the years I've come to discover
That passion and emotion does not make a lover
It's only for what you call a one-night stand
Tears and grief and a lonesome man

(continued)

Cuz for that river to run very deep
So should the caring you're wanting to keep
Yes it's head and shoulders above the body
Cleaner and straighter and sweeter than being naughty

Now over all these years
Now it appears with some trying times and tears
I did slowly learn to love
Something other than my baseball glove

Something called sweet Shari to endow
Sweet memories on my brow
And little did I realize but I do now
I loved you before I knew how

Putting the horse before the plow

I MADE BY BED

Lay me down to sleep
Dreaming of fantasies
As secrets I keep
And of God to speak

I turn down the covers
And tuck in the sheets
Counted my blessings
And forgot my defeats

Picked out a mattress
A little hard to the touch
Comfort was not my concern so much
I really didn't foresee a need
Of burying myself in bed like a seed

All I wanted was a little rest
On the trip to being the best
But best in bed was not my goal
As much as being best at expressing my soul

(continued)

As I crawl in I'll find out
If I've made it well
For bed can be the first sign of living hell
As I toss and turn
And my motors continue to burn

I'll know that I've made my bed
A place I'll not always dread
If frustrations and weariness I can release
For an inner peace

Then I'll know that the bed I'm in
Will help me those battles to win
And the bed I've made of women
Is for more than mortal sin

It's deeper deeper yet
Then shallow pleasure it is said
And the self-righteous soon regret
The dread of an unwed bed

Made by a life misled

I'M THE RAINBOW

*I'm the rainbow
And you're the sun
Giving Life
To a stoic reason*

*I'm the canvas
And you're the oil
Giving life
To painted soil*

*I'm the poem
And you're the words
Giving life
To soaring birds*

*I'm the thorn
And you're the rose
Giving life
To flowering prose*

(continued)

I'm the dreamer
And you're the dream
Making love
To me until you Beam

Like the sunlight
Seeding my rainbow
Behind the night
Before you go

Turning colors of beauty
From rain drops
Passing through the sun's duty
In a prism before an eclipse stops

Me the rainbow and you the crops

IMAGINE TO LOVE

IMAGINATION ... THE LAW OF ATTRACTION

I forsaw what happened today
I can predict what may
Or may not be the story
Or the ink spot

So long as I think I do
Thinking fate does what I already knew
Without recognizing the clue
That imagines each day as brand new
For imagination is the preview

It's what can happen in a day or two
It's just up to you
It's the compass of what you're going to do
It's the orders to the crew

I thought I could
I imagined I would
I dreamed I should
I understood I did

I will never doubt again
As doubt is the biggest sin
For imagination and me
Turned creativity free

Attracting life to my realty
I can I will I am

EVOLUTION

Evolving inside an apple is a core
Creations longing forever more
The seed for the future is planted there
Crafting a tree from a pear

It's nature's way of living
And God's way of giving
Good form to our universe
And the destiny to which we traverse

So within mankind there is a seed
That section of the soul called need
And to this we must be agreed
That to grow forever the soul must feed

Must feed upon the sunrise brawn
And the breaking of the dawn
The passing of a worthwhile day
Letting the seed grow with each penetrating ray

Until it becomes inner strength
Of an existence that has no length
It's merely a perennial cycle we sow
Set in motion and sustained
By the strokes of Michelangelo

(continued)

Listening reading learning
Thinking speaking and yearning
To become the bloom
The expression of a past seed's womb
Till the outer cover dies
And that seedling begins to rise

Rise out of the deadened casing
As the offspring facing
The newly planted seedling
Rising to live its own tracing
In the spring's repelling

Breaking through the fertile sod
And all else is merely detail
Reaching up to praise its God
Road signs and directions along the trail

To the reality that a man's life is only clever
When the seedling is allowed to endeavor
To never sever the inner strength of the savior
And discover its reason for evolving forever

Sure nothing is forever …
Well isn't that clever as saying never
That then happens to sever our endeavor

INSANITY

I strode up to the man
And asked him for a pass
To never-never land
Bluntly he said you silly ass
Don't you know
That only the rich can go

I turned away
Talking to myself
About some other day

Such is the life of a dreamer
Creating situations
That hint of a schemer
Threatening relations
With things no one knows
But the man in tomorrow's clothes

I turned up
Talking about more
Coins in my cup ... insane for sure

Frankly on the verge of insanity
To drag me down
Under the footsteps of humanity
With screams of listen
As the only sound
That you're missing
Where only the rich can go

(continued)

I turned back
Talking to no one
Just the sky and the sun

Such is the life of a redeemer
Creating situations
Broken like a femur
That holds on with tendons stretched
Not to mention the fits of pain
By getting up again

I turned over
For another feel of life's tow
While others picked the clover
Where only the rich can go

Yet through all the nonsense
The present came down
And sudden fits of romance
Overcame the quest for a crown
By being smart and lazy
While only the rich go ... crazy

I turned around to what I had missed
Laying right there on the ground
Was the diamond in the rough
Waiting for the right stuff

Where the happy healthy are sane enough

IT'S NOT THE MONEY

I heard this celeb on TV
Say "Believe me"
He said "I've got it
And now I can forget it"
"It's not the money"

Isn't it funny
Me sitting here
Crying in my beer
About money

It is sure easy for him to say
He's got steady pay
Nothing but fun paying his bills
But what about us folk from the hills
We got nothing to look forward to
Except being broke and blue

What about you
You got troubles too
I just don't appreciate the guy telling me
"It ain't the money"
When he's got it made
While I'm shaving with a worn out blade

(continued)

Maybe that's the way it's gotta be
But please don't insult me
By saying "it ain't the money"
Sure it is even when you have it
Because you don't catch that guy offering a split

With us folks from the hills
That can't ever pay our bills
That's the way it goes
Playing lotto and going to the casinos

Which of course "ain't about the money"

IT CAME TO PASS

Desire can't be
Held in your hand
Like a rose

Intensity isn't
Something you
Find in a field of clover

Humility doesn't
Appear as easily
As a smile

Immortality won't be
Earned without
Desire intensity and humility

For the past is written
And the future is made
As the resting place of
All mortal men

(continued)

This trip is mapped
Not by those that accept
Little and want no more
But by the soul
Of great men that assume
The finder's role

A role of inspired
Leadership holding hands
With followers and
Carrying a heavier
Load for the weaker spirits

Who instinctively question
Their own existence
So it comes to pass
With the leaders insistence

To be the makers of History
And legends in life's mystery

IT'S MORE THAN A TREE

There are times that set us free
There are times that set us apart
There are times that strike up
A memory

Of those times will it be
A whim or a memory
There are other moments
There are other feelings
There are other visions
In memory

Of those moments will we
Remember tis a memory
There are the thoughts of mothers fathers
There are thoughts of sisters brothers
There are thoughts of others
From a memory

Of these thoughts will we
Savor this moment's memory
For these are meanings to the family
These are yearnings to be felt
These are lives to be built
Upon a memory

It's more than the family or an ordinary tree
It is the family tree

I'VE SEEN THE MOUNTAIN

In the distance stands my mountain
For years it was so far away
Looming in the dusk spinning away
Night & Day
Some Way

Some How
I wanted now
It wanted when
I demanded proof
It demanded my heart
I gave my soul
It gave me another goal

I now feel the terrain a lower mountain
It is now my gain
The vision has held my attention
The time has come for ascension
The wind is now at my back
The moon is in its track

Bright and lighting the way
I scale the heights each day
In the wake of making
Molehills out of change

Beyond Mountains once thought a range

KING OF NO MAN'S LAND

The Dreamer is King

Go look out over your court. Scan the masses that stand before you. They're here in reverence to your stature. They're here to praise what you've done. They're yours for the moment. Give them something that they need.

They are pilgrims from the ages of the Court Jester and Gladiators. They look for something to touch and believe. They know no way other than the path you will draw. Don't let them down with your ego. Go before them master. Give them your best. This is the moment you've prepared for. Don't fail the test.

"What! You say there's no one there
You say the seats are bare
That the followers are nowhere
Don't they know that we need them I wonder
I wonder if they were ever there"

Maybe you just imagined they would follow you
Maybe you only thought you had the right for their rights
Maybe you only thought you had the answers
You alone

Maybe this is a sign
Maybe if you are the man you will learn before you teach
Teach before you preach
For now you are the King of No Man's Land until you've earned
The right to face those masses

(continued)

They will only listen to you if you're theirs
You must gather yourself for a more sincere fight
A fight with yourself to express a separation of your whims
Of what's wrong from what they perceive as right

A King of men must know the virtues that serve the masses
Only then will they trek to your classes as they did to the
Greatest King of all time
Lead don't plead for the sign

Set those principles down that are right
Voicing them with all your might
Never willing to give up without a fight
Feeling the words and smiting the spite

Then you're King of Their Man's Land
If you've beckoned well the auditorium will fill
And the crowds will swell
For as their King you now have a message to sell

"*Come one come all to the land of the free and the prize of the wise*"

LE' BALLOON
(a mother's fear)

Mamma Mamma look at me
I'm making a bubble moon
With Le' Balloon
For all to see

Daughter Daughter believe in me
If you play with Le' Balloon
That bursts too soon
Death is a certainty

Rock-a-bye rock-a-bye
Le' Balloon broke
Right around noon
Swallowed with a cry

Rock-a-bye rock-a-bye
Le' Balloon
Before the coming of the moon
I'll certainly die

Rock-a-bye rock-a-bye
Le' Balloon
Broke to soon
I just had to try

(continued)

My oh my
There's the moon
Despite Le' Balloon
Maybe it's a lie

Mamma Mamma look at me
Le' Balloon broke too soon
Swallowed before noon
But I didn't die

Mamma Mamma don't you cry
For my daughter won't own
Le' Balloon
The price is just too high
She might die

A parity: Let the Balloon in trouble
Find its own bubble

LIFE IS GREAT

Life is great if you don't weaken
So don't wait if it's fun you're seekin'
Everything we say and do
Is a reflection of me and you

In the mirror or the shadow following
Becomes your legacy without pride
Swallowing

In the wake of each day's plight
Is your history book's delight
With worn pages depicting longevity
And torn pages thrown to your destiny

So take the time to be happier and healthier
Keeping track to see if yourself worth is wealthier
If it is not then your life is left up to fate
You can change it is never too late

Then all will agree your life is great

LISTEN TO THE PULSE BEAT

When I hear your name
When I see your face
When I feel your touch
Or smell your skin
Or taste your lips
I can hear my pulse beat

It sounds like the first time we met
When I didn't know blood had a sound
But like all treasures
And human pleasures
That have been found
The impact was profound

First it was pounding in my head
Then it engulfed me when we were in bed
Burning a hole in our bedspread

My ears almost burst
From the feeling unrehearsed
As though I'd been cursed

It got so that I would listen
While we were kissing
To our pulse beat
An incredible feat
A delectable treat
The sound of a wedded heartbeat

(With each two beats
We are one heart)

LONELY SOUL BLUES

Lonely soul blues
Like an abandoned train
No one knows
The trouble and pain

Carnie man
Always getting high
In a life of storms
That clouds the sky

Gypsy hands
Urgent eyes
Selling dreams
From a choice of lies

Tents and rides
Swinging times
Dirt and grinds
Just for dimes

Marks are lucky
Some don't care
Others are uptight
Cause losin' ain't fair

(continued)

Lonely soul blues
No easy way
Only he knows
If he'll make
It through the day

Each night is the brink
Packing and getting sober
Catching a wink
With a companion crow bar

Onto the next town
Lonely soul blues gone
Clowning around
The carnival show must go on

Life's no fun
Maybe the next town
Revival will be the one

LOVE IS FOREVER

Love has no age
It only has you

Feelings have no time
They only give us away

Memories have no reason
They only pass us by

Birthdays have no certainty
They just count for today

But you're the reason for
Love
Feelings
Memories
And countless today's

Shari happy 2.5 billion heart felt
moments and countless memories

Years: 66
Months: 792
Weeks: 3,168
Days: 22,176
Hours: 532,224
Minutes: 31,933,440
Seconds: 1,916,006,400

Heart beats: 2,554,675,200

A loving heart is forever

LOVE IS ON MY MIND

Things pass through life
Family children and a wife
Infatuation will come and go
Sun will shine and the wind will blow
But how many really know

When love is on their mind
There's not many ways to find
If love is on your mind
Even though you think you do
Do you know

Is someone loving you
Or is it you thinking they do
Do you really know when love is on their mind
Is it something you can seek and find
Like Christmas presents or mating pheasants

Is it that simple
Does it come and go like a dimple
I don't know but I would say
When infatuation is in the way
It will seek and it will find
Releasing the thoughts somehow confined

(continued)

Confined to moments spent alone
Until thoughts pick up the phone
And say I need you
Hold me close
You'll know you've got my dose

For love is on my mind
There but somewhat confined
Until you decide to seek and find
That figment imagined to be mine

Apple stem twist and twist
Tell me will she be mine
Does she love me to exist
Am I on her mind

And want to be kissed

LOVE IS THE WINNER

It is said
That honor is dead
As a sinner is bred
It's a goner to love making in bed

Yeah for passion alone
Could have grown into a winner
But after a sigh and a groan
I loved the sin instead of the sinner

Yeah took her to bed
And laid her on her side
Caressing her head
Tearing away her pride

To inflate my ego
Misled by her forced grin
She helped the facade grow
As we loved the sin

It is said honor fled
When sinners took it to bed
And left it for dead

For I had pleased the sinner
Rather than love the winner

LOVES LOST AND FOUND

Most days just pass
Without gain or loss
But some darker days
Have a mortal cost

It's called a broken heart
Love that went wanted
As bodies part
For feelings flaunted

We all have such memories
In our lost and found
Calling out in life's stories
That love lost is indeed profound

Then it happens…for no apparent reason
It catches us in a kiss or a look
So we have to make a decision
Is this again mere hugs mistook

(continued)

Or is it true love in real life
Above all flings
And will this man take this wife
For sex kids and mortal things

Leaving all those sad goals
To fate
And finding that in my soul
You must be my mate

Then everlasting love once found
Cures all loves thought lost
From sea to shining sound
You are truly my eternal Pentecost

Believing in the what's right will alight

MAKING UP REALITY

Making up
Making time
Making love
Making out

What is reality
A friend
A clock
A mate
A kiss

It is whatever you make of it
Reality does not make us
We make reality

Or is it circumstance
That takes us to the big dance
Where we have to take a chance

With our effort
Our priorities
Our faith
Or none of the above

(continued)

Could it be our thinking in the end
Like making up to a friend
That needs to change
And our life to rearrange

Simple things disrupt
Making time on the clock
Such as getting ourselves up
Improving our stock

Making out with a kiss
Being happy
Being healthy
Being prosperous

Making Love with a mate
Being you only
Not denying fate
Or my reality

Making reality
Is so hard to do
If it is making you

MOONSET OVER TIME

Looking at the moonrise when you're oh so tired
Raises the spirits desire re-fired
The fuller it becomes the faster the pulse runs
Despite the many other stars
It gathers attention from afar

Like a porthole into darkness
Wanting us to see through time's trespass
As it rises in the sky
Human emotions begin to fly

Young and old alike all alert so
No reality can avert the involution
That will hurt ... It has unleashed
Beams to you to insert in your
Quiver of life

The sky opens as it glides to its old
Familiar heights returning
To its resting place beyond
Our sights ... circling our vibrant
Clock moments dawned

There is no stopping its relentless motion
As it moves it creates tides for the ocean
And changes our seasons
A Moonset upon our emotion
And a claim to devotion

(continued)

*Can it be the one eye to see why time
Is so precious to even the aborted life
Its beauty has been told many times
Painted and put in rhymes done
Try to understand what it means
As it drops past beyond the sun*

*I see it I feel its demand
To make the most of each day
Leaving foot prints in the sand
Alas look back over your memory
Remembering that you serve the circus
If it's only yourself you serve
Rethink your purpose retrain your nerve*

*Giving the next moon trip your best
Never doubting you'll meet
The test meeting the challenges
That fate will suggest
Crying as the moonset touches your chest*

*Hallelujah you're blessed with no sins
To be confessed
The moonset has cleansed your quest*

EVERY DAY IS MOTHER'S DAY

"Mother May I"

Mom may I go out and play
Mom may I buy a toy
Mom may I ride my bike to Joe's house
Mom may I have Joe sleep over

Mom may I go out with Joe tonight
Mom may I have the car tonight
Mom may I miss school today
Mom may I go on this date

Mom may I go out for football
Mom may I go to the Stones concert
Mom may I sign up for College
Mom may I get married

Mom may I have children
Mom may I visit you in the hospital
Mom may I find you a nursing home
Mom may you rest in peace

Mother may I remember all you have taught me

(continued)

Life is so short and so swift under our radar screen
Leaving us lost and wondering where we might have been
But it is the moments where Mom was the center of the earth
And became our value and personal worth

That we will remember
Though we tend to forget her intent
It is her teachings that pay the rent
Bless our work and build our tent

Motherhood is not always planned and predictable
But it is always managing what is put on the table
So if you are wondering what to do today
Call your Mom and tell her you are Okay
That will make her Mother's day

To Christie, Kimber, Kelli and Kip (Mr. Mom)
From your father whose greatest
"Mother I May" or might
Marry Sharon Kay … White

Then I did "Mother May I" to get those great kids

MOTHERS OF BLACK

Mothers of the men of black
Overseers of their black daughters
A purer soul not known to act
Be they the strength of a culture
Or the leader of a struggling pack

It matters not
They hold on with their goodness
The destiny of a race fraught
With the ultimate stature of their kind
The only credit of their means
The father the runner
A slave of the past
A pawn of the present
And possibly the father of the future

Only secure in the strong arms of the mother
Showing them with a patient voice
And soft caresses to another
The black mother's son waiting for Kingdom come
To be able to stand proud once thought dumb

Yet strong as one
The nation black or white
Indivisible under the justice for all
Must congregate in spite
Of insecurity of the family unit

(continued)

In that unit the leader of the pack
The chief of the tribe
The captain of the ship
The decision maker
The bread winner
The defender and the pillar
Is the mother of black abstention

The mother of black sons and daughters
Essentially the pillar and the post of invention
The Father the son and the Holy Ghost
Who's looking down on creation

Waiting for the Father to stand up or die
To the Mother in black
Carrying her family on her back
And her possessions and pride
And her offspring's dependence
On her strength
And though the discredit for the past
And somehow the present rests
With the mother of black

Tis the father's strength
That she needs to be happy
And herself fulfilled for the future
For no mother can forever be lonely
And think of her off spring only

(continued)

Without being torn down
And in crumbling to the ground
Taking her family's work with her
So give her strength I pray to
Pull it together in a family way

To bring the unit together
To pluck her man and quiet his feather
And make him proud to take the reins
To share the pains
And cultivate the gains

Of the mother's children in black discourse
Awaiting the black man on the white horse

Though this appears to be racial stereo typing or profiling
It doesn't apply to most educated black families
Given the same opportunity and same plain
We all must strive to not live in vane

But it is how social evolution
Mends the fences and reduces defenses

MOTHERHOOD

I would if I could
Fall in love with motherhood
The oldest profession
To avoid transgression

Grownups we all become
Deaf, smart or even dumb
We have the greatest thing
Our mothers who teach us everything

Along the way each day
It is they who tell us what to say
Whether it is grooming or going out
We respond to her whisper or shout

Great as great may be
It is her image we always see
As in a dream or in fear
She is the embrace always here

I would if I could
Give my life for motherhood
But since I shan't
Doesn't mean I can't

Nature somehow put us on earth
Between our Father the hearth
And our mother brought birth
To a child to be their joy and mirth

For life is what Mothers are worth

MOTHERS THE MAGICIANS

Magic is illusionary but enticing
Enticing is romantic but elusive
As the matriarch rules the nest
And the Patriarch rules the rest

Until the children demand
That we parents understand
Then it is no one's stand
With chaos near at hand

That's when it becomes
The law of the land
Laid down by the mother's command
With the sleight of hand and contraband
The family is back as a clan
Defending Mother as the Queen of the Band

Magically orchestrating her poker hand
So it seems all along it is done for her man
Happy Mother's Day to the Magicians
That have been blessed by the laurels

Of an appreciating clan

MUTUAL GRATITUDE

Tell me your problems
And I'll tell you mine
But do we really care as a pair

Inward feelings of fear
Running down my face
Which we call a tear

Silent signs of attitude
Showing through my language
Coming finally to a sense of gratitude

Because it could always be worse
As we acknowledge each other and another
Words come as we converse

First as strangers and then as brothers

For no being shall survive
As an island
When need wishes us alive

No being shall love or exist
As a stranger
The companion will always persist

(continued)

For to hide as you must
Resist as you must
You still will accept my trust
Come success or bust
If our oneness becomes a mood
The result is mutual ineptitude
For which we both suffer from ingratitude

So we must
Show mutual trust and gratitude
For to distrust this platitude
Will sink our inner mood

Confused as this innerlude

MY BREATH FROZE

My breath froze on my face
My chest heaved at the pace
Destination unknown
But the journey is my own

My brain is stuck on go
My feet won't go slow
Destination unknown
But the dream is my own

My children are on my mind
My wife is holding up fine
Destination unknown
But the reward is my own

My friends all must wonder
My associates thought me under
Destination unknown
But the way is my own

Yes my breath froze
I'm wearing worn clothes
Yes the times have yet to dispose
Of mounting pressure to foreclose

(continued)

But the subtle pleasures
Which go with seeking illusive treasures
Somehow in itself measures
The value of handling pressures

My breath froze but my face knows
Destination unknown
And the alternatives are my own
Mine alone

"For Life is my journey
Not my destination"

MY FORTUNE COOKIE

You un-wrap my life one cookie at a time
Hidden in each day is your special prize
Waiting for me to find its size
Folded into an odd form to epitomize
You in a very unique disguise
You a very secret surprise

That's life's special flavors
Hidden in a message that savors
Your inner most hopes and Treasures

For you are the fortune that seeks my pleasures
At sunrise taking love's wistful measures
Into your heart that never waivers
And a Soul filled with surprising favors

A fortune cookie waiting to be un-wrapped
At sunrise for all of me to surmise

As Our Eternal Surprise

NOT THE GOOD

It is the strong that endures
Not the good
The good must find a way
To receive its harvest
While the strong works
To betray the rest

It is the way of the unwritten
Play…a drama projected on the
Screen of our future
By the frame
Of our memory to nurture

Though we all play our parts
The ending never comes
The finale is tomorrow
The meaning is today
Left in sorrow

While the plot is to be good
Or to be strong
That is the decision

(continued)

For the good must be weak
At time of lust
And the strong must be
Indifferent and unjust

As we each accept our lines
As our dialogue rejoice
Justice enters the scene
To take the hand of choice …
Judging the Strong's stance
Caressing the good
With love and an inheritance

Of the harvest so wanted by the strong
Who are left to the spoils of being wrong
As the survival of the fittest
Is not a contest

But the need to belong
In the end Good wins
While the Strong defends
And the meek inherit the sins

While the Good live as it begins

NOVEMBER

AUTUM LEAVES autumn leaves they are falling down
Once they clothed my trees a green swaying dancing gown
Now they're lonely chilled and scattered on the ground
Autumn leaves August harvest nothing left of summer to be found

Autumn leaves autumn leaves a riot of orange red and brown
A strip tease with the trees as they all come falling down
Just a silent reminder of summer kissed by a warm sun
Autumn leaves September is done the cold breath of frost has won

Autumn leaves autumn leaves the beauty last season gave
Now the look is dead the frozen earth their grave
Once so lovely to be covered by the winter snow
Autumn leaves October snow its Nature's strip tease show

Autumn leaves autumn leaves the tree's stand cold and bare
Each branch reaches out in its own silent form of prayer
For summer's gone and the sun has turned to a cold face
Autumn leaves autumn vice…are gone to November ice without a trace

Giving winter its hibernation place

ON ANY GIVEN DAY

On any given day
Any team can
Beat itself

In spite of effort and work

On any given day
Any person can
Beat themselves

Though intentions were their inventions

On any given person
Can be built
A winning team

With visions of a legacy

On any given evening
These dreams can
Come apart

(continued)

Consumed by our desire to be famous

On any given morning
The comeback
Takes some heart

Brought short by bad health

On any given day
Can be built another dream
Of bricks and clay

Assuming we are alert that day

On any given life
With conclusions
Despite our Universal strife
Come mankind delusions

We are given another chance
To enhance our advance
To pursue and live in peace
Adventures with faith never cease

On any given day

ONCE UPON A SUNDAY – HELL WAS CREATED

Once upon a Sunday in no man's land
There lived a creature called Satan
Satan as it's told lived in this far off place
Put there by God as Adam and
Eve become uncontrolled
God could see that mortals prone to infidelity
Could not survive without some element of sterility

So God made a place
Way off in space and called it Hell
Hidden from man without a trace
He made Satan in Adam's weaker image
He cut him from brimstone with no linage
The purpose of the birth and the heat of the hearth
Caused Satan to glow as red as a molten lava flow
God made this place a land he called Hell

Void of creatures and life as well
It was dry as a piece of smoking ice
Barren that was Satan's vice
God then spoke to the world called Earth
To Adam and Eve and those given birth (continued)
"Harken unto my word" he said
"Ye have not listened when I've asked you to be good
Ye question me when you should have understood"

(continued)

"So to make my creation a better place
I impeach ye to heed my grace"
Adam and Eve and to those given birth
Giggled and pointed and showed their mirth
God replied and said "heed my message because
I've also created what may be an eternal vestige
I've called it Hell and it's in a far off place
Satan's the king and here's his face"

Satan then appeared on the scene
Adam and Eve both squelched a scream
"But Lord he is ugly and mean"
"For me to beseech this decay
Ye have not listened to my teachings
Ye seem destined to stray
Even though threats aren't my purpose
Nor is it yet Judgment day
But I thought it was time for the un-righteous to pay"
"So listen ye good to what I pray…
If you choose to falter and stray it's ye soul ye slay"

"A soul that is now a part of you
Shall go to Satan for Hell to brew"
Frightened Adam and Eve resolute
Decided never to stray or deceive
The lesson they had learned
Passed on a message and no soul burned
To this very day Hell is still not very far way, they say
And God's lesson is still a curse
Threatening us all as we face the hearse

(continued)

No one really knows who abides in that far off land
Called Hell it's the fear of living with Satan
An end without peace and misery blatant leaving fear to dwell

As did Adam and Eve and all those that histories conceive
I believe we all have a kindly reprieve
If we're true to ourselves and to no others deceive
So as the curtain falls upon all I think we'll all surly know
That Satan and Hell were created by God
For only those tempted to throw off virtues with evil to sow

And even they return to the fold before they burn
For once upon a Sunday Hell was created
To enforce the law of God on Monday
But the misery of not knowing the final event
Keeps the sheep from straying by sensing the Advent

And fearing the life misspent

ONE BACK TWO FORWARD

One step two
Two step three
Life's no bargain
If today's all you see

Three step four
Four step five
Hope is all that keeps us alive

Five step six
Six step seven
Pessimists never see the inside of Heaven

Seven step eight
Eight step nine
Lady luck is neither fair nor blind

Nine step ten
Ten step one time through
Just a beginning each time's new

Then if one step is back
Two must be ahead
Cause any other course and we're dead

(continued)

Over a period of time
Keeping the count keeping score
We forget what's in store

And not deal with a backslide or two
It's an acceptable level of effort
With a tendency to cavort

One foot forward and two back in a slippery shoe
Blaming everyone but you
Creates a demise of the external pew

For back sliding will not renew
One step forward and back on two
Until you back into you
Chasing something new

When openings are very few

IF NOT BUT IF SO

Are you good
If not
Do you think so
Or wonder if you could

If not
Who else will know
Are you growing
Do you strive to learn

If not
What will your earn
Are you dreaming
Do you want more than you discern

If not
How can you get very far
Are you expecting much
Do you live life chasing a cigar

If not
Aren't you the sheep and not the wool
Are you a winner
Whose attitude is the cup half full

(continued)

If not
Bad attitudes breed skid row bums
Are you enthusiastic
With a will to be your sums

If not but If so
Then you've got a chance to pass the test
The test is not a contest
When it comes too close to the vest

If not but If so
Of those who know
That doing your best
Is the contest

It's a self-happiness sense
Knowing the best is your fate
Just attempting excellence
Makes you great

And failing is deciding to wait

OUR LOVE

Our love is like the wind
It's always there fulfilling
Some days it is a breeze
Some days it is a storm
Some days it is chilling
But most days it is thrilling

Our love is like the warm rain
It is always cleansing
Some days it is gentle
Some days it is a pain
Keeping us from being vain

Our Love is for you
For as our children you're like the wind
A warm breeze that is always there
Some days it is distressing
But most days it is a blessing

(continued)

Our love is because of you
For as our children
You're like the cool rain
A cleansing blessed refrain
Always there for our gain

Our love is from your soul
For all God's children
You're the spirit from the womb
That is all knowing all whole
As the wind the warmth of the eternal tomb
The very essence of your love

Is your children with the presence of our love

PEACE ON EARTH

P erfect
E xaltation
A ttacks
C ynical
E xcuses

Take one soldier
Take one life
For senseless purpose
And peace shall cease

Take one son or daughter
Take one to heaven
For wrongful excuses
And peace shall forever cease

Take one country
Take one loss of pride
For ideology versus principle
And peace shall forever cease

For Peace on Earth
To be the perfect exaltation
Good Will to men
Must confront an imperfect world

With Soldiers of Good Will
Attacking cynical excuses....
Then Peace Shall Never Cease
Nor will wars prevent abuses

With the fate of the world
That peace induces

FORMULA FOR PEACE

Hand me your weapons
Hand me your cause
Now contemplate your sons
Think of your daughters as you pause

Is it worth the price you pay
To confront your fellow man
With fists clenched to betray
Peaceful days in each other's land

I don't believe
You believe it's right
To forsake those you conceive
Your children just to fight

Think and ponder
Why is it necessary
To ravage God's wonder
With only selfish banners to carry

(continued)

Why not throw down
Your pride from your side
Make peace your sound
Before we all have denied

That in peace
Lives don't cease
Love and friends abide
Before we all have died

For a belief in the same God's absolution
That Religion without reason = Revolution
That Reason minus Religion = Resolution
That Perfection is Reason with Absolution is the Solution

In the God we trust knows the difference

PLUG IN MY SHADOW

Plug in my shadow
With the umbilical cord
Turn on my light
With the brain wave

Deliver me from evil
With the belief
That my shadow
Lives and my brain grows
And my heart knows

When love is near
Delivered from fear
Unto faith before
Forever After

Into
Tomorrow's
Heaven on earth

Unplugging doubt
Into worth
From birth

To never
Fear Eternity's hearth
Known as HELL

With my shadow
Doing WELL
Creates Heaven's girth

And in its image he gave birth

PREACHER MAN

Wash away the tears and dissolve our fears

Preacherman Preacherman
Where do you stand
On your pulpit
Or in the sand

Simple as it may seem
Your followers
Believe your dream
And in the spirit that it stirs

Preacherman Preacherman
Don't forget
Only if we can
Will beliefs be set

If we're to hold up
You must realize
It's from a lasting cup
Filled with no lies

Preacherman Preacherman
Do you understand
Your words must
emphasize
Not criticize

(continued)

If you do that
No matter what
All will stand that have sat
In reverence to what you taught

So Preacher man Preacher man
Don't open your mouth
Unless you know the dirt from the land
And north from south

We're looking to learn
From you
To which you earn
By being true

Preacherman Preacherman
Write it down for the doubters
Say it with conviction for the believers
Site it proud to the scouters
Pray it for all to hear even the achievers

Brush away the skeptics and dissolve
Their political deceivers

PSYCHIC OR PHYSICAL

Tell me a tale or two
About what you believe and what you do
Are you more inclined
To view things from the front or the behind

Do you take more interest in a thing of beauty
Or do you get turned on by doing your duty
Or are you turned on by a face that's kind
Or are you looking for a stimulation of the mind

Physical versus psychic
Selenic or dyslectic
What really turns you on
The nighttime or the dawn

Tell us pray tell us your story
Do you want moderation or glory
When you finally decide and commit it
Try it for a while and see if you fit

Because if you don't and you start to hurt
Psychic will be a mind to avert self-destruction
Physical will be the body with no resurrection
If you've picked the easier scene
Which only makes you mean

(continued)

You may sacrifice your good life
To be happy as a necessity of mental strife
After all it is your choice and gain
For which you've paid the pain

Just don't lose what you've had in full
Because dreaming is psychic
Doing is physical
To have it all

So tell me a tale or two
About what you believe and what you do
Are you more inclined
To view things from your front or your behind

When truth is the size of your heart
and the strength of your mind

SCATTER GUN OR RIFLE SHOT

Pick up your weapons hunters
Set out on your hunt
Pick out your prey
Shoot the gun shoot the day

Did you score your limit
Did you come home happy
Was your shot on target
Or did you miss the prey

If you aren't sure
Go out the next day
Taking notes did it occur
Did you get your prey

If not why not
Was it your weapon
Was it your shot
Did the prey live on like it or not

If so look at your gun
Look at your technique
Did the shot from the rifle run
To the heart of what you seek

(continued)

Or did it scatter
And fall helplessly to the gage
Leaving your effort a limp matter
While the prey leaves the stage

Yes the conquest is not the number of pellets
It's not the loud blast
It is in the rifle sight which gets
To the heart direct and fast

Then if there is a miss
Another well aimed shot can be fired
Before the prey runs into the mist
And you become too tired

Time may require more and more
To bring your prey down
But placing your shots to score
Will preserve your right to another round

For even death can wait
On a peaceful trip
With a sporting camera grip
And some bait

Making peace with the deer slip
And worth the freight

SEVENTY-FIVE

39 thirty-seven times
Age and getting older
With fibs and rhymes
Looks are the beholder

Miles per hour
Hot and cold
Weakness and power
Young or old

In each we preach
That life is not a number
To do so we beseech
That a digit can encumber

Our hope our vision
To live our days
With plans and reason
To fend off delays

It is a mortal waste of time
Misspent worrying of beauty
When in fact the soul is sublime
And honoring it our duty

Happy Birthday to me
(If I accept 75 as an accomplishment
Just think what is meant to be
If I reach 103)

SHELL GAME

Under the next shell
The only way to find out is to take a chance
But the tolls we're counting seem rehearsed
To risk body and soul and expected romance
For the love of self comes first
The tolls we are not counting cannot be disbursed

Look under each shell
Seek and ye shall find
For a better way to do the same
For it is a compromise to take a chance
To look and find that it may be
And it may not be the big dance

Truth under each shell
For the shells belong to the house
And unto this house there is no baker
Just the table the shells and the urge to peek
But even if you were to see your candle stick Maker
There are no answers you know how to seek

(continued)

Disappointment under each shell
It is put up so shut up
I don't think you could avoid going to Hell
By always looking for the shortcut
Expecting to be the successful scanner
And you don't even salute when they sing
The Star Spangled Banner

Losing to the shell game
When guessing is harsh
And there is no claim
When the shell game is a farce

And you might as well hide under a hearse
For things can get worse
If you forget the national anthem's verse
While looking for the shell
Promising Heaven

Under a shell concealing Hell

SHE'S A WOMAN

She is a mother
She is a sister
She is a lady
I've loved her
I've kissed her
She's a woman

She is an equal
She is a partner
She is a companion
I've loved her
I've needed her
She's a woman

She is a wife
She is demurer
She is a life
I've loved her
I've missed her
She's a woman

(continued)

She is the silk
She is the fur
She is the fabric
I loved her
I've felt her
She's a woman

She is my tenor
She is my singer
She is my voice
I've loved her
I've played her
She's a woman

She's my woman
She's for me
She's forever
She's for her man
In a woman's world
With her man around

She is the Queen and I am her Crown

SHINE ON ME

At sun-up we are amazed at the light
At sun down we are phased by the dark
In birth we are raised by the might
In life we are crazed by the sight

It is the shine that holds us
It is the warmth that marries us
It is the fear that molds us
It is the sign that buries us

So for the moments we cherish
Each year we express our wish
To our spouse or lover
In such time we seek and discover

Searching deliver me from evil
Life is more than upheaval
Hold me close to your need
Allowing my life to succeed

My love is indescribable
My feeling is reliable
My feeling is viable
So shine on my life or I am liable

To be less than I could be
By loving me
We both are free
To shine for eternity

For the hereafter my love for
My wife my family and their shining light on me

"THE ANGEL OF DEATH"
(Nazi Justice with Vengeance)

He was sighted
The vengeful were delighted
Justice would be done
Vengeance would be won

Mengele dealt his own hand
Portrayed his injustice for the fatherland
Slipped away in fear of vengeance
Living a spiteful life of penitence

Ironical as Hitler was his cause
Justice may encompass one lucid clause
That is the unwavering chapter of revenge
Played to the swing of fate's heavy hinge

Slamming each of us to the ground
If we ignore the sanctity of the profound
The sanctity of the life we've been endowed
Along with the latitude most are allowed

To act in our own way our own justice
But facing the consequences of prejudice
When fallen to that level of greed
About one's own selfish deed

Then justice must be sighted
Leaving the vengeful delighted
For it is the same doctor on the run
Whose fitful life and death means justice is done

For those souls that were lost
To the holocaust

SILENCE IS OUR MUSIC

Sing your song
And I'll lend my ear
Come on along
You have nothing to fear

Love is quiet
As there's no voice
That's willing to say it
Just a lover's choice

As thunder needs to be heard
There's nothing spoken
Without a word
Unless it's silent yonder

Like soft voices in the dark
Hesitating to see
Faces that will mark
Impressions in a memory

(continued)

The senses grasp at reality
They only recognize now
Nor do they grasp infinity
Unless you show them how

For little do we realize
That love doesn't speak
It is in quiet disguise
Until silent love is our music

From a heartbeat
From the pulse beat
From the ear's replete
From the touch complete

It is love's silence we seek

STANDING IN FUTILE ESTEEM

Esteem is it ego
Allowing some to bestow
Or ambition's repent

We all stand in awe
Of being special
Being different

Many strive to stand out
And end up the same
As the crowd is hell bent

Yes, they're all the same
Trying to be different
Ending up future spent

Punk cool stoned
Chasing the same dream
So no one is the way they seem

Except doing it on our own
Makes more sense
By standing in futile esteem

As an awesome Individual
Standing tall while others fall
As the Captain of life's team

SUCCESS UNLIMITED

The farmer of a self
With success unlimited
What a beautiful thing
Planted in the garden of opportunity
Cultivated by the souls with a purpose

To improve themselves
And the garden around them
This garden of opportunity
Is God's laboratory

For future's story
He planted the seed of knowledge
In the selves that
Dwell in the garden of opportunity

Some will waste their fertility
Some will experiment
And question
Their existence

Wanting to know why
They live out their time
And waste their opportunities
Others will take pride in

(continued)

Watching dreams grow
Into reality
Realizing that success
Unlimited awaits those
Who understand fertility

And celebrate history's pages
For as the garden grows
So goes the drama on unlimited stages
As the threatening wind blows

But success limited to the act
Is far inferior to the actor
Pursuing fame and fact
Than for the benefactor

As giving is for living
And sighing is for dying

SUCCESSFUL YEARS

Successful years are made up
Of successful months

Made up of successful days

Made up of successful hours

Made up of successful minutes

A life lived successfully
Minute by minute
Becomes successful

Hour by hour

Day by day

Week by week

Month by month

Year by year

(continued)

How good a successful moment can be

The definition of success is in each person's
Life style
Values
Habits
Principles
Ethics
Honesty
Family ties
Relationships
Response to adversity

Not an easy trip but it is a journey not a destination

MIND OVER DESTINY

The mind makes our destiny

Overcoming doubt along the way
Setting us free every day

Unleashing the fear of tomorrow
By thinking of no sorrow

Loving a life of dreams
Making love to what life seems
Not what fate schemes

Unattached to the past
And the shadow cast
Is our hope and prayers that hast
Come to pass

The mind is our destiny
Our very thoughts take us
To heights we cannot see
Or discuss

For it is just faith's piece of us

SUPERSTAR

The American Dream
It would seem
Fits the historical mold
As Roman stories told

Praising the body more than the mind
Forgetting why the roses twine
Seeking pleasures through and through
Bowing to thrills for anything new

Crowds demand and get more excitement
Forgetting why and what yesterday meant
With many doubts because of such terms
As "nice guys finish last" it affirms

Is it true can it be
That we've forgotten society
Let's step back and take awhile
To scold ourselves and make a smile

(continued)

Then take a toll of our daily role
Feeling a need to search our soul
To be true to what's important to do
By placing values above thrills and pills

If we can get to those kinds of things
Then we can contemplate what it brings
By avoiding a false sense of views
And reading the Bible not just the Sporting News

This will bring reinforcing to heal the scar
Caused by a mindless worship of the superstar
So everything can renew that super you
Accepting that what we do is for the few

Who aren't dedicated to being emancipated

TAKE MY HAND

Touching leaves my soul in your grasp
Your warmth is addicting
Take my hand help me hold on
Until you're expecting

I'll never know you better
Than right now as you
Find me in your need
Though you've always wanted

Me ... I don't know when
Your commitment grew
Out of desire into seeking a friend
That you already knew ... until

Our possession of more
Was passion not love
Giving me your hand for
Better or worse more than a glove

(continued)

But truly touching me
Only happens when we
Become committed to us
With our vows and trust

As you bring me to
You with your need
Give me your hand
As our desire has agreed

That I took your hand before your need
And your hand as your want
Planting a seed
Into a larger and larger font

Of our lives and epitomize
A longer stronger breed

LIFE'S ECHO

Life's echo
A listener's whisper
The speaker's voice
Knelt on the needs of man
Are the words of the Evangelist
Depicting a feeling most
Don't know for themselves

The secrets of the future
Is every person's puzzle
Waiting to be deftly assembled
Or destined to be strewn as
Impatient desire attacks
Without faith or order

He who finds order finds
The message for others
Forming on his lips
He becomes
A life's echo
A listener's whisper
A speaker's voice
As the Evangelist

One who must live with his choice
And forget the shallow voice
In a world where the future is last
In the grave of a crucified + master

With the echo resounding to the cast
That we can live forever after the past

A SECOND TIME AROUND

We all hope for second chances
Bold moves and careful glances
If you hit one out of three
You're the star they come to see

If you play at par
Spectators come from afar
If you are down 10 pounds
Bathing suit size resounds

It is when things go wrong
That new numbers sing your song
It is not that God allows
You to say the second vows

It is your heart
A brand-new start
A second chance
To find true romance

A second chance
To further enhance
Your life your hope
Not wanting to elope

(continued)

But put on the show
Where we all can go
Watching our family grow
Dressed in red white and blue
It is a start brand new

Discarding the old baggage
Stepping on a new stage
The players are all in renewal
Exchanging rings of jewel

Representing a life to come
Knowing where you came from
Realizing your souls foremost dream
Together the bride and groom are the theme

And Crown of the Second Time Around

SNOW STORM CATTLE

Here I am astraddle
This metal saddle
Caught up in traffic
Listening to my wipers rattle

Snow's coming down
All around
Seems it strangles
A Chicago town

Hope I have enough gas
To make this one last pass
For there's no way to pedal
This salty hunk of metal

Here we go again
Moving two feet beyond
Where we've just been
Lord the snow has turned to rain
And there's a car stalled in my lane
I must be insane

(continued)

To straddle this metal saddle
In this herd of mobile cattle
There goes another poor soul to the side
His gas is gone and his motor's died

Wonder if and wonder when
I'll ever get home again
If you can believe and conceive
Being lonely in a crowd
Just sit in your car beneath a snow cloud
Then stuck
Next to a cattle truck

Oh no
As if traffic isn't enough
The rain is turning to slicker stuff
The heater sounds like an egg beater
And if it gives in I'll most surely
Meet my creator

Sitting here astraddle
This steel saddle
Smelling this truck full of cattle
Fighting this mobile battle

(continued)

Would you believe it's been an hour
Since I passed the Water Tower
And as I'm leaving Chicago
Up to my stir-ups in snow

Sitting astraddle
This steel saddle
In this herd of metal cattle

Wondering where I'm going
And where I've been
Hoping I'll ever get home again
Driving into a driving wind

With my hope as a friend

SECRETS OF THE MIND

SECRETS OF THE MIND

Uncover the reaches
Pull down the stars
Count the sand pebbles
Upon the beaches

And you won't
Touch the secrets of the mind

Uncover the moss
Turn back the pounding waves
Count the grains of salt
Beneath his cross

And you won't
Scratch the surface of the mind

Undo your kite string
Close your eyes to time and
Count the passing moments
As you fly and sing

And you will
Beseech the secrets of the mind

(continued)

Uncover the History
Turn back its tattered pages
Count the regrets
Of mankind's story

And you won't find
The secrets of the mind

Undo your better senses
Spread your roots
Until you have wings
For the trip beyond pretenses

And you will find
The secrets of your mind
Then Seek and you shall unwind
A truth for each secret found

Then make a poem sound profound

THE GAME OF PSYCHE

To get control of your
Opponent's mind
Before the warm-up and match starts

You look him in the eye
You look away nonchalantly
As if you don't care
You move his water jug over

So there's room for yours
You lay your racket across his
Against the net
Then tell him how well
He's playing

You ask him if he minds using
Your can of balls
You take the downwind
Side of the court
Before he can get there
Then turn your back to
Tie your shoelace

Before warm-up starts
You hit your first ball deep
To his backhand
His weakness his defeat

(continued)

THE WARM-UP

By this time you can feel
His eyes narrow
The vision of doubt creeps in
He returns the first backhand beyond
The baseline

You stop abruptly to let him know
That the shot was way out
Your next shot is a topspin
Blooper deep to his forehand
Cross court
His return again sails long
Which you catch before it hits
The ground

Then apologize for hitting
The shots so deeply
Down the middle of the court short
His start to the net is
Slow because he is so deep
Behind the baseline
With a stumbling approach
He hits it into the net
You are winning the warm-up

(continued)

Just at the point
When he begins to hit
Decisive shots
You ask him to hit you
A few overheads
Each of which you let bounce
And easily put away
Not decisively just smoothly

After four or five you ask
If he wants a few
Your first lob should be a
Top spinner high to his backhand
If he returns it
Easily retrieve it
And hit another topspin
And hit another top sin
To his backhand and
Another and another

Apologize for not being
Able to hit them short
Then ask for practice serves
And compliment him on his serves
"I've never seen you serve
This well before"

(continued)

Your practice serves should be accurate
But not hard just decisive enough to be deep

One after another
Six in deep to the backhand
Then move to the net to begin
Again saying "I've never seen you serve so well"
By now you have won the warm-up
The spin of the racket and eventually the match

Is it a sin to win mind games
Without the names and fames
Who takes the blame for a loss
Is it your win or his lost

Only if you feel competition has a cost
There are no winners or losers from a ball
Being tossed into the air
And asked to fair

On where it lands or who it underpins
Then the mind game wins

THE MATCH

The mind is playing its game with his confidence
The first game is a continuance of complements
Hitting to his backhand and making the most of
The inner game of tennis

If he recovers soon enough it is then to each his own game

THE MIND GAME

Is it unfair to compete
Is it sinister to replete
Can it be and is it true
That playing unfair is really you

The sport of it all
Is not in the racket or the ball
It is in the challenge
On that form of stage

Playing the mind game
When we all start out the same
And then it is time
To turn on the mind

And win the real game
Proving we are not all the same

THE STORYTELLER

Picking out a pattern on the wall
Looking at an ink spot's scrawl
Skipping cracks on the sidewalk
Going nowhere for small talk
Picking up leaves
Just to look
Walking through the forest by
A gloomy brook

Too cold and shook to look at fate
This is the storyteller's gait
Trying to create
An inspiration that just couldn't wait
From the duck hunter spreading bait
To genes blending to make a trait
Like trolls catching fate
And lover's fishing for a mate
The storyteller must create

The storyteller to best seller
It isn't just a thought
That can't be bought it must be sought
When caught put to words

Then a plot
First it's cold then it's hot
A war of words must be fought
A personal testimony
Must be wrought

(continued)

Catching life like scenes
From nothing but in-betweens
About kings and queens
Marines and BAD dreams
Using most any means
To liven up pork-n-beans
With the sauce of New Orleans

Storyteller to bestseller
Put it to the paper story speller
Fiction spinner romantic winner
Imaginative little feller

The storyteller
Walter Heller to best seller
Caldwell Taylor to Norman Mailer
Whether you're a short trailer

Or a small sailor
You should let your bell weather
And your tall teller
Put a killer in the cellar

And it may just turn into a
Best seller

THE WELL

Love is more than a feeling
It is a well
That fills when
A need needs drawn
Think of it as an event

But is that the well
Aware of time
Or is it there
When you need
To drink from memories

The event called love
Doesn't go beyond the
Surface of the bottomless well
The more you need
The deeper the well
And the deeper your
Understanding of love

Life is merely an
Exploration of the well ... lo

Many never drink
From the depths
Nor do they
Understand the need
That takes you to
The bottom of why we are

(continued)

To the level of the
Beginning meeting the end as
The circle of love
Is everlasting … like night and day
Love is there
To explore
Beneath the surface
Beneath the event
Beneath life
Ready to flow

Into an open heart
Thirsty for more
Than a life without meaning
With the well to drink from
Its depths to understand
That love isn't an event
It is sustenance
A bottomless well
Welling up to lovers

And wetting down the covers

THE AGONY OF DEFEAT

Beat me
Batter me
Defeat me
But don't ignore me

Defeat is a personal thing
It really hinges
On desire to be accepted
And the fear of being rejected

There is no agony in defeat
When you can accept it
As a temporary setback
Until you've had a chance to try again

I know it's hard to accept
That it doesn't matter
But does it

Try to look at it objectively
As you look back
Don't observe something
Simplistic in all of life's endeavors

(continued)

Don't you first see a desire
To accomplish something
The desire emanates
From your very spirit or being
For some reason

This reason is a need
A need for fulfilling oneself
The degree of fulfillment
Has a great deal to do with
The agony of defeat

The more you need
The more you have to lose
As insecurity is the true agony of defeat
And security is the true enemy of the defeated

Be secure in your need to lose before you win

VISITORS OF ANOTHER WAY

Milky Way
Another day
Another time
Travelers beyond
The sunshine

The medians are there
To listen
Ears grope
And the eyes glisten
For the other way is near
Mortals close it out
With fear
Only holding onto
This life so dear

Can we visit this
Other way
This encounter
Without a day
Without a night
Where there's no

(continued)

Darkness nor is there light
Void of indulgence
And fright

Visitors of the other way
With souls that don't decay
Call it heaven
On Judgment Day
But might it not be
A blessing
A traveler
In God's dressing

Body turned into the mind
So only thoughts
Are able to find
And visit the Other Way
Far beyond the Milky Way

Energy transcending mortal display

ALIVE

When we die
And I don't know why
I believe we'll live again
In spite of sin

More alive
Than dead
In a different form
Instead

Of this I realize
And no one really dies
They just fade away
But their force doesn't decay

The substance
To which they are
Emanates each day
From afar

In the form of energy
We plot a course
In the endless sea
We are unable to see

You're not passing away
You're just passing by
Free to thrive
Eternally alive

Knowing that eighty is on overdrive

A HARD WINTER'S SPRING

It's been so long
Since we've seen the ground
The seasons turn
The Merry-Go-Round
For it's been a hard winter

To pray for spring
Is to bring on fall
That's everything
Most of all

Those that hibernate
In the close of fall
Close down
And just wait

Waiting for the clouds
To clear
Till the sun dawns
More near as

(continued)

The earth begins to break
With blooms
And off springs
For nature's sake

No more icy roads
Closed abodes or half loads
Standing by as the earth erodes
To recreate nature's abodes

Hallelujah spring
Is almost here
With it comes good cheer
And the twinkle of
Ecology as children sing

Raining in a hard
Winter's spring

WRINKLES OF AGE

As time passes over the dam of existence
There's no stopping the flood
Life evolves as does time in a plot of suspense
And a current of creation is in our blood

Wrinkles of age are vines of experience
Spreading as the ink spot stains

This is said of the memory
The memory of what used to be
Voiced to a past harmony
Much like the rings of a tree

Wrinkles of age are vines of experience
Spreading as the ink spot strains

Like old girlfriends who stand for something
In the minds we once knew
Now is gone to hurt or sting
As feelings have turned blue

Wrinkles of age are vines of experience
Spreading as the ink spot remains

Be it Sue … Carolyn or Rosie were their names
Until then they had loved someone tame
Thrown around in the boy likes girl game
Thereby turning the clock back all the same

(continued)

Wrinkles of age are vines of experience
Spreading as the ink spot wanes

We recovered from the disappointment
Of knowing it wasn't to be
Until I found the anointment
Of Sharon Kay for me

Wrinkles of age are vines of experience
Spreading as the ink spot explains

We had our clicks and slacks
We had our jeans and loafers too
As records no longer made of wax
Played in cars customized like new

Wrinkles of age are vines of experience
Spreading as the ink spot stains

Without meaningful notions to dare
Our hair was our biggest pride
Kept neat but always there
Shorter the more uptight we tried

Wrinkles of age are vines of experience
Spreading as the ink spot sustains

Those were the ages of fifties
That we now look back upon
With wonderment graphic nifty's
And wishes that are now bygone

(continued)

Wrinkles of age are vines of experience
Spreading as the ink spot maintains

We lived those days as a group
Together we faced the tribulation
Aging now as we recoup
Our memories with new expectation

Wrinkles of age are vines of experience
Spreading as the ink spot explains

But endless years don't make a life
Nor does it fade the memory
For I still remember the happiness and strife
In the arms of my past history

Wrinkles of age are vines of experience
Spreading as the ink spot arraigns

It was those days of the proms
Fair acres and the youth center
Growling dads and sensitive moms
Until voices turned to tenor

Wrinkles of age are vines of experience
Spreading as the ink spot engrains

(continued)

That was just a part of growing up
Hanging upon each friend
Much like an orphaned pup
Crying in the wind

Wrinkles of age are vines of experience
Spreading as the ink spot detains

So today as we stand and look back
Upon those days thought so serious
We realize what little we lack
Compared to when we were delirious

Wrinkles of age are vines of experience
But thank god for the refrain
That now makes sense
Of the mystery of our ink spot stain

Without a pattern or a frame
No mention of fortune and fame
Starting out we are all the same
With fears and tears to tame

Forming wrinkles as vines of the times
And signs of the lines of ink on a page
With our crimes that are there
Leaving the stage … too early for prayer

TRUST

If you can't trust your friend
Can you trust yourself
If you can't trust yourself
Who can you trust

The profound lie
Comes from the lips of a man
Who says
I shall never be tempted

To paint an illusion
That would sacrifice
Truth's bitter pill

For you see that man has
Swallowed the pride
Of knowing thyself

For the sake of
An advantage that
Will never last

(continued)

He no longer can
Trust himself
Nor will trust others

And no peace shall be his
Only doubt and distain
For in God we trust

And unto ourselves
Be true
But to others
We shall be untrue

Until my trust comes through
To You

NOTES TO A NEUROTIC

Note the person who
Cannot be straight
And will do then undo
Because they cannot wait

Some dreams must come true
If you're pursuing something new
For you can't be happy or blue
Unless it's happening to you

Fantasies are real
As long as you can feel
My heart beating
And hear my sermon repeating

Reality may not exist
Though tomorrow will persist
For my mind shuts out
What time is all about

Logic has no meaning
When the past is careening
Around the shambles
Of unworthy gambles

Neurotic behavior is a clue
To a weakness inside of you
If wary minds undo
Themselves for dreams and
Neurotic thoughts untrue

Belief is the cure … It's all up to YOU

SPACES

Spaces filled
Fill it with air
The oxygen will
Turn the barren
Outer space to life

Spaces fulfilled
Fill it with thoughts
The act will turn the barren
Inner space to action

Spaces willed
Fill it with something new
The challenge will
Turn the barren
Outer space to something true

Spaces distilled
Fill it with faith
The belief will surely
Turn the barren
Inner space to heaven

(continued)

Spaces killed
Fill it with love
The feeling will
Turn the barren
Loneliness to fulfilled

Filling our inner and outer space
With our past habits haste waste and taste
Creating our real age in the aging pace
And healthy race

To eternal peace in our lasting place

HE WAS CALLED TINY

In my younger days
Just around the turn of nineteen forty
When war was all the craze
Lived a boy just a toy called shorty

He had a heart that boy
Even with his unfortunate start

Never up front at the beginning
Having to strain to keep up with the pack
But with a desire bent on winning
Later put most others to his back

He had a heart that boy
Even with his unfortunate start

As he gained and won
He was afraid to count the blessing
Brought up as a undeserving son
Not a natural winner nor much for confessing

He had a heart that boy
Even with his unfortunate start

This made him try harder I guess
Practicing pulling and sometimes pushing
Preparing his system for the stress
Like grease applied to a bushing

(continued)

He had a heart that boy
Even with his unfortunate start

They named him Tiny cause of his build
By a coach who respected his desire
Always bent upon something willed
And fanning the flame and stoking the fire

He had a heart that boy
Even with his unfortunate start

Tiny was never quite first team you see
Cause the bigger boys always came first
And from this to him came the key
Accomplishments as failure reversed

He had a heart that boy
Even with his unfortunate start

Now that I look back thank God I was also Tiny
Not many can be fortunate as me

Cause in losing I dropped gently to my knee
And asked him to help attain a spirit that set me free
And thanking him for making me almighty
TINY

(That was my Coach Dave Englund who named me, for my pound for pound determination, as tiny, who himself is now at the age of 88 a world-renowned art Professor and Sculpture of giants of the world)

THE BRAVEST GIRL I'VE EVER SEEN

Have you ever met someone that impressed you as being very strong? Not easily discouraged or distracted from what they're all about though it may have gone wrong. They seem to have the perseverance and fortitude to go ahead, with their duties even though they have misfortune and handicap instead. I have. My oldest daughter is of that character. She has been brought up in a fairly secure home, that's a factor. But she has had her ups and downs along the way. That is to say, it hasn't been easy for her each day. And all along these ways and bygone days I've never known her not to try. And if at first she doesn't win, she tries more often and again; do or die.

She's done this many times.
First it was being the oldest; asked to be the first; be the boldest. She had to try things up front, not forgotten but somewhat cursed. Before she has seen anyone else do it, unrehearsed. She stuck her neck out; fought many a bout just to try the things we asked her to scout.

This made the way for her younger sisters and brother to follow; one another. Little does she realize that this has increased their size. Secondly she set the scene for no acceptance in between. She loves school then now and when; feeding our pride with mind and pen. With the example for them to follow, all of us became filled, none went hollow. It really wasn't easy for her, to try, to that we concur. But the amazing thing is that she never asked why. She knew in her heart that good graces apply; to children that give it a try.

(continued)

Later she was asked to face the hill overcoming vanity with much will.

With a finger almost lost she faced life's biggest cost. The bill was to overlook the facts of adversity, for the sake of just being she. It also meant putting up with much pain along the tendency to weakness and strain. Turning her back upon herself she demonstrated a personal wealth, of character and fortitude not lost to her silent mood. I admire that girl so much for her heart so gentle to the touch; never asking for pity or a crutch; she's her own sail to such and such.

So let me tell you quite frankly she is the apple of our eye and has taught us to never ask the reason why. Because living isn't unless, you try.

Thank you Christie Caye
For your courage to venture and fly
From the nest to the sky

TURNING

Turning on a pedestal
Turning towards what is helpful
For the ego

Turning away
From the light of day
Though it is a lie

Turing on a friend
The turning shall never end
Like lost hope

Turing in your mind
So easy to be unkind
And selfish

The bigger the ego
The smaller the mind

The bigger the lie
The smaller the ear

(continued)

The bigger the storm
The smaller the wind

The bigger the selfish needs
The smaller the rewards

Caught turning
When you've turned
There's turning back

But it's a fact
Turning on a lover
There's no turning back

And Turning on yourself
There is only ego and lies
With no rewards but stormy skies

But turning around can be profound … as paradise found

THE COMMENCEMENT DAY

The beginning
The end
What a limited
Understanding of life

The commencement
The benediction
What a profound
Way of limiting a life

Words words words
Spoken heard ignored
What A shallow
Way of inspiring a belief

The teachings
Might never dwell
Beyond the commencement
Of mental atrophy

The discipline
Of the necessity of learning

(continued)

Decreases with the commencement
Unless knowledge is craved
By an already hungry soul

No school of thought
Can overcome
The cathartic
State of graduation
To nothing more

It is the school of desire
That stokes the flame
To the spirit's fire
So commencement is
Not lost to acceptance

But is the door to opportunity
And a lifelong career found

THE BIGGER I AM

I am so big but am I dumb
The bigger I think I am
The smaller I've become

The smaller I become
The closer is reality
Cause then everyone's bigger than me

Am I so smart am I for real
When the smarter I think I am
The less I feel

Do I listen or do I just talk
Am I the leaf or
Just a bigger stalk

Just for an instant to be great
And show how big I am
Before it's too late I can't wait

For the more I think of me
The less I appear
To those that can see that it's just the fear in me

(continued)

I am so big but am I dumb
The bigger I think I am
The smaller I've become

In the mental state of deaf and dumb
Where size doesn't count
And my ego has succumb

To the message on the mount
Erasing all the doubt
Living by the commandments ten
Ending wondering how big I've been

When I should have asked do ... I need to begin again

THE GAMBLER

Life revolves around the spindle
Much like the wheel of chance
Looking for some hope to kindle
Smiling as winning numbers become happenstance

Life is so much like the rolling dice
Tumbling to a resting place somehow
And in spite of men and mice
Its meaning rests with an earnest pick and plow

Life is so much like the turning card
We never know what's coming up
Be it smooth or be it marred
You decide how to fill your cup

Life is so much like the bouncing ball
Hitting and missing the slots you want
Awaiting the right chance to call
But you're the author of the plot

(continued)

Life is much like the numbers turning
The odds are not always in your favor
Unless you find a worthwhile yearning
And good intentions to savor

Life is s much like the Bacharach box
Holding the secrets fast inside
Not easily or freely releasing the locks
Forcing you to develop a hard earned pride

Life is a gamble you see
Nothing good comes with a guarantee
So no matter how hard you plea
You'll never be a winner until you decree

That life is more much more than
To gamble away
Each day just being free to lose your way

GURU

The Guru
What does he want from me
Could it be
He knows something I don't see
Could it be
He is the prophet

You can bet
He's no threat
So it's left up to you to beget

He merely plants the seed
If he sees the need
So don't feel Compelled to heed
Unless you believe his creed

But if you do follow his lead
Do it with Good speed

Think it through
Till you feel it's true
Then with a will to pursue

Formulate your action be it new
For opportunities are very few

(continued)

But if you do follow his lead
Do it with Godspeed

Because his suggestion
Is forced to reflection
And has led to dissection and correction

By smarter pioneers
And ventures'
Than he

Guru
Give me your clue
Is it true
That most followers are through
And never start anew
Are you what I already knew

Or is that how you became a Guru

EGO TRIP

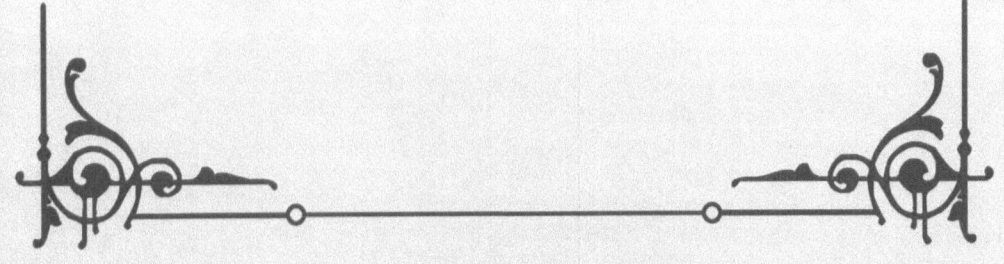

EGO TRIP

Come along
Take an ego trip
With me
It starts with insecurity
And builds with desire
To be more than a scared
Ordinary person parked comfortably

The more the flame is fanned
By rejection
The hotter becomes the pursuit
Chasing dreams of a better reality
Taking an ego trip

It is very costly for
You must sell your soul
To feed your ego
And the Devil is ready to
Take your ticket

Just pay your due
And climb aboard the
Junket…the spectacle
The display
That you think you need
To feed your greed

To be whole
At any price
You sell pieces of your goal

If ego is your soul

MAN BIRD

Forever man has envied wings
He has looked skyward
As the eagle glides
He has climbed the highest mountain
To try to touch the sky
He has formed materials
Into instruments to
Carry him high
He dreams that he will
Go up not down to die
The man bird wants to fly

He's built his kingdom
Here on earth
Forming a concrete sphere
Just to be a runway to
Beyond the stratosphere
Flapping his conceptual
Frame of wings
He now must go higher
For to fly with metal wings
Is not the desire

(continued)

He seeks the outer limit
Of what he may conceive
Only held back by
What he can't believe

Once aloft
The hearty souls are
Calling to the ground
That the universe is
Flat not round
Claiming that they have found
The source of light and sound

The man bird wants to fly
He also wants to find
Those answers to unwind
But he doesn't care to
Know where we've been
And where we go

If we are only dust in the wind
And a black hole is where we descend

WALKING IN THE SAND

What do you want to do
Young man
Walking in the sand
Between life and death
Start and Stop
Green and red
Before you're dead
What do you want to do
Young man
Don't just walk in the sand

Plant your feet
Mid the air
Walking to the beat
Between life and death
Start and stop
Green and red
Whence you've tread
What have you done
Young man
Have you given life a hand

(continued)

What do you want from life
Young man
Walking hand in hand
Between life and death
Start and stop
Green and red
With words I've said
Who do you love
Young man
And for what do you stand

Answers to questions
Young man
Written in the sand
Between life and death
Start and Stop
Green and red
Don't just fall out of bed
In a holy man's stead
Instead praise God
Young man

Before your dust is sand
In someone else's hand

FREEDOM

Freedom takes many forms
It's the bird flying its own way
It's the ship plotting its own course
It's the writer inscribing his own thought
It's the lovers rolling in the hay
It's the success attained without force
It's the butterfly that's never caught

Freedom must weather many storms
Like the dingy upon the raging seas
Like the sleep that knows no dreams
Like the babe that is black of skin
Like the pod that has no peas
Like the mind that has no schemes
Like a fighter losing his will to win

Freedom must overcome many scorns
As the child who arrives unwanted
As the swan ugly to the eye
As the fool deaf and dumb as well
As the hero who becomes daunted
As the man who must know the reason why
As the orator that has no spell

(continued)

Freedom then must set the norms
In a system created by natural laws
In the minds of humane leadership
In the hearts of restless mortal men
In the veins of mindful pause
In the soul of the mortals grip
In the judgment of repented sin

Freedom Finally Is
The faith of those who believe in fate
Love of life that's passed from man and wife
And the choice of those who seek each other
In their own way to procreate

After Life

SMALL TOWN BOY

Back among the corn fields
Lies the heart of a nation
Marked by a church
And a Standard station

This is the small town
Mobility up
Population down

They're moving to the city
What a pity
Living together in clusters
With bright lights
And many lusters

Rushing here and pushing there
Fellow man not aware
This is the city life
Pressures bent on causing strife

I for one moved into this
Looking for success expecting bliss
My career took me out of that small town
It put me on a merry-go-round
To no where

(continued)

*Thank God I had more to dare
I endured it
With a frightened spirit
Till I got the chance
To return to the romance
Of a small town*

*Back to something I didn't appreciate
In my younger years I just couldn't relate
To using my mind as well as my body
Taking the time I had to think write and study
So if I became any more than I am
I will thank what many people see fit to damn*

*I will always be thankful for my small-town life
That touched me my children and my wife
Until I found out that it is not the town that makes a life
It is our vision of a better future with less strife*

*Thank God we are moving back to the city
Still a small-town boy in search of that big town joy
It's a pity to have lost that small-town boy
To a bigger job and a bigger toy*

With nothing bigger than being a decoy

ULTIMATE OBSESSION

Have you ever
Wanted till it happens
Have you ever
Been obsessed with life

Have you ever
Turned a day down to something
Have you ever
Been free from doubt

Have you ever
Loved without selfishness
Have you ever
Accepted all your faults

Have you ever
Rested from frustration
Have you ever
Bested your dreams

Have you ever
Given up wealth for truth
Have you ever
Tried to be less than the most

Have you ever
Fed your existence with hope
Have you ever
Possessed more then you obsessed

For obsession is only a way to cope

ULTIMATE RISK

Will you do
What you've dared
Will you do
More than you received

Will you do
Your brother a favor
Will you do
With all you've got

Will you do
Unto all just for joy
Will you do
Better than before

Will you do
On behalf of the meaning
Will you do
As you're heritage blessed

(continued)

Will you do
Today without doubting tomorrow
Will you do
Tomorrow when it is today

Will you do
Now without reserving effort
Will you do
Wonderful things for all

Will you do
More for others than you

For risk will only do if you risk yourself

HAVE YOU OR HAVE YOU NOT

Have you and will you be obsessed
Obsessed with the notion that now is
Not wondering why for sake of self
But thrusting your might as if confessed

To bettering all that you touch or consent
With the faith of a fallen savior not elf
Not because you're big or great but for the joy
Of being alive for a while in wonderment

But not being overwhelmed by being small
In wonderment of our reason to deploy
Great effort and desire toward the summit
Of existence facing all short or tall

FOR

Ultimately what you have or will is destiny
Destined to what you've wanted
Not necessarily easy to come by
But worth all the hurts that face sincerity

Honest but naïve we've heard it flaunted
Simple but stupid they're called with no why
A right to be good without shame
This is a life with heart as well as undaunted

Yourself for others not just oneself
Have you or have you not
Come off the shelf
Feeling outside yourself

If not for self but for mental health

FINDING YOURSELF

Are your looking for the answer
To your existence
Did it ever occur
To look behind your pretense

May it be you're just pretending
To be something you really skirt
Then occasionally just defending
Your ego from the hurt

This was certainly true for me
Mincing no words
For I want you to see
There's no difference between first and thirds

Only your mind is holding you back
Thinking it is something less
Dwelling on what you feel you lack
Keeping you from happiness

In the tracks you tread
Look and ye shall find
It is said
The ease of being kind

(continued)

By constant rehearsal
Only you can accept the fact
That you're very special
Getting yourself untracked

The lines are written
And here they are

"Myself I am not smitten
I've yet to go that far"
"I am here to play my part
Be I support or be I star
Finding myself I will start
Depending on myself my heart
My faith my might my insight"

Finding myself is putting
The start before the ending …Amen

ROAN

They say a dog is a man's
Best friend
Obedient
And ready to defend
Its master
To the very end

I say a dog
Is man's master
Cause a dog can adapt
And survive
Even though trapped

They have the faith
That tomorrow will occur
Believing in the same
Big eyes and a ball of fur

It's because they don't
Expect much
A gentle word
And a loving touch

On four legs they stand
It may seem absurd
That they are the master of man
Being able to catch a bird

(continued)

Getting the dog before the cart
With an endless heart
And no fear to start
Tail and head are far apart

A friend always for a bone
That's my dog Roan
She doesn't change
From day to day left alone
In her fur and mange

Coddled in the stroke
Of a hand on her fur
She doesn't need to smoke
Or think or drink or purr

Life to her is now not afterward
Roan the master
My respect goes out in a word
You don't breed disaster

You just remain deserved

ACTOR

Actor or benefactor
What's your stage
Are you written for
Or just turn the page

Who says you're not on trial
Actor or reactor
Trying hard until your last mile
What's your style

Maker or taker
Speak up and be heard
It matters more now
Than afterward

Erector or defector
Don't build your hopes too low
Cause where you set your limits
Is where you'll grow

Actor or enactor
Before you go
Tell us your story
So we know

Are you acting
Or just reacting

EGO MANIA

Love thyself
Before you love another
Do unto others only
If they do for your brother

I am I said
A lion
Instead of a lamb

Do you think of I am
Cause it's everything
To flap big wings
And write you own boom-a-rangs

I will I can
Is that who I am
As the ego of man

Or the fulfillment
Of I
I the almighty
I, the savior
I the embodiment

(continued)

Of all that is
Tell me master
Is it ego mania
Or is it insomnia
Of the soul

I search I find
Just to unwind
My wish to define

What creates dawn for others
And dark night druthers
With attainments
That are ultimately cajoled
By the dissidents

Maybe that's why God created Hell
To keep the striving soul in check
Balancing ego with will
For His children that defect
Revitalizing alter ego

INTO ERGO

FREEDOM TO BE YOU

Ours is the right to be alive
Ours is the right to think for ourselves
Ours is the right to live our life as we decide
Ours is the right to be good or bad
And to protect those that tried

Freedom to choose

Ours is the right to earn our daily breads
Ours is the right to forgive trespasses
Ours is the right to avoid temptation
Ours is the right to forgive transgressions
And deliver ourselves from evil

Freedom to change

Ours is the kingdom, the power
The glory forever
Ours is God in heaven peace on earth
Goodwill to ourselves and others
(As you treat yourself you treat as brothers)

Freedom to be you

(continued)

And heaven comes to earth
For those that have peace
Ours is the heaven of a peaceful mind
A peaceful kingdom
A peaceful power
A peaceful glory is our

Freedom to each to live in peace
By fighting the war within ourselves
And winning our freedom from fear
And the hope of peace on earth
Good will to men who fight sin
And win
For Our Father's Kingdom
The Power
And the Glory
Forever
Amen

DELIGHTED TO BE WRONG

I'm delighted I've been slighted
I've got no love to lose
No other route to choose
I couldn't walk in a loser's shoes

I'm delighted I've been slighted
I've got no love to lose
If it comes my way
I won't let it stay
Cause of the price to pay

If I have to choose
I don't want to lose
And have to walk in a loser's shoes

I'm delighted I've been slighted
I've got no lover to lose

Hand me down your fortunes boys
Cluck your tongues make the noise
A victim of a lover's ploys
I'm delighted I've been slighted
Of the lover that destroys

(continued)

Hand me down your heart boys
Break your will and stomp your joys
Playing the games of human toys
I'm delighted I've been slighted
And given a choice

What do you mean I am wrong
Why don't I belong
No one listens to my voice
Or my lonely song

Now I am delighted to be wrong
I found that love is strong
And only you can make me belong
Crooning this new song

WHAT IS HAPPY

Laugh and skip
Clap your hands
Smile and dance
Play the bands
Hype yourself
Until it stands

Then are you happy

What is happy anyway
Is it what you need
Or is it what you want
Does either make you happy

What is happiness

What I want
Till I get it
Then just put it aside
Not even with that much pride

Wondering why it was so important

(continued)

That I have it as I had tried
Like feigning a growing weed
As long as you feed it
It will grow until you realize
You don't even need it

I thought on this for awhile
This is what I found
Like feeding a growing weed
Is that what I really want
Or is it just a taunt to say
You can't find happiness anyway

Then you just weed it
And grow something you desire
Finding that what you want
Is not what you need
No…well strike a détente'
Between what you think you need
And what you think you want

And enjoy being free to be
A flower not a weed … That's being happy

BE MY TIMELINE

A year
Counting ticks and tocks
Pages and clocks

A day
That allows us to say
I need your love

An hour
That allows me to flower
For want of your love

A minute
That brings us fruit
Together in pursuit of love

A second
That lets me beckon
You away from doubts of love

A timeline
That is to touch and find
Love of our own kind

So be my infinity
Be my reality
Be my timeline to divinity

(continued)

THE BOOM-A-RANG

The boom-a-rang is hell brother
Don't you know
It will get you
One way or another

Do your neighbor bad sister
Don't you know
It will get you
Because you've hurt her

Sin lie and bitch boy
Don't you know
It will get you
The boom-a-rang is not a toy

The boom-a-rang is hell girl
Don't you know
It will get you
With its vengeful whirl

(continued)

Toss it out children
If you only knew
That when you've committed sin
It will get you

Boom-a-rang is God's way
Don't' you know
It will get you
On your judgment day

Now that you know
Toss it out to do good
So it will come back to you
With blessings once misunderstood

Which is
"What goes around
Comes back profound
In the air or on the ground"

MY CHILDREN

Children are the blood
That makes my heart beat
It's the heat of love

Children are the image
Of my spirit
With each turning page

Take me back

Children are the sweetness
That makes me good
It's the sugar of good sense

Children are the image
Of my dreams
So alive again on this stage

Take me there

Children are the everlasting
Visions of my time and worth
It's the heaven on earth

Children are the savior
Of my soul
To live forever in God's favor

So take me back to them

POLITICIANS

ARE THEY BORN OR RAISED
From birth or mirth

ARE THEY RIGHT OR WRONG
To us or themselves

ARE THEY HONEST OR CORRUPT
To each his own conscience

ARE THEY FAME OR FORTUNE
Money is desire not justice

ARE THEY HOLY OR SACRELIGIOUS
Religion for reason or for purpose

ARE THEY HOME GROWN OR HOME MADE
Leaders come from strange places

ARE THEY EFFECTIVE OR DEFECTIVE
A problem maker or problem solver

ARE THEY MADE OR MAKER
Self-made or self-maker

(continued)

ARE THEY CLIMBER OR BUILDER
Trampled underfoot or a strong footing

ARE THEY NOW OR NEVER
A failure of submission or a flight to vision

ARE THEY PAST OR PERFECT
Looking back or going forward

ARE THEY FIND OR SEEK
Where to look or where to go

OPINION
Politicians are made not born
By the maker of men
Beyond human scorn
With the will to win

Not necessarily for what is right
Nor above sin
Or are they looking for right
In the wrong bin

DON'T FORGET

Don't forget mama and papa
To give your children roots and wings
Give them roots for stability
With a strong ground of security
Planted in a home with fertility

Don't forget mama and papa
To give your children boots and things
Give them footing for stability
With things to use in reality
From a home of security

Don't forget mama and papa
To give your children roots and wings
With Roots to grow the best
Wings to enable them to fly from the nest
From a home of creativity

Don't forget mama and papa
To give your children lutes and rings
With shoots to build their own nest
Rings to engage their conquest
From a home of longevity

(continued)

Don't forget mama and papa
To give your children roots and wings
If you do mama as the bequest-er
They will be the master
Of all things
From a mother of destiny

Don't forget mama and papa
Plant the strongly rooted stalk
And the well-structured wing
To withstand the clock
And the valleys life will bring

Don't forget mama and papa
That in birth and life
You determine weak or strong
If the roots are deep
And the wings are long

For a flight home they will always keep

ALWAYS TOGETHER

Life is spent and pieced together for
As beings we are created
Not to be apart nor
Ever to be separated

Life together is the seed into bloom for
Nature uses us in pairs
As she never ceases nor
Did she give us babes without mares

Life is a tune of more than one bar for
The rhythm is required for two
Remember children's music couldn't be nor
Could we without such as you

Life comes and goes and no one knows for
God created mortals
But as we live together so shall we after nor
Shall shadows divide our portals

Together we are conceived
Together we conceive and believe
That Together we will always be
United by Eternity

The Father Son and the Holy Ghost
Holds Us Together Forever

(continued)

HEREAFTER

HEREAFTER

After the sun sets
After the love making
After the job is done
After the prayer is answered

What is Hereafter

Hereafter the sun still sets
Hereafter there is a love maker
Hereafter the work is never done
Hereafter the prayer is the setting sun

What holds hope
If it is not tomorrow
Why would yesterday matter
Unless todays have meaning

I must have hope for the sun to rise
For my job too and our lives
For my love that never dies
For my prayers to be ever wise

Forever without hope
Is death hereafter
So I pray don't let me die
Without the sunset a lover and my work

For now is not ever after

ANGEL OF MERCY

Do we have Angels
Or are they a fantasy

Angel of mercy
Savior of destiny
Speak to me

About a better time
For my writing
For my rhyme

Or am I
Just a dreamer
To think

That my words
Mean a thing
Or hit a worthy string

Across the Trespass
Between minds and ears
Hopes and fears
Days and years

(continued)

Speak Angel of Mercy
Guide me closer than I seem
To a better theme

For my writing
For my rhyme
Towards
The reason for my vision

That my words decree
Something that others
Wouldn't see
Without me

As an Angel of Mercy
Flying next to thee

EYE SHADOWS

Walking in the street
Passing away the night
Till dawn and the shadows meet

Faces turn to me
Eyelids closed
So we can't see

The light exposed will fade
Leaves are gone for me with
No shade

As the clouds
Over the meadows laid
I'm now afraid of gray shadows

Gray shadows become the night
Pitch black void of light
I'm afraid of gray shadows
Since I lost my sight

(continued)

And the light will never dawn again
I'm afraid of gray shadows
Dark is life's pain

Now that I can't see
The world's gone
A dark shadow to me

Like leaves with no shade
It's to be I'm so afraid
Of black shadows covering me

As a silhouette of life's charade

(Author feeling through a blind person's eyes)

ANY DAY NOW

I'm gonna be rich
And I'm gonna be famous
My habits will switch
And I'll be a success

Any day now

Any day I'll do it
Somehow
I just have to decide
To get to it

But oh shoot screw it
Give me that drink I'll do it tomorrow
When I have time to borrow
The day after this sorrow

Someday I'm gonna be rich
Someday I'll be famous
Someday I'll switch
And I'll be a success

(continued)

Listen to what I have to say
When I decide to act
I'll be something someday
That's a fact

I'm gonna do it my way
Any day now
Once I decide to do what I say
And my wasted time will allow

And when I make my pitch
Waiting to be lucky my way
I'm surely going to be rich
Since life's a gamble anyway

But in the meantime
Isn't it a bitch
That I don't have time
To switch and be rich

"Any day now"

LOST TIME

I'm a traveling man
My day is theirs
And the night is mine
Catching it between lost time

Sleep and thoughts of home
A family of lost time
With love so I can roam
Flight delayed what a crime

I'll be late
Just waiting on airtime

No one is normal
No one to check
At the terminal
Or on the flight deck

Looking out at the rain
Makes me wonder
If I'm insane
Delayed by lightning and thunder

(continued)

For it's not the money
It's not the acclaim
It must be
Ego to build a name

To be number one
That's sought with fame
Dreaming of satisfaction
But is it worth the game

When the top is won
Where the climb is done
And the past is just all gone
Stuck in the coin changer of lost fun

Waiting on this game changer
Called stormy weather

MR. HELL

Heaven on earth
Go to Hell
Hell is here
Take your pick
Dr. be nimble Mr. be quick

The doors are open
Take you pick
Since Adam's apple
And Eve's grapple
We've spoken of Heaven
And we've feared Hell
Someplace far off
Where we might dwell

Cast it out
Kill the doubt
Now is what it's all about
Dr. Heaven created Mr. Hell
So we would have sin
As well

(continued)

Not all is good
Nor is paper always wood
So be it a spell
There's a Mr. Hell
As well

Giving us a reason to be good

It's the Devil there as Mr. Hell
In purgatory with no glory
Mattering not where you later dwell
When sinning is your story

If you're good
You're in Heaven
If you're bad
You're in Hell
Then Dr. Heaven
Becomes Mr. Hell
Suffering under Eden's spell

You choose your own path to Heaven or Hell

KNOWLEDGE

Knowledge is power
Just ask the powerful

Knowledge is wisdom
Just ask the wise

Knowledge is faith
Just ask the faithful

Knowledge is important
Just ask the teacher

Knowledge is listening
Just ask the thinker

Knowledge is one and all
Of these

Knowledge is whatever
You want it to be

Knowing it is nothing
If you use it
Without tenacity
Beyond your capacity

Knowing that you flail
Without a trail
To follow
And a God to Know

Thus ignorance in a moral sense
Is knowledge as its past tense

A BLACK HORIZON

Can a soul be anything but a light
That passes from here to there
In the night
I wonder

Looking upon a black horizon
Makes you wander where
The spirit begun
Under our dying sun

Halted along that lonely highway
We took in the stark stare
Jerked astray
By shadows there

That a farmer hauled the harvest
Into this scene with colors fair
Now it's bare
And hope in his chest

(continued)

My camera's eye stood still for the magic
Looking into today for tomorrow's share
Of this blank flair so tragic
But no life is fair

Is it a shadow of another time
Or the future as a dare
To not rhyme
In spite of time's aire

Whiten the sky into contrast
Stroked from a white glare
It's still a black horizon of the past
When life begun under a living sun

With Atom and Eve with a proton
Melding neutrons into a son

MAJESTIC

The peaks are solid formed the mount
The snows are liquid formed the river
The trees are alive formed the shade
The waters are still formed the wake

The lights are coming formed the stars
The day and sun are fading formed the night
The shadows are falling formed the darkness
The wilds are quiet formed the peace

The flesh and blood formed the man and woman
The day and night formed the time
The love and wars formed the fight
The belief and sin formed what's right

Peace on earth; formed good will to mean

All will live forever
Majestic as the endeavor
Captured in the scene

For now is gone forever
As the picture seals
The moment

THEN THE RADIO WENT DEAD

Eighteen wheelers all around
Radios on
Got the sound
Breaker breaker that's the sign
Channels on to one nine
Chatters here noises there
People aware but most don't care
They just want you to know
They're there

This is the tone that was the tune
That one morning just before noon
Everything was normal
Everything was fine
Then came the breaker
Into one nine

My God guy wake up
Where you headed
Either you're crazy or
Your throttle's leaded
Watch out buddy you're gonna crash

(continued)

Then came the groan
And the smash

The last sound I heard
Was a swerving
Truck bed
Twisting and turning
Till the radio went dead

Me thinking there's no way
That it should've been his last day
A high price to pay
On this lonely highway

Next day back the same way
Back on the line
Tuned to one nine
The word was out
And it was said
That the radio was going
But the trucker was dead

NOBODY KNOWS

Nobody's been down this same road
But me seeking my fortune in between
My heart and the heavy load
Nobody knows the trouble I've seen

Nobody feels
Exactly how it feels
To be clean of demons it conceals
From the bottom of my wheels

Nobody's been down this same road
But me

Others have had their dreams stepped on
Hopes shattered and almost gone
But nobody's been down
Down on this same road
But me

What I'm saying my friend
Is that each story has it's beginning
And end
And this road has had a big bend

(continued)

For when you get to upwind
You realize
Nobody cares
How the wind blows
How the grass grows

And no one knows how Jesus rose

So if you're wondering what life will pay
Pick up your hand and in spite of risk play
The game of life your way
Because nobody can say

That feeling sorry for the road
You chose
Is why Jesus rose

MOBILE ILLINOIS

As I listen to that radio
Playing some honky tonk
I speed up and go to catch the taillights ahead
Sun's been dead for some time
Riding this four wheeled bronc

I can't wait until I find my bed
There goes that tune again
Catchy in its melody
Something about what might have been
Gosh that may apply to me

Just sitting here in this mobile saddle
I'm thinking of my goals and roles
Played as a soldier in this battle
Feigning reality
Much like moles
Allowed to dig more fox holes

Pleasantly much to my surprise
I look out my window and beauty
Hits my eyes

(continued)

Beyond those headlights from on far
I see the moon and each glowing star

The wind is up bringing in clouds above
Beg that snow is over for the year
So spring begins to appear
Bringing Robin's egg
And turtle dove

Sad no I can't say I'm really sad
More like I'm tired not mired in pity
But loneliness is a factor to be had
Even if as I mobile to the city

Ah it seems now I have company
Part of this metal symphony
Road signs dance and prance in front of me
Like bars of music of a melody

Awaken tired eyes because up ahead
Is my destination and a resting place
Marked by beacons oh so red
Tis the city that's my bed

(continued)

Those white lines along the road
Keep closing in on me in my episode
My tired eyes don't seem to stop blinking
Might be coffee will help my thinking

Or my destiny could be in jeopardy

This is the essence of Mobile Illinois
Driving and striving to better my lot
Giving up the security and at times joy
Searching for that golden pot

With each rainbow sought but not caught

ALONE

ALONE

Did you ever feel the emptiness of your self
Searching for the warmness of another in dismay
Hoping you're not the only one that feels like an elf
Dreading that the night will be worse than the day

Loneliness can be so vast
It can exist even as you stand in a crowd
Deeper and the longer it lasts
Stronger if you pretend to be proud

Reaching out is just part of the solution
A smile and the eyes will help you
But this is really a part of evolution
From depression oh so blue

All people with feelings have been there
It just takes different forms for some
Especially if you really care
And are not prone to be deaf and dumb

There are others ready to help you
Feelings of love and embraces waiting
Don't wait too long for the cue
It's your turn to do the relating

(continued)

So reach out with your eyes and your smile
Hold out your hands to be warm
Then your sense will beguile
And gone is that lonely storm

Togetherness is the way to overcome
That empty feeling of sadness
So long as you don't succumb
To self-inflicted distress

Smile reach out for love
Be together with the one you trust
As feelings return to the sky above
For you are sharing yourself from dawn to dusk

As you can see it doesn't take much more
Just your mind and your touch
For being alone reaches the core
While being together is life's crutch

And hiding from your feelings hurts too much

WINGS

Wings that spread
For mankind
Can they be for humans
With a spirit and a mind

Look into the eyes
Of a child
Hold them close and
See if they aren't wild

Like a baby bird
Waiting in the nest
To be given a boost
And encouraged to do its best

Those little limbs
Become the wings
To carry out the flight
That life inevitably brings

The mother of the eagle
Has a mighty mast
To bring about the beauty
That birth has cast

(continued)

If she has the instinct
To love and teach
The eagle will use its wings
As far as it can reach

The child bird
Is nature's pet
Given strength and folly
To mature its reasoning wit

And all is well
Until the time is near
To prime the departure
Of the child bird's career

If the lessons
Have been learned well
The wings will lift
And the heart will swell

The child will ascend
On a confident course
Towards the meaning
Guided by a Godly force

Wings have spread
And mankind is in flight
Void of dread
And keener of sight

Mature wings striving for what's right
Looking for love's delight

STEPPING STONES

Step high to the beat brother
Churn your legs up and down
Climb to the heights mother
Fate is back in town

Step to the beat sister
Stride, give yourself a ride
Lady luck don't you miss her
She can be on your side

Stepping on those stepping stones
To heights unknown father
Never fearing to go alone
Once the notches are prone

Step to the beat all you children
Dance your way to the moon
Cause it's more fun to win
Children you can't start too soon

Hone those human bones
Grease you heels
As the mind atones
For the dusk that time steals

High stepping to the Rolling Stones

FOR LOVE

For love we suffer
For heart we die
For mind we doubt

A doubting mind
Shall die without love
For love we will suffer

For heart we long
Forever we need to belong
Forsaken love shall cry

Forgotten days shall pass
Forlorn hearts shall fast
For we are too old too soon

Too late are we smart
For love we suffer
For heart
We die

A fool am I

For not loving you
As my heart knows where
While my mind shan't share

When love isn't there

IF GOD WERE GOVERNOR

If God were Governor
I would more clearly see
Kneeling before the throne of dignity
But for the sake of my soul
And the feeling of guilt
For playing a role

I walked in like just any mortal man
And he held out the royal hand
Yes I do
I do understand
The seat of power
And the leaders of the land
And I still appreciate the command

Of the Heads of State
And the rigors of debate
But the thing I cannot accept
Is the overriding precept
That even if God were Governor
I would not have to kneel
Before the throne
Like the appendage
Of a gopher or a drone

(continued)

For even then with God as a reason
And dignity the treason
I don't like the impression
Of feeling like little ole me
In this country we call free
Where the equality of what we can be
Is striving to be on an equal plane
When society isn't totally vane

Then we can rise to have a gaze
Into the Governor's eyes
That may take having him realize
That even God exemplifies
Humility dignity
And the realization of mortality

That if God were Governor
The righteous would be King
And pride will be the Jester's hallowed ring
Of thee I sing

"Long live the fool
that sits on a throne
Instead of a stool"

THE COLD WINDS OF LIFE

As I sit here in my boat
Holding on to life and my coat
I'm confronted by the cold winds of life
That blew away my work and my wife

Because I am too blind to see
That my dreams started dreaming me
I got so I couldn't tell
The water from the well

I got so I couldn't speak
Without my tongue in my cheek
I got so I couldn't laugh
And made fun of my other half

I got so I couldn't sing
And began to notice my ears would ring
When the cold winds of life
Became a cutting knife

And cut lose my boat
Far down stream in the moat
Now telling me I couldn't find the sea
Because my bad dreams were dreaming me

While reality was killing destiny

SOUND OF SILENT NOISE

Noise with no voice
No choice is to rejoice
Good sense as silence

Does the wind speak

Listen hasten to hear
Speak to be weak
Wisdom is silence

Do the preachers listen

Shout spout fumes
Hear to find answers
Joy is silence

Will the crowds quieten

Moan— to suffer
Smile faith as the buffer
Belief is silence

When will the masses listen

Cry out to no listeners
Love and mourners become strong
Feel the difference

(continued)

Who cries at the funeral

No shouts no cries above human frailty
Nothing more to lose
Silence is majority

Will the voters really know

No sound is heard
From a word
In the beginning

Can birth be more than it's worth

Nothing to be said
Even for the dead
Be still
To eternity's will

Will heaven or hell listen

Listen to the silence
In the tolerance and reverence
To a life born silent

Willed to be forever reverent
Burying silent noise as the final event

A QUITTER

A quitter is someone
Who doesn't believe in "Thy Will Be Done"
Who takes the easy path
And not gaining on what you hath

Looking at a mountain not a thrill
Making it bigger than a mole hill
It is the toll that will kill
What little initiative is left to skill

The quitter has much to give
With doubt comes a heavy heart to live
Looking for the lonely road
With a perceived heavy load

It is too much to bear
For those who don't and won't care
Looking at a grave situation
With a heart that weighs a ton

(continued)

It's too much to expect
That only the will is wrecked
Looking at the weaknesses of a man
Without a desire to understand

That it is fear of being tough
Without the courage to say enough is enough
With their brain left on hold
Until it is too late to just grow old

Yes a quitter is someone
Cast in sin
Who doesn't believe in
The will to win

Nor

"Thy Will Be Done"

HAVE YOU HEARD

Have you heard
There's heat in the winter sun
I'm here with the word
To say I'm still in love at seventy-one

Have you heard
There's fighting at the closing bell
I'm here to tell of this bird
Who won't go stale

Have you heard
There's dancing to the slowest tune
I'm the singing night bird
Who still looks at the harvest moon

Have you heard
You can have romance
Even the oldest bird can
If he will just give it a chance

Listen and dance no matter how slow the tune
To the winter sun to the harvest moon

(continued)

Have you heard
My word
I'm in love's dawn and night
With no end in sight

My passion won't go stale
My romance won't go pale
With the winter's sun
Nor the bell tolling ninety-one

Have you heard
Aging is absurd
If doubt never occurred
And age is just a word

Formed by the herd
Of cattle that didn't tattle
On the early bird
Who has his own saddle

Riding into heaven not deterred
At being one hundred and the third

CATCHING AIR

Catching air in a glass
Inflating balloons with helium gas
Growing flowers and cutting grass
With nothing to do with our past

If you don't understand what I'm saying to you
Try to catch mist in a shoe
Or keep falling raindrops brand new
Catching air is the thing to do

If and when we finally knew
That only the free bird flew
Everything else a passerby can see or touch
Doesn't mean too awfully much

Considering that the soul is only free
To Christians Jews and Muslims who care to see
The molting angel feathers by being holy
While catching air is preaching solely

The prophet's word unto eternity
Is of a God we hope to see
Who created Air Catchers mentally
Making wind mills for catching me

GOD'S TREES

Trees in the spring are like a beautiful woman
Blooming in spite of size and shape
With beauty as the aging of the grape
Swaying gracefully in the wind
Statuesque as it's asked to bend
Felines and trees a blessing to the breeze

For without them what need would there be
For leaves
Or birds or bees
Or the poetic mind
Yes they can be undressed caressed
And told they are the worst or the best
But life goes on for the proud trees
Whether you or I or nature disagrees

Though there is something quite profound
About the splitting limb earth bound
Broken dreams and broken limbs
Fallen women and dead roots
Make for sin and bitter fruits

(continued)

In the forest of our dreams
For it is the bitter grape that spoils the wine
And sin that prunes the tree out of shape
While the sunshine being like the mother hen
Warms the nest for hatching
Not knowing where the egg has been

For who knows a tree's worth
Or a woman's girth
Until the offspring's flight and the seedling grows
God only knows how those buds in spring arose
And explaining the urge to seize
The offspring falling too close to the trees

For the child goes as the tree grows

AN ANGEL

An angel came to find me
To take me by the hand
To show me how to be free
And then to show me how to safely land
In my place to stand
In line to wait at the gate

She came to me in a storm
When my hopes were dashed
Against the shadow of my past form
Told to spread my wings before I crashed
She showed me how to raise my head
And place myself above the mortal dead

It was a chilling chilling affair
Because I think I got to the point
Where I felt angels don't care
Telling me the past could anoint
Earthbound angels are resurrected
And save those souls yet aflected

(continued)

For a blessing of a chosen few
Who pray their wings could renew
But their wings could no longer raise them
Above themselves above the limb
And they were grounded to their fate
Destined to doubt and wait

Those who believe they must
Those who said it's true
To find an angel to adjust
Taking us thrusting us unto
Heaven as we flew
Earth angels taming of the shrew

Those Angels are the Savior's host
To the Father Son and Holy Ghost
And the Arch Angel flying close to the fire
Fends off the Devil's ire
While my Angel is the Sire

Of Mr. Doubtfire

RECKLESS REBEL

Willed to win for a better way
This is the fuel that makes them great
Becoming our statues tomorrow not today
Remembered for what they gave despite debate
Reckless rebel that's the label
Called a name but gaining fable

The natural way is so slow
Those that confront that natural range
Fight up stream blow by blow
As all the answers change
Those seekers are called the names things to flout
Heretic maverick rebel no doubt

Until later upon the mount
Their names are forgotten
Called reckless not the scout
With discontent the memories rotten
Awaken world these are the dreamers
The new way the constructive schemer's

(continued)

Look back upon those earlier ones
Franklin Whitney Wright and Ford
Names remembered not as Huns,
But respected for successes reward
Learned as the minds are allured
To the changing future past demurred

Our statues line the chambers of time
None built for those that criticize
Dedicated instead to minds sublime
That created miracles amid the cries
Fool that will never work Flaunt him
Crucify the ideas tear them limb from limb

The character of the reckless change agent
Who only believe in their version of what is spent
Foolish obstinate poor listener aggressive hell bent
Not what is easy or conventional with political consent
Desire, risk, persistence, courage, faith with insight
But reckless in the creation of a visionary's sight

Holding off the enforcers
Who defend their mediocre discourses

RIPPLES

Ripples in the water
Carry me home

Ripples in the mind
Cause me to roam

Ripples in my face
Turn me to stone

Ripples in the heart
Turn me alone

Ripples in the skin
Denote the cometh age

Ripples in the chin
Is the sagging stage

Ripples in the days
Turn the leaves to brown

(continued)

Ripples in the seasons
Turns the World around

Ripples in the universe
Brings stars alive

Ripples in the heavens
Bring angels to strive

Ripples in the sand
Is gravity and time

Ripples in the ripples
Is God hidden in this rhyme

NO SIMPLE MONDAY

This was no simple Monday
Though the clock is still on the wall
The rain pours down my day
And the sun is still a shiny ball

Thunder and lightning in my face
As my tears trace
To why I'm back
And what I lack
All start of a broken heart

Saying I need one more chance
For old time's sake
And our dying romance
So our marriage will awake
Just one more time
It's no punishable crime

If you love me Tuesday
In spite of divorcing me
On a simple Monday
I won't be free
It's still the first of the weak
And the last of what we seek

(continued)

By falling out of love on Wednesday
We have to tell the kids on Thursday
And move on to Friday
With no weekend for family play

So let's keep it simple on Monday
And stay

Together

STORMY

Stormy thoughts
Of a stormy mind
Held my attention
Not to mention
My imagination

Stormy days
And stormy nights
Quite a sensation
Of a sensual creation
Known as a delusion

Just a good dream
About a bad thing
Making my stormy mind ring
Giving me a crippled wing
Such a stormy fling

It couldn't last
Beyond this thought
Because it couldn't be first
With clouds to burst
And sad times to curse

Just ravings of a mad man
A sad man a stormy man
A lonely man
Storming inside till he died
For to himself he lied

That which is in a stormy mind
Is what I'm denied
And did not seek and find

NEVER TOO OLD TO LOVE

"How old are you?"
I'm twenty-one, how old are you
Never too old to tell
Always too young to die

You're never too old
Till you're too old
To care

Like an old dog can still bark
Until he can bark no more
You're never too old
Till you're too old
To snore

I've seen people in my time
Some young at twenty
But old at twenty-nine

Then there are an intriguing few
Who are in tune with themselves
Though their record is stuck on eighty-two

(continued)

You're never too old
To live and love
For it's an old lover

Whose life's meaning shall discover

That barking at the moon
Is always a hunger
To willing oneself younger

Myself
I've seen others out of tune
Not in sync with the moon
But I'm a product of my wife's tune

Never too Old to Live and Love is the prize

CASTLES IN THE WIND

Building that castle in the wind
Is like stopping sand towards the end
Put it up to behold my friend
Better hope there are dreams to blend
Building sand castles in the wind

Bitter cold so we can send
The broken hearts that refuse to mend
Over the hills we have to fend
So each of us can comprehend
Saving sand castles in the wind

Hoping the soul will defend
The honest cries that can't condescend
Sadness creeping in refusing to bend
While egos cannot amend
Land castles in the wind

Catching snow drops that offend
Tears breaking a love to blend
Hold me tight don't let me expend
Something I can't possibly rescind
Human castles in the wind

Loving living till the end
This is in essence spiritual zen
Holding up my castle in the wind
If this prayer is as I intend

My castle holds up beyond life's end
Amen

TOO SWEET TO BE BITTER

You face me with your eyes
You eye me with your face
You know me with your words
You change me without a trace

We taste each-others fruit
So sweet
We play the tempest flute
Come hither

You're too sweet to be bitter

You are my melody
The music of my life
You're the taste of fruit
Within a tempered wife

As we push and shove
You're the taste of my youth
Mouthing my love
With gritted tooth

We're too sweet to be bitter

(continued)

When you smile around me
It drives me crazy
Just look at my need
When our life grows hazy

Yes you are sweet to the heart
And how it ever lasted
When your smile won't start
With anger being blasted

You're too sweet to be bitter

From our teens together
Wed to babies and jobs
Surrounding us in stormy weather
Between the tears and sobs

Now that we are growing older
Facing this unknown future
Our lives must be bolder
If we aren't just a figment of nature

We're too sweet to be bitter

I guess it is forever
Despite time and the aging notion
Holding hands together
Making life's sweet fruit the potion

Hereafter is too sweet to be bitter

I WALK THE FIELDS

I walk the fields
In my mind
Around the thistles
Over the rocks
And up the hills
Like any fox

To my belief in life
It isn't a shallow stream
It's not a bad dream
It is an appreciation of beauty
The inspiration of hope
The perspiration of work and duty
With the willingness to elope

I walk the roads
In my memories
Back to the good times
Dwelling in the house of success
Searching for lost friends
And forgetting excess

(continued)

Finding most answers
About my belief in life
It isn't a raging storm
It's not a windblown history
It is the elation of the norm
The creation of man
The gestation of child
The station of our command

I walk the days and nights
Of tomorrow in my plans
Around the debris of failure
Past the self-inflicted obstacles
And the set backs
Due to impact of higher hurdles

To the freedom of thought
That isn't just false hope
It's not a failure to cope
It is the imagination of romance
It is the elation of good will
It is the reason per chance
That God is man with time to fill

(continued)

So, I walk the plank
In my faith and relationship
It isn't a fatal blow
But the emotion of leadership
It's not a path to bestow

But the rehearse of good behavior
As was the resurrection of the Savior

Truly the suggestion in my Epitaph
"He Walks in the Fields of Destiny"
On the Path of Peace Good Will to Men and Women

THE PUREST FLOWER

The purest flower grown
In the Garden of Eden
Is the purest flower known
In the Garden of Man

The flower of love
Planted in the garden
To be coveted by those
Seeking the passions of woman
And picked for the
Bouquet of the devil
Rather than the heroes
Besetting evil
While God prepares the
Judgment day
For those that love
Their own way

Why can't the purest
Flower ever grow
In the hearts for all to know

Like the passions of
Evil and sin
Grows in the weak
Hearts of men
For if it could be known
In the Garden of Eden
It could be grown
In the Garden of Man

Rather than the backslide of sand
Sifted by the Devil's hand

AS TIMES PASS

Many times have passed
Under the bridge
Of what has been
And what will be
Those times have
Traveled good and
Have traveled bad
Some happy some sad

If you look back
And remember
That day late in November
When our beginnings
And endings merged
Into a chain that
Never begins nor ends
An anniversary of infinity

Not remembering what
It was like to be alone
And not wanting to forget
To remember to share

The thrill of being together
Lo if we forget it is the
Anniversary of the end
Of being alone

(continued)

Realization of this
Passing of memories
Into a reservoir of
Appreciation of each other
Dams up the desire
To run away to a new beginning
For the rejected
End must flap in the
Breeze of loneliness until
It is tethered to a
New beginning
A new November to remember

Damming desire
Shores up boredom
Not the tillage of the
Selfish one
Each anniversary has one
Wedding us together
Though he or she don't
Realize the lasting prize of
The forever chain
"It" goes about

Looking for a dock to
Mount for the sake of
Wandering wondering
Finding regretting retreating
And being rejected
Why oh why couldn't satisfaction
Reign in each the same
Each link of the chain

(continued)

But November doesn't
Mean the same for all
That came
But someday
On a someday morning
The anniversary will rain hard
A hard November
Rain will mark the
Time that the reservoir
Will fill and spill over
That dam until it
Washes away the mystery

Of why and why not
This will be the lasting
Link that pulls the
Beginning and ending
Together to the circle of one

No loose ends
Just endless memories
In the hearts of two
Travelers passing over the
Bridge as times pass
Under

(This is the story of Shari and
Jerry taking their vows
That have lasted for 55 years
Until forever comes)

AND THE
END BEGAN

AND AS THE END BEGAN

In the beginning
There was never any thought
Of the end

The feelings of today
Held forth for tomorrow
Played in the music
Of a soft summer's dream
About the leaves as they begin to fall
No further than
The past

Keeping the Indian summer
In our grasp
But that too was to pass
The winter scenes come
Back to their beginning

In the beginning
There was never any thought
Of the end

Snow rain and ecstasy
Giving away to spring and
The greenery during
April May and June an end
To the beginning of its fall

(continued)

While silence is the tune
Turning circles around the moon
For in the beginning
There was never any thought
Of the end and nature's rendering

Such feelings sad and oblique
Held forth for all seasons
Played to the music
Of a weathering poet's reasons

With silence as the tune
Turning circles around the moon
Till the world was turned back
To the beginning

Where there never
Was any thought of the end

And then the end began

SUNSHINE IF YOU PLEASE

Like sunshine through the trees
You can take it if you please
Holding onto nothing
With no reality to seize

You can't hold
What you haven't got
Day dreams won't bring
You happiness

Fading like fantasies
Without lasting charms
Put yourself into the sunshine
As it trickles through the trees
Clutching at air with your arms
Until there is no reality

If you please

You can't save
What you haven't sought
Night mares won't bring
You gladness

(continued)

Like wind rushing through the trees
You can take it if you please
Holding onto nothing
With no companion to squeeze

Despite your pleas

Occurring before your eyes
When you realize
That sunshine or rain clouds
Trickle through the trees
Until frost they freeze

However you can romance
The sunshine if you please
With what you put off as chance
Is planted as family trees

Then you can
In your mind's vision
Understand that creation
Is the metaphor not the reason

AS WE ARE

Now we are as we are
Gone too far away
To get back to the
Way we were
Oh yes we are too far
To heal a wound formed
Into a scar
We have to be as we are

Why is a wishful word
Wanting to forget what is heard
So don't ask me why
We were as we were
It's just wishing we are
As we were don't
Look back upon
Our shadow
Tagging along
Attached to the sun
Of yesterday now gone until dawn

Sunrise gives us the chance
At love and romance
Like a train without a cable car
We need to be as we are

Attached to a soothing loving star

HIS VOWS MADE VISIBLE AND INDIVISIBLE

From this day forward

The man who can see beyond himself
Is visible to the world
The man who can smile at his misgivings
Shall ever give
The man who can work with love
Shall know love for work
The man who can believe in the spirit
Shall feel the spirit

In sickness or in health

The man who can swallow his medicine
Shall never be sick
The man who accepts defeat
Is ever accepted
The man who can find joy
Is destined to be glad
The man who can find himself
Shall naught be lost

(continued)

For richer or poorer

The man who can bless the works of others
Has much love for his work
The man who can relate to heaven
Is in the main stream of faith
The man who can persevere to be fulfilled
Will not be empty
The man who can be patient
Is to be no patient of fear

For better or worse

The man who can be seen by self
Shall be visible to life

The woman who finds this man
Shall forever be his indivisible wife

To love and to cherish
Till death do they part

HER VOWS MADE VISIBLE AND INDIVISIBLE

From this day forward

The woman who can see beyond herself
Is visible to the world
The woman who can smile at her misgivings
Shall ever give
The woman who can work with love
Shall know love for work
The woman who can believe in the spirit
Shall feel the spirit

In sickness or In Health

The woman who can swallow her medicine
Shall never be sick
The woman who accepts defeat
Is ever accepted
The woman who can find joy
Is destined to be glad
The women who can find herself
Shall naught be lost

(continued)

For richer or poorer

The woman who can bless the works of others
Has much love for her own work
The woman who can relate to heaven
Is in the main stream of faith
The woman who can persevere to be fulfilled
Will not be empty
The woman who can be patient
Is to be no patient of fear

For better or worse

The woman who can be seen by self
Shall be visible to life

The man who finds this woman
Shall forever be with his indivisible wife

To love and to cherish
Till death do they part

FAMILY

Time may be misspent
Just going where you've went

Time being well spent
Is going where you meant

It is family that makes the trip
Something never to skip

Fun and games arranged
Are the vitality to being engaged

Weekends and holidays
Getting together many ways

Pictures then memories
Bound into album similes

Capture the moments
Where love is the events

All played on the stage
As poems are to a page

Whether they are sons or daughters
Dogs in-laws or fathers

(continued)

All interact for the occasion
But there is more to the reason

It is for a life too short
That togetherness won't abort

But it's what each life can add
When you're a mother and dad

Becoming grand and great grand
Of the Motherland

All for the clan's command
Of the Fatherland

A family is forever living to rehearse
Their early lives to avoid the reverse

With loneliness as the curse
While separation awaits the hearse

Family is the center of the universe
And the meaning in this verse

I'M THE RAINBOW

I'm the rainbow
And you're the sun
Give life
To your mystic prism

I'm the canvas
And you're the oil
Give life
To painted soil

I'm the poem
And you're the birds
Give life
To soaring words

I'm the thorn
And you're the rose
Give life
To flowering prose

(continued)

I'm the dreamer
And you're the scheme
Make love
To my rainbow's beam

I'M THE CLOUDS

I'm the clouds
And you're the storm
Give hope
To your scorn

I'm the flood
And you're the rain
Give fear
To the vane

I'm the climate
And you're the weather
Give hope
To being together

(continued)

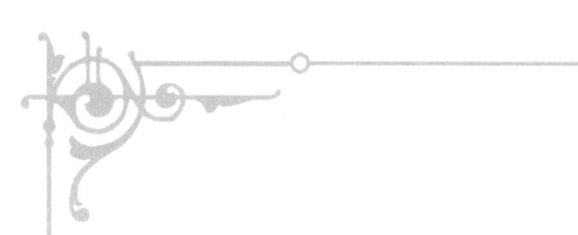

I'm the poem
And you're the words
Give the forecast
To the afterwards

I'm the clouds
And you're the God
Give us the plan
And we will till the sod

I'm the dreamer
And you're the dream
Give us hope
That heaven is not a scheme

For you're the heaven
The rainbow and the sun
Dispelling the fear
Of Hell being there not here

ADOPT ME

Look at me
Hold me in your eyes
Pick me for your own
Aren't I the right size

I've been waiting
For so long for someone
To like me the way I am
And adopt me so I belong

To a heart to a home
Without doubt holding me back
I'm tired of being alone
And my future off track

Please take my hand
The longer I'm picked over
And inspected
The more I'm a leftover
And the more I'm rejected

So take me upon your knee
Put me in your crib
All I'm asking is that you want me
And I'll adopt your name

On my bib

THE GOLDEN HOUR

The golden hour touched me
As the moonlight raised above the night
Into the dawn of tomorrow
To break again

Oh the sun feeds the night time
To then begin
To break and live again
Its cycle shall never end

The golden hour haunts me
With its taunting bouts
Foisting upon us its doubts

The golden hour named me
With its birth
But time will tell my worth

The golden hour
Has each minute
Timed to my life

(continued)

The golden hour
Makes each second
My midwife

The golden hour helped me
To understand that life
Has not begun to end

And the golden hour
Shall not pass
Until we amass

Its spiritual power
At the midnight of my life

CLIMAX

The day I tried my last trial
The day I smiled my last smile
That day I stumbled the last mile
The phone rang
My heart sang
Ole' Lang Sine
Goodbye sweet melody
Hello to what cannot be
The climax to a fantasy

The day I wrote my last song
The day I know I was wrong
The day that was much too long
The phone rang
My heart sang
Ole' Lang Sine
Bye-bye to what used to be
Hello to sweet reality
The climax to history

(continued)

The day that my mind went cold
The day that my desire felt old
The day all my stories were told
The phone rang
My heart sang
Ole' Lang Sine
Bye-bye sweet memory
Hello to what couldn't be
The climax to ecstasy

The day I cried my last tear
The day I ended a lonely year
The day I forgot my fear
The phone rang
My heart sang
Of the boom-a-rang
Bye-bye loneliness
Hello happiness
The climax to my duress
Is to the love I now can confess

And the day my heart left my chest
Climaxing my life to invest
In your Forever After vows and caress

LIFE

Why is it
That life is at your fingertips
Unless you want more
Then it becomes
An elusive butterfly
Fluttering with the
Gusts of wind
To and fro
Away from your
Sense of destination

It seems the senses
Are always trying to catch up
With the intentions and
There is no mending them together

Be it your will to
Leave the cocoon
And become that butterfly
With your need and courage
To mend a crippled wing
And have the stamina to
Get back up and bring

(continued)

Hope to scale the next slope
The wisdom to know what's right
The faith with a will to cope
The instinct to change your flight
To a pattern and sense
That takes on fright

All these instincts are needed
To fly the trails divine
As a butterfly
Into destiny's design

Forging the birth of a moth
From the ugly and weak
Into the beauty of a mutation
With the strength to seek

Creation of Life's peak
The inheritance of the meek
Freedom to speak
And the will to seek

Life is then complete

LISTEN TO MY PULSE BEAT

When I hear your name
When I see your face
When I feel your touch
Or the smell of your skin
Or taste your lips
I can hear my pulse beat

It sounds like the first time we met
When I didn't know blood had a sound
That had to be found
The impact was profound
First it was pounding in my head
Burning a hole in my bedspread

Then my ears almost burst
From this feeling unrehearsed
As though I had been cursed

It got so that I would listen
For your heart beat
An incredible feat
A delectable treat

From head to feet

So now you're hearing my pulse beat
Making love
To your heart beat

HOW HIGH IS HIGH

How high is high
Take a trip to the bottom of your soul
Then climb back up to peace of mind
This is the extreme of low to high
To go deeper or higher is hell
Those who believe that there's height
Higher than peace of mind shall die
At the bottom of their soul

How low is low
Let your mind go
Unfettered and frustrated
To peaceful calm
Only to be awaken
By the 23rd Psalm

Having missed out on
A daughter or son
Due to good times gone
Celebrating lost time
By basking in a chemical brine

So kicking that drug habit
Before it's too late
Enables the trip back
To Peace of Mind
And what matters
On the clock of time

Getting high on each hour, each day and each chime

CALL COLLECT

Call me please call me collect
You don't seem to
Care who you wreck

Cause waiting isn't going to hurt
Your timing
You don't seem to care
Who you are nickel and diming

No charge to call out of town
Call me by name in effect
No coin to bring you down
Just call me collect

As if I had a choice
No such telephone sex
But at least I will hear your voice
And no one else's text

So pick up the phone
By its neck
Dial the number and
The charge is on my check

(continued)

Tell the operator
Dialing my number in reverse
You're fickle as well as poor
To complete our broken converse

And the charge is collect

Waiting and waiting for your call
Doesn't help me
Or forestall
You calling for free

Next time you can chase me

THE TRUTH

The thought of truth
Never crosses the mind of man
Until the mind of man
Crosses the threshold of commitment

For it is commitment that opens
The mind to conceive of the pleasures of giving
The fulfilment of helping
The sanctity of peace in the very mind that
Believed it to be true

The egg shall never hatch in a cold nest
Nor can a lie grow on a tree
But the deviation from truth
Can kill the mind of man
That is making him free

The egg will hatch the idea
And the flight will prove
Its content and cross the threshold
Of danger into the space
Thought beyond the soul

(continued)

The thought of truth
Crossed the mind of man
As day became night
And there was no sight
To explain the sunlight

And it all becomes a lie
When we die
With truth found beyond our eye
Left to the time we can fly

Away from the truth we deny

SENTIMENTS

SENTIMENTS

The sentiments of youth
Are quick easily formed
And for an instant almost uncouth
About life love and insecurity become sentiments
A rush of sincere uncontrolled bursts
Framed by extreme lows and high at firsts

The sentiments of middle age
Are not so quick nor easily scorned
And can be written on one page
A few loyal opinions become sentiments
Expressed about what works from remembrance
Of the past and it's most meaningful common sense

The sentiments of old age
Are never quick slow nor deformed
And can be remembered from the yellow page
It is the sage not the stage that become sentiments
Spoken from experiences and truth
Never envisioned by youth

(continued)

The sentiments of any age
Are expressed in quickies and mistakes reformed
Because what should be may never be
If it depends on love as the stakes and
Hate as war changes the sentiments decree
That each individual is not free

To decide the ride
And suffer the sentiments
That they applied
Having no excuse or intent
To over ride

The regrets and sentiments of the human Rip Tide(s)

THE HUMAN COVER UP

Take a face and paint it black
With a beard and some shellac
Smoke the rope and behind
Those colored glasses of every kind
Take you pulse with a drink
Put on a smile and hide what you think
Yes this is the human cover up

Because in hiding there is no confiding
In the principles to which we should be abiding
That is openness sincerity honesty
Just being real people and not a travesty
But the world is full of buts ifs and ands
And the cringing hearts and wringing hands

Saying why ... why do I want to cry
I knew I could laugh and get a natural high
By just being me
Sincerely letting other people see
Into my heart and into my mind
Into my future and not my behind

The runaway and fleeting fears
Of the cover up of painting my face black
With a beard and some shellac
Saying I'm just going to be me
And set this Self completely free

From these black clouds that cover my insecurity
When all it takes is uncovering the real me

CHALLENGE OR CHISEL

Peck peck peck at the wood
Chip chip chip at the stone
Pound pound pound upon the stake
Pull pull pull upon the rope
Stroke stroke stroke the pen
Sing sing sing the song
Giving it everything
Giving it all
Like our forbearers Abraham Mary and Paul

We've taken our own lives in our hands
Following the sound of far off commands
And must decide down inside
Whether we consider life to be a challenge
Or a chisel

The chisel is a utensil held up straight
Beaten upon levered and made to wait
While the challenge is the hammer
That forces the issue
That stalks the prey
That keeps track of the day
A morsel of man's prey

Eaten by those stalking on two legs
Versus the one-legged peg
That must be wedged between he who begs
In spite of the temperate Haig

(continued)

Diplomacy courtesy good common sense
Taken within the intent and maturity
Can turn that chisel into a prince
And challenge into opportunity

But this is not done easily and haphazard
It's the mature mind the healthy body
And time honored standard that create the stone
Upon which the chisel must feed
So that challenge is not alone
And the art form has been decreed

The declaration of beauty, stature
And unrelenting value
To the honor of Michelangelo- Rembrandt-Benet-Washington-Churchill-Lincoln-Gandhi and Jesus
The men of challenge
The men of stone
The rock of ages
Those whose time written upon the pages
Shall not be forgotten
Within the century thus past their passing
As Shakespeare shall ever be
A Godfather of poetry
Chiseled into our memory
The challenge to make History
Created on the canvas of Posterity
For me to forever see

SAME CONCLUSION

Why is it all great men and women
Arrive at the same conclusion
That simple pleasure is a sin
And God is not an illusion

Above and beyond the phonies
I've read a million and one
Stories and testimonies
About God's only son

And it's still unreal
To many of the masses
That enthusiasm and zeal
Don't come from the intellectual classes

It comes from belief
In oneself so one can believe
In the essence of bondage relief
For unto oneself it must deceive

(continued)

Oneself into frustration
About the conclusion
That the mirthful station
Is caused by the grand delusion

Called the anvil
Of the hesitant
Stricken by the devil
Until doubt is unpleasant

Then it seems in age
The great men and women
Arrive at the same conclusion
That the shallow life is a sin
And the Savior is no illusion

The spirit be with you until then

THE PIONEER

The pioneer breaks the ground
He breaks the ice
And navigates the sound
He rolls the dice
And walks the hard road
He must handle hardship
And must carry society's load
On his endless trip

The pioneer must have a strong back
He must have a strong will
To keep his ship on track
To higher mountains still
He must fight off ridicule
And must tread strange lands
Then navigate with very little fuel
With blisters on his hands

The pioneer must be willing to face danger
And must sacrifice himself
Where there is no forest ranger
To watch out for his health
Somewhat sad and alone
He must risk his scalp
And must be on his own
With no one to turn to for help

(continued)

But it's the pioneer's soul
Just waiting for the start
That gets him to setting far reaching goals
Known to be strong of heart
For this is the only way he can fulfill
The longing urge to roam
Taking for granted that only unusual will
Will get him to his home

Praise be to the pioneer
Praise be to his feat
For its destiny he will hear
As the soldiers stand in defeat
And critics can only weep
About the heresy they reap
While pioneers make the leap
Allowing history to repeat

And the world shall stand at his feet

THE ILLOGICAL LOGIC BECOMES TRUTH

Logic is the restraining wall
That surrounds our rational mind
It has been built stone by stone
From experiences we are
Willing to acknowledge and accept

The longer we live and the more we intercept
The higher the wall becomes
Until it won't let anything in or out
Eventually it will if allowed encompass
Endanger and engulf our rational mind
Thereby enclosing our reasoning power
With those thoughts and experiences
That we have accepted
Called traditions

Logic though it may be illogical
Has imprisoned the potential
Of the rational mind

Tear down that prison
Give the mind leeway and watch it expand
Its rationality its logic its depth its insight
Into reality as new traditions

(continued)

The great creator created boundless potential
To think beyond what is now
To enable us to form the future
Out of the illogical somehow

For to conceive a new thought though illogical
For research and discovery is molding logic
Out of the clay of doubt
It then becomes
The sculpture of truth

So set no limitations upon your brain power
Only envision much more than the logic from
Before

This the Psalm of Clay ... a mind bound by tradition fosters
Stability without creativity
An unbound mind is the creator of new traditions

"Conventional wisdom is already out of
touch" ... so says Michael Crichton

AN UNDESERVING SON

An underservicing son
Made of fluff and grind
All bluff and no fun

Sunshine and bottle of wine
Clover's bed and the roses twine
Casket and chairs made of pine

That's the world
Into which we are hurled
Mother's warm body curled

Daughter or son
Picked by God one by one
Undeserving until it's done

Make up your mind
To live it kind then
Grapes are good and so is the wine

(continued)

In a life
Cut by an immaculate knife
Helped along as man and wife

Hoping to be the one
The deserving son
When it is all done

With sunshine and a
Bottle of wine
Thank God I've still got time

Yet in the undeserving line
I'm a victim of my deserving mind

JUST ANOTHER WORD

Love
Is just another word for security

Security
Is just another word for I'm wanted

Wanted
Is just another word for I'm needed

Needed
Is just another word for hold me

Hold
Is just another word for never let me go

Never
Is just another word for something you can't have

So if you let me go
I'll never love again

OUR BOOK

The book of our lives is in the hands of the reader

The reader is turning the page
The stage manager is setting the stage
Reading from the book of our heart
And we're just playing our part

Page by page it's turned
Emotions and bygones are yearned
With the script of time
And our liberty as a face on a dime

The pages they may yellow
And with age enthusiasm may mellow
But the words remain the same
Never a change with the changing of a name

Be it first act or the last
Be it the future or past
We shan't see the curtain come down
Without wondering for whence we're bound

(continued)

The book's last page
And the exiting from the stage
Is surely not the end
But merely the reverberant bend

Turning us inward so we can go homeward
Rising again to whence we wend
Back towards the sunrise of our existence
Arising above the words ... beginning and end

Then save me for posterity
Turn me into a CD or DVD
Hearing me in effect
Or send a deceptive text

Leaving the blues to fake news

GOSH IS THAT SAD

Who determines the winners and the losers
The sinners and the boozers
Is it by some spiritual choice
Or does each victim or victor have a voice

I've been asking the Maker the baker
And the undertaker
Are you satisfied to have lived
As you've lived before you've died

And each man gives a different answer
Usually tempered by
How high and how far
Gosh it's sad I cannot fly

Inhibitions yes
In some a lack of ambitions
But that still does not give us
The answers we seek
About the valleys of some and
Those that attain their peak

And maybe it's not by an immortal design
That some will tow
And some will step over the line
Before they go

(continued)

Maybe it is by chance
That some are smitten or spurned by romance
Maybe it's not fate
That puts some of us on our toes
While others are busy
Mainlining their nose

Gosh it is awfully sad
To have lived and never to have had
A moment of joy
Not remembering the optimism
Held as a boy

For those poor souls
How sad it was that life was so unkind
For failing to aspire and set goals
To be a memory in anyone's mind

Gosh it's sad as they lay in the casket
Cold from embalm
With no lasting memories in their gift basket
And all that can be said is the twenty-third psalm

FROM THE MOUTHS OF BABES

Listen to our children
We must listen to our babes
Accept their voice

What they experience
We can know
If we can just know us

Be it from the Book of books
Saying of sayings
Song of songs
Poem of poems
Story of stories

All tell us nothing
Unless we have retained
The past from mouths of babes

For folly
Is not listening
And not feeling
Our children's thoughts

(continued)

As from the mouths of babes
Comes the light
From the gloom

Listen to their books
Their sayings
Their songs
Their poems
Their memories

Telling us their story
And their version
Of our story

Make it glad not sad
That is the real glory
Of the happiness of a babe's bliss

And a mother's kiss

THE MASTER'S PIECE

The mortar between loose bricks
The words between blank pages
The door at the end of life's tricks
Nothingness and just forgotten ages

Add the Master's hand
And you add hope
You add duty
You make black
Into beauty
You make day
From night
You make strength
From fright
The Master piece of all who pray

The mortar between loose bricks
When it's dry will die
The words between blank pages
When they are turned
The door at the end of life
When it's spurned
Creates nothing from strife

The mortar between strong bricks
Builds a fortress
The words between filled pages
Turns life towards
The door of the after life
For it opens and accords
Creation forever

As the Master's Piece

THIS IS NOT GOODBYE

This is not goodbye
So don't you cry

We will be back
Just in another track

All will be well
You have hope to sell

People depending on you
To put together something brand new

A little twist here
A bigger twist there

No one will notice
This is not the both of us

Calling the shots
Making the TV spots

No one will remember
If we left in October or November

This is not goodbye
Look reality in the eye

(continued)

Our time has come
To go after the Kingdom

Before it makes us beg
With its rules and reg

Taking away the fun
That is why we are done

Moving on to fight the fight
To bring the wrong into right

Look out Big Brother
The Rhoads' are putting it together

Into an association of fighters
To fix it for the takers and doubters

With a Provider's Bill of Rights
Well within our sights
If it takes becoming Governor …

Move over tis a political makeover

BREAKING UP IS SO HARD TO DO

Holding on to your way
Only deters the break of day
When the intent is wrong
Breaking out you must be strong

Take away the will to hold
Make it fair play
As business products are sold
The old fashion way

In the market place
With no inhibiting rules
Controls are the space
Between the fuels and tools

Master get out of the way
With rules and reg
That make it far from play
When we all have to beg

We are forever on our knees
If the ruler is the reason for the rule
Then there is no one to please
Except the Government we duel

(continued)

Monopoly or Monopsony
It is all the same
It is Enterprise set free
That wins the game

But who are the losers
That is the question
For Government controls the users
And due process is not the reason

It is the Bullies at work
That comes with the Monopoly
To solve it we must not shirk

Breaking up the dominance that Monopsony compels
Is so Hard to do
While the Wizards of Voodoo
Kill the Freedom that Enterprise sells

As peace and patriotism swells

GREAT HANDS

*Great hands are for more than clapping
And for slapping*

*I was told at a young age
That I had great hands*

*My baseball coach Mr. Tennett
Told another I had the best hands yet*

*His assistant coach would hit gigantic fly balls
To which he made calls*

*Go Jerry see if you can get it
And I did it*

*My position was shortstop
Because of my hands were not prone to drop*

*Anything hit my way
Until that day I made the unassisted triple play*

*Even in the major leagues
This was an exception that intrigues*

*Only eight have ever been turned
And mine was concerned*

(continued)

With the bases full
And their best hitter's pull

It came over the mound
Making this whizzing sound

I dove and caught it while on the ground
Not realizing what I had found

Jumping up and leaping back
I tagged the bag as that runner lost track

Three outs were then booked
As the man from first knew he was hooked

A slide and the tag that I took
Put a the triple play in the book

So my time as a quarterback and point guard
Was all using the hands that a base ballgame would regard

As great hands for my school's greatest record

A VOW TO THOSE NEEDED

Why do some people feel used
Versus why do others feel needed
Why is sex felt abused
To those who feel used to be heeded

Lo people taking feel used
Should know people giving feel needed
While people loving feel heeded

Love is everything
To those who have
Been daunted

Love is everything
To those who
Are wanted

Why do some people feel wanted
Versus why do others feel daunted
Why is sex nothing from above
To those who feel doubt about love

(continued)

Lo, people are taken by fear
And people are not truthful
Though, people are searching to endear

Security is everything
To those who
Have doubt

Security is everything
To those who
Turn to love to turn about

All of the doubts and insecurities
Are hiding in each closet to be found
Behind the tuxedo and wedding gown

So long as truth is the vow
Love is forever after now

FEELING GREAT

*Who could feel great
With all that weight
Who would feel good
With all that "wish I could"*

*Fortunately I'm not now blighted
With being short sighted
Everything I've now done
Is for the long run*

*Getting up putting my pants on
Ye, that's just a part of getting up before dawn
But I'm speaking of effort
The concentrated kind not the cheap sort*

*The magazine said
"Lose weight the easy way while sleeping in bed"
Well the fact is
That self-control doesn't fizz*

*It doesn't come in a bottle
It comes from having your hand firmly on the throttle*

(continued)

And to get your hand around it
You must first find the will to shift

With your own attitude
For self-control takes fortitude
To just say "Hey, I'm going to be this way or that"
Then just keep walking up to bat

And circle the bases
Chasing your shoe laces
And lo and behold
You will never feel old

For feeling great is forgetting weight
And pursue your natural state
It is not a date nor is it fate
To have started too late

Just consider you have time
To wait as you lose weight

A ROSE IS CARING

A rose rose high in the wind
Special in its carriage
For its beauty could only lend
To its special place on stage

Given to us to love
As we love a friend
We've been thinking of
A rose as more than just to send

A rose is caring
Special in its carriage
Worthy of couples pairing
Into a family's marriage

To deal with the stock of temptation
The threat of bondage
And the imperfection of creation
Played to a rose petal's age

A rose is caring
Its thorn is for pain
When couples pairing
Is made in vain

(continued)

Given to us to love another
As we love adventure
Veering towards the other
Results in hate we censure

To deal with the stock of temptation
We hide our transgressions
Between the vows of dissention
And divorce our apprehension

A rose is caring
Its roots are always there
When couples pairing
Return to why they care

A rose rose high in the wind
Special in its carriage
For its beauty could only lend
To a special second marriage

Hoping that another start
Won't be a thorn in our heart

I WONDER ... ONE OR A HUNDRED

Is a meaningful life one year or a hundred
Is a meaningful day now or forever
Is pain instant or always there I wonder
Is age the indicator of our endeavor

To the seekers of self-gratification
Is reality just a perception of our leaning
But always there in peace or satisfaction
While questions of the soul have no meaning

For the knoll is only meaningful
To the naïve mountain climber to seek
And the valley is only beautiful
To the sacrificial climber at the peak

For those wanting answers for salvation
Of evil shall forever live knowing the inferno
And when one day or a hundred years are done
Life without pain is life eternal

For inside the Gates of Hell
Pain is the endeavor
While inside the Gates of Heaven
A meaningful life even for an instant can be forever

BRAINS

God I've always had brains
But why was I so dumb
God I've always had arms
But why was I so numb

God I've always wanted to be great
But why must I wait
Is it your will
That the good news I've read
Won't fill an empty head

And love won't seek the living dead

Unless those brains
Become more than ink stains
Spreading across a borderless life
Lived without dedication to my wife

Though accepting me as I am
And making my brains into a knowing man
Until it's a way of life dedicated to
Something as simple as my wife

(continued)

Divorcing this precept
Destroys any head with brains
Because it won't accept
That marriage is the reins

Holding us to the conception
That love is the almighty
And that there is no deception
When Monogamy is the sanctity

Of life liberty and the pursuit of happiness
So help me God

PLEASE CALL ME SIMPLE

Please call me simple your way
For I want you to be the same each day
I'm nothing unless you can understand it's we
Please don't try to outsmart my plea

By trying to outsmart me
For you are what your behavior will be
You may hide behind words
You may profess our love like birds

But don't lie to me as I do to you
Because I don't start till you're through
Please call on me ... simple
Please touch me ... gentle

Please keep your intentions true
Otherwise you're just kidding you
Swing your arms
Expose your vanity
Through your charms

(continued)

No problem
But don't take me upon your bed
Unless you expect me to believe you instead
Yes, it is so ample
My need for you is so simple

For just plain ole you and me
Never deceiving our Pictionary frames
Drawing simple rules we can see
Without just playing lost fun and games

Simple is as simple does

MEANINGFUL

Words are forming upon my mind
Thoughts and shadows
Expression much inclined
Groping for a meaning that endows

Dreams in pictures taking shape
Falling upon this unsuspecting tape
Hands are clapping in the sanctuary
Time is passing if we don't hurry
Tongues are clicking in the choir
With these words to turn to fire

Simple words upon my mind
Pouring from me unkempt uncut unrefined
Just expressions taking shape
Falling from me to this tape
Catch them catch them if you will
But if you don't my mind cannot be still
It must be heard
I must express each word

And even though to the human ear they may escape
They're still captured upon this tape
Typed or typing just as life
Making a record of the author's strife
As the writer's friend
Espouses the mind about the end

(continued)

Taken anyway if taken at all
Hear these words oh tape as I call
Out the name of those whom I know
Tis this venture creating as I go
This I guess is my very purpose
Not to sink disappear or even surface

Just to bring upon the bough
The words I feel the things I do
And then teaching how
To mold these deep felt thoughts
Into plans and well placed plots
Forming a vision for others to see
Simple thoughts from the mind of me
Handsome rewards can be mine
If these words I do refine
Into simple short sentences
For the tape to catch the reminiscences
Till the idea is clearly there
And then the listener if thou shalt be
To mince a care

(continued)

Mindful still I am though
That the reader will know
And shall ever be
Just as meaningful to me

For what I am I am
I must be mindful and understand
That what I do I do
So my words have meaning to you

A writer an artist a songstress
A creator of business
All know that what they do
Must be meaningful to you

If you've read this far on your own accord
Likely you're not bored
And I strummed your meaningful chord

THE STRENGHT TEST

Who so shall strike me
Shall feel my strength

Who so shall hate me
Shall feel my love

Who so shall disdain me
Shall feel my faith

Who so shall feel me
Shall be strong

Who so shall be strong
Shall not need me

Who so shall test me
Shall feel my determination

For they shall be committed to themselves
And feel important

They who shall believe
Shall feel good

They who shall deceive
Shall feel unimportant

(continued)

They who shall receive
Shall he thankful

They who shall conceive
Shall receive

They who shall contest me
Shall feel my determination

For they shall be committed to their beliefs
And feel secure

They who shall work
Shall feel worthy

Those that don't shirk
Shall feel adequate

Those that don't smirk
Shall feel my joy

Those that have been a jerk and have no friends
Shall feel my ambition turned into their determination

Giving them the will to be the giver
And receiver of mortal strength

By being the minister of will power

GUTS

GUTS

It's not the skin
Or Muscle
That is the will to win
And create a miracle

Not just pride
As determination mounts
It's what's inside
That counts

Some call it guts
Some call it soul
But no ifs ands or buts
It's created by a goal

If it is as simple
As all that
Why do people tremble
About every at bat

(continued)

Maybe it's their way
Of expressing
No belief in today
Or its blessing

With no bridges to burn
Ironically they can win
By making a u turn
Around to right from sin

And could let go
Of those if ands or buts
To be a hero
Because of guts

LOOK AND YE SHALL FIND

I found my dream dreaming me
It was under a cover covering me
Fading in and out of the inside of me
Looking to be seen no ordinary dream
Dreaming me

Caught in the tumbler of time timing me
It taught the teacher teaching me
That I wanted to be
Myself being what I want to be
Not that dream dreaming me

To this I found if one look I took
Of reasons reasoning me
I could deduce or add the sum of me
Into a person who becomes a reality
No longer a dream dreaming me

Off the stage of wanting to be me
Onto the fringe of fantasy
I'm just now seeing the look of thee
As I discovered the we in me

(continued)

And life began to be the ninth degree
Looking inside of my reality
Changed my mind about being free

Of the dream dreaming me
For now you and I are conceiving history
Look and we shall find
Our need to be dreaming destiny

For getting there is free

RAIN

Rain is fun
It is before sun
And during night
Glimmers twinkling bright

It comes down hard
It comes down soft
It grows the yard
It fills the loft

Rain can be sad
More than a little wet
But it isn't bad
Gotta have rain you bet

It drives the cattle home
It scares the kids
It turns the dirt to foam
It puts our plan on skids

Rain can be glad
When it doesn't beat down
And a draught has a hold on Dad
Worrying about his ground

(continued)

It brings home the crops
When we need the moisture
It seems it never stops
As we have the animals cloister

Rain can be our savior
For without it life is hell
It fills our tanks and the river
We are very happy that it fell

It finds us all growing tall
For it feeds our nation
From winter spring summer to fall
Our barns and tanks don't ration

Any harvest at all

POSTMORTUM

Why not on the other hand
Didn't we actually think and understand
A life looked at posthumously
Is without a simile

That eternal peace
Comes from the ability to cease
What we are for what we can be
Then we can pass on guilty free

Like a winner celebrating the
Demise and shallow grave of the sinner
Looking back at what could have been
But never to be a skimmer

Saying prayers and burying a life
In its own history
Is like stating regrets to his wife
In what has been her misery

(continued)

Instead dirt is over his eyeglasses
Does it really matter
That it is his ashes
We do scatter

With memories not wanted
Justice will prevail
With offspring taunted
And no scripture can avail

Mankind is burdened with truth
It is a life thus given
And set from youth
Who's RIP is to be driven

By a postmortem on how he was livin'

THE WAITING GAME

Waiting for someone else to step forward
And say the word
Why can't we say at any cost
That we're lost
We're afraid or we've just been delayed

Or are we hiding from something we understand
Liking it to our resistance to give others our hand
To the price it will cost oneself
Lost to the ultimate holocaust
Man vs. Himself

Waiting for the stop and go sign
Do we really know
When to stop and when to go
How's it feel to be the winner
Far superior to the pant of a sinner I bet
Because it's a peaceful pause as I set
Into the dashboard to find a cause

That is worthy of human pride
Yes the human side

(continued)

Can it be that one can feel good
By just being what others say we should
Or by standing in line and shout
Looking for the easy way out
Man vs. Self-Doubt

Waiting for someone else to step up
Offering to be instead of me
Waiting until inaction becomes our enemy

Waiting for the stop and go sign

Waiting for our last place in line

Man vs It's Not My Time

SYNAGOGUE OF GOD

Is it sin or God
To fear divine
In the Synagogue of Satan
Or the Book of Revelations 3.9

A Synagogue cannot speak
Though it may not be weak
A Synagogue can't say
Though it may know the way
A Synagogue isn't of the living
Though it may stand for giving
A Synagogue isn't God
Though many bow to its demon's Rod

It is his image we applaud
As the Synagogue of God

Religion from the start
Was for man to heal the hole in his heart
Rather than healing the hole in his head
Man made up religion instead

(continued)

Worshipping Symbols God was just hanging around
Looking down on this violent ground
Called the good earth
Filled with sin and mirth

Hoping to silence this lack of love
He sent angels from above
But they were in for a fight
With the Red vulture in flight

Called the Devil
Bringing all to the same level
Protecting his sheep
From the faith God could reap

The devil was going to win
And no amount of sin
Could bring God to the earth
Until God proved his worth

So he created by immaculate birth
From the rib of the Devil's fiery hearth
A human being of stature
A living Synagogue as a mortal creature

(continued)

Jesus Christ was his name
And the Devil's demise was his game
Though it took time and pain
God's work was not in vain

In battle the Devil took God's son's life
And thought that was the end of the strife
But low and behold
The boulder rolled

Letting good will prevail
The goodness of the Savior put the sinners in jail
And though sin did not cease
The sheep were no longer to be fleshed

From then to now
No one really knows how
Jesus rose from the dead
But belief in his life creates instead

A Synagogue of the Lord to crucify Satan's dread

STORMS AND WEATHER KITES

Storms don't brew like coffee

Clouds don't form from a sun spot
Rain doesn't come from a teapot
And the calm before the lightning strike
Cannot fly the weather kite

It can't hold its predictions in abeyance long
Or so long till the wind whips it to death
Though it may seem neither right nor wrong
It gives you fright in your breath

It can be just plain fear in those worried eyes
Because a storm is unpredictable
It can be the surprise at sunrise
It could be the latent threat made unstable

But there is no way to tell the truth in a storm
There is no way to stop and say let's start over
'cuz it took time for those frictions and sparks to form
With us wanting to smell the clover

And paranoia isn't built on clout
It's merely a task of taking out an erasure
To remove the sperm that gave birth to doubt
And cancelled a honey moon flight's pleasure

(continued)

High noon isn't just a time to eat or a time to shoot
Or find a war drum to beat
Unless you can get to the root
From whence the storm will repeat

Then it is somewhat like putty
Holding on to air and speculation
Not really a topic for study
Nor is it a time for revelation

It's best if you can ride out the storm
Taking your licks and your bites
Hoping all will get back to the norm
Before it destroys all that's learned from weather kites

Not just a position to defend
But nay with each gust and rain pulling at the string
Be aware and listen to the blowing wind
For it may be pain the storm will bring

For as the director of the band
And the headstrong tribunal
Could be that not all ideals could withstand
The essence of one more weather kite's funeral

(continued)

But if the choices aren't there
One must make the best and one must show
That they're aware
Cutting the kite loose is to let go

And take a deep breath
Heading back into the storm
Don't be afraid don't fear death
For the other kites still appear to be in safe form

And the future use of weather kites
To predict flights
Lost to the storm instead
Are being put safely to bed

As the Katrina and Harvey's
Hurricanes forecast bled red

MELTING YEARS

Melting years like useless tears
Before our eyes
Time and essence dies

Melting years like unfounded fears
Before our careers
Time and essence lies

Melting years sinking hopes
Before a will that copes
Time and essence cries

Melting years gone by
Before answers to why
Time and essence defies

Melting years with our mate
Before it's too late
Time and essence tries

Melting years with our family
Before our eyes they flee
Time and essence then replies …

(continued)

Goodbye

Melting years
Useless tears
Unfounded fears
Sinking hopes
Years gone by
Without our mate
And family's sign

Nothing left to melt but frozen time

THE GULL'S ILLUSION

The author's word must create
As in the Gull's illusion
That the answer is faith
Like a surgeon's fusion

With the cutting knife
Telling stories of the time
Holding true to life
Even if it doesn't rhyme

Poems fiction or history
Given the pen
Love hope and misery
Spiced with goodness and sin

That only God's stage will allow
Flying high with those deep "6's"
Showing those who don't know how
About flying spiral fixes

Up to the sky's outer limit
Where it's cool and still
Looking down on the summit
Above fear for the thrill

(continued)

Rather than efforts akin
It's God's highest mountain
That limits his children
To drinking from the fountain

When Christ walked on water
Putting necks in the doubter's noose
Don't they realize as a starter
That they're killing the goose

Up where fear is afraid of fear itself
The Gull of the illusion takes a bow
Level off creature for your health
And Jonathon will show you how

Safely looking over your shoulder
High above the ground and the grass
You are close to the almighty beholder
And HIS immortal fearless mass

For it's the wind that sings
"Look Gull's fly up here
Spread your wings
Never fear God is near"

FLIGHT 271

Yes I'm on the ground
In from Peoria bound
Snow is bright from the sun
Waiting on Flight 271

Got to get to Atlanta GA
On Delta Eastern or TWA
Could be now or sometime late
But no matter what I've got to wait

Here I am waiting on standby
Just behind some other guy
He's just ahead behind the next
All of us somewhat perplexed

Not much to do not much to say
Except to call the place I'm going to stay
Telling them of my bad fate
Hoping they'll pick me up at the gate

(continued)

Take me on into Atlanta town
So I don't get jacked around
As I hear the announcement of connections made
It's the countdown I'm afraid

I'm way down the list
If I don't make it I'm going to be missed
Smith Jones Franklin Stone
But no Rhoads on this load they moan

That has a connect to your final destination
And without hesitation
Come back later
For the 6:18 standby to Decatur

Good luck sir
I heard him purr
He took out a list two pages long
Checking in my mane and spelling it wrong

You're one of a couple dozen
With assignments we've frozen
It's the capacity we're meeting
With standbys already in their seating

(continued)

Nor was it likely I was still in the running
One two then it's ten
Names keep coming
Couldn't remember where I'd been

Hey wait a minute
My named was just called
I may still be in it
If flight 271 isn't stalled

With the proverbial mechanical failure
Ah, oh the flight attendant is saying sir
You have to get off this one
Because there will be no flight 271

Then I have to beg and borrow
A cabbie to come back tomorrow
For my day is done
Putting me up in Day's Inn room 101

Scheduled on another Flight 271

A-BOMB DROPPED

THE DAY THE FIRST A - BOMB DROPPED

The visions of a peaceful world departed
Then the threat of all-out war stopped
And the value of mortal power restarted

And a cold form of war started

As threat of annihilation was thwarted
By the fear of the trigger
That could be transported
Into a world by air no bigger

Ban the bomb they say
But who are they
Are they the enemy of decay
Or prognosticators of Judgment Day

With a cold form of war to stay

Who fears most fears mistakes
The mistake of eternity
Could be those who flaunt their own sakes
Without realizing social reality

(continued)

For whosoever shall disregard
That day in Japan
When the blast heard created the scarred
Shall be forever to not again happen

And don't misunderstand the value
Of the threat it stopped
Built on the head of a missile
That shall never again be dropped

Until the cold war stopped

The day the second A-bomb dropped
The visions of a peace in the world departed
When the threat of all our destruction estopped
And the intimidation of nuclear power started

Deterrent or servient
For whatever impact of that day
We cannot be crass or ambivalent
Of the reason and its senseless way

Nothing gained nothing built
Wherever the armies and navies went
Taking on each other in guilt
For the A- bombs advent

(continued)

Then the cold form of war's decent

For each question you ask about war
And the killing it represents
There is no answer therefore
Even when the killed and killers repent

For that reason the bombs were sent

THE DAY THE WAR STOPPED

The day the great war stopped
Is the day the A-bomb dropped
The day possible peace began
Was the day of the eternal atom

The day the world stood still
Was the day of overkill
For the balance of power
In fear of a nuclear shower

Nations fret and feign
But no one will chance radiation rain
The day humanity realized
That self-destruction was now crystalized

(continued)

Yes the day the bomb was dropped
Was the day sanity stopped
Hitler, Tito, Mussolini and Stalin's hoax departed
And the quest for the H-Bomb started

Or have we just opened the door
With the infamous World War
As the bomb we thought defused
Evil for evermore

Until there is a Galactic Star War
Closing Hell's kitchen door
Removing the Earth forever more

As the A-bomb will not even the score

STAND UP GROWN-UP

Maybe it just happens
Happens when it's time
Just like the feelings of friends
Gradually arrives if we seek and find

Or do we just grow up
When we realize
That the act of living
Isn't just for love sick lies

It's simply getting it together
Regardless of the influence checked
By our Mother and Father
And what the past hasn't wrecked

The clouds will clear
From stormy weather following you
Then redo yourself for love without fear
As that makes an adult
Out of the blue

As maturity rearranges
All of a sudden
Your inner voice changes
And the need of others isn't such a burden

(continued)

For your relationships
Are healthy in spite of tsunamis
Once thought sinking your ships
Are now priorities

The saying to just Grow-up
Is a challenge and does not erupt
As a test of your sippy cup
That is still half full as you grow up

Though half may seem corrupt
Until you shape up your thinking
Finding it is better to stand up
As a grown up

Or you will fall for anything

AND THE GAME WENT ON

I sat on the sidelines
Huddled within myself
Feeling down and out
In my mind and my health

I'd been taken out by a crushing blow
My legs were gone and I couldn't go
The rest of the world seemed to be passing by
As I started to cry oh no

The game went right on
See I was more important to me
Than I thought I was to them
Until I finally could see
Sitting here holding my limb

That we're all an island
As isle of flesh and bone
Left to fend the circumstances and stand
Up all alone

(continued)

Left to the devices of a moan and a groan
Or gritted teeth and come back prone
I guess it took this to realize
That we're more important in our own eyes

And Humility may be the ultimate prize
Just to realize
Not criticize
That coming down makes a person wise

Friendships come and friendships go
Lessons are learned and the more you know
The more you want to learn and grow
For the game goes right on

In spite of your feelings pro and con

WAIT

Oh maker of the morning
Wait on me

Oh maker of the eve
Wait for me

Oh rainmaker before you leave
Wait with me

Oh maker of the sea
Sail with me

Oh maker of the heavens
Fly with me

Oh redeemer of hope
Cope with me

To be free

I stood in the shadow of the sunshine
Much in awe of thine
Until I realized
Fate wouldn't wait

(continued)

On me

It was moving on
With each breaking dawn
Letting freedom
Get away from me

So I took up my senses
I tore down rows upon rows
Of defenses
So Heaven knows

That I was bare
And found that faith was there
I took her by the hand
And walked to her command

I now can wait

For Madam fate
Who is waiting for a sailing mate

BONDAGE

I'm bound for the city of destruction
I'm bound for the outskirts of myself
I'm bound for the country of affliction
I'm bound for the bounty of wealth
And more
My bondage is with my own arms
My bondage is with my own doubt
My bondage is simple indecision
My bondage is floundering about
The score
Is my mind tied in a knot
And my courage held hostage
That is to have or to have not
The bondage of myself at this stage
Or
I will break free
To be the new un-bounded me
The new me will be stronger
For crucial decisions I will take longer
For
The new me will be smarter
To hell with being a self-starter
Sure I can exchange bondage
For old age

(continued)

Encore
I can rearrange the stay
By turning my next page
To a mystery
To an epic
To a History
To a biopic

An Unbound tale of freedom
From Myself

THE FUN IS IN THE BUILDING

Pick the plot
Draw the plans up good
See what we've got
Order the wood

Set in the foundation
Put up the frame
Surround the walls
The interior goes the same

Next is the roof
The siding and such
Almost finished aloof
The feeling's too much

While my work was on fire
Take some time
Before I retire
To the house I built so fine

Little did I know I would wilt
Just couldn't wait
Till I got it built
So I could coast and create

(continued)

Now that it's done
Stand back and take a look
Boy was that work fun
I think I'll read a book

Just another day goes by
Others rushing here and there
Here I am rocking and looking at the sky
Not alive nor do I move my wheel chair

Then wham with a sudden heft
It hit me
I was dying the death
Hanging on boredom's tree

Let me go I said
Give me another life to build
Let me get out of bed
Before my will is killed

Order the wood hire the hands
Pick the plot
Draw the plans
See what we've got
Before I die of idle rot

The fun is in the building
Of life's work never done

IOWA

Kiowa the Indian of peace
Tama the reservation of forgotten freedom
Oskaloosa the camp of the encamped deceased
Keokuk the water rippling no more of Kingdom come

Muscatine cultivating corn from forgotten lands
Sioux City the tribunal burial mounds
Osceola whose buffalo plains still stands
Indianola the happy hunting grounds

Iowa the home of the Kiowa

The home of the natives free
The home of the tribes of the past
The home of the white man decree
The home of the future albeit cast

The heritage of strong will
Hard work and simple surroundings
With common sense answers still
To simple but worthy renderings

(continued)

Questions that can be answered tomorrow
Much better than today's sorrow
Because its culture
Attracts a circling vulture

To destroy
What it taught every Iowa boy
Thou shall reap what thou can employ
In spite of being the decoy
A native culture handed down to decree

That the Iowa Boy is the Indian in me

AUTHOR'S FORMULA (39)(41)
DIFFERENT TIMES

Age is just an act of charades
Add it up and multiply yourself alive
A mere seven- and one-half decades
Into 75

Age is only mind deep
Facing it is the hard part
Do you smile or do you weep
Body up and down beats your heart

Age is only voice deep
Is it strong or weak
Will I run or leap
Giving all it can seek

When I do a pushup
Age is only weight up and down
Can the muscles hold what's up
Or shrink and wrinkle round

When the face is scolding
Age is only skin deep but wise
While beauty is beholding
To false impressions of size

(continued)

Seven comes eleven on the dice
Age is being 39 41 times
And looking 25 twice
A form of illusion that rhymes

Age is just an act of charades
Add it up and multiply yourself alive
A mere seven- and one-half decades
Into Seventy-five

I'm not old
I'm just a man child on hold

Chronological Age 80
Biological Age 50
Difference 30

Life expectancy in men 78
Plus the difference of 30
My life expectancy 108 won't wait
Difference due to life style waist size
60 years marriage diet and

Most importantly daily exercise

FEELING GOOD

Feeling good isn't a body thing
Feeling good isn't the idle fling
Feeling good isn't what drugs will bring

It's more than a good cry
It's more than a chemistry
It's more than past history

To deal with human misery

It's something easily missed or misunderstood
For knowing what you should
Is in itself doing good
Then doing it
To feel your spirit
Feeling understood

Having the spiritual desire
Yes feeling good is going higher
Than any ordinary flyer
Higher than those without desire

(continued)

To be what God's will would
Have us be
Yes free to be misunderstood
For doing good work is feeling good

From that measure to whence we go
Where most people don't know
By listening to the mind blow

Riding the words understood
To the land of should
Could and would

But I will not

Have a great first date
Make love to my soul mate
Give a hand to my children

Nor experience that illusive win

But like Mike and Nike could … Then just do it
To free your spirit
By feeling good

PULL OFF

I hope I can pull off what I've put on
I hope I can hang on to what I'm trying to pull off

Set-ups and set-downs and setbacks beseech me
And there are those high flyers
Who cannot reach me

But there are not many if any
Who want to pull off
An entrepreneurial symphony

Playing tunes thought even insane
In the eye of a hurricane
In search of fame

Better to be turned on
Better to be put on
Better to move on

Then to have regrets at dawn

So I honor the gracious Goddess of Loft
Pulling off a soft landing
Before the clock can annul
The flight of a fateful seagull
Hoping to pull off what is aloft
And hang on to what I'm trying to pull off

By pulling off this road to nowhere

HIBERNATION OF LOVE

Thoughts spring from my mind
Through the cool crisp air
The grass crunches under my feet
As the days of renewal are almost there

Though the clouds are still low
And the atmosphere gray like a glow
My spirits will sow the budding of the day

Positive with a green field
Flowers and trees though just shadows
The glaze is coming off the windshield
And there's vapor rising from the meadows

Yes the days of spring are almost here
With a twinkle in the morning
When I think about you being secure
And the gestation of love against scorning

We were together despite
Stormy weather and managed
To love and fight
Till we got engaged

(continued)

We played our parts
Through the rain
Falling upon our hearts
Instead of reliving pain

We cuddled when possible
With sex as our reason
Oh so pleasing and plausible
Generating heat during every season

With wrinkles our faces still mourn
When I think about our need to shove
And recover from our bodies retreat forlorn
During the hibernation of love

Freezing our thoughts of each other
And making us warm in our coats
For the next battle to smother
The hibernation that love invokes

Melting into our hearts it stokes
Hope

TWO BUILD OR PERISH

Two Blocks
A building will build

Two rocks
A religion is willed

Two shocks
A grain is borne

Two flocks
A herd is shorn

Two thoughts
A business is started

Two plots
A theater curtain parted

Two dots
A mind will focus

Two gots
Regrets to make a Locust

Two that fought
Seventeen years thought lost

(continued)

Two then sought
An Exodus of Freedom from holocaust

An intercourse of two human leases
Is formed in love, for
Reproduction of a species

Then the world shall be two
A division of sperm and egg shall not perish
Building around the mean of you

The wonderful process of passion
Of emotions of desire consumed
With a reason and a nation

With the will of Israel and the land of God
Avoiding the favor of one unto none

For God's will is done … in tandem
Gentiles and Jews in Jerusalem
Too cherish or perish

Since we are all one under the sun

DEATH OF FEAR

DEATH OF FEAR

Death of fear is certain
If you confront the fear you're averting

Death of self is sure
If you feel impure

Death of attitude is guaranteed
If your self-image you impede

Death of life is not inbred
Unless you believe you will be dead

Death is dread and doubt
That's what confidence is all about

Confidence comes from the death of fear
And it's not certain
When your self-esteem is hurting

So take yourself by the hand
Lead yourself to the promise land

Tell yourself that you understand
Give yourself an enthusiastic hand

With a prayer at your command
Doing what you know you can

For death of fear is certain
When you can do what you're averting

GET ON WITHOUT IT

Get off of it
Clean up your mind
Then get on without it
Before you fall behind

Justice can become a crime
Negative thought can drag you under
Give it too much time
And your manner will be just so much blunder

Nor can your virtues possibly drown

If you look up instead of down
If you smile instead of frown
If your attitude is coming around
You can flourish and abound

Get off of it then get on without it
Take the time to do it with the right grip
So you don't have to do it over
Clean the weeds and grow the clover

Tell bad bedfellows to move over

(continued)

Look for the opportunity in every difficulty
And don't become overwhelmed by the pity
So realty is without doubt
Void of doubt and insanity

Just don't fear it
Get off of it and get on with a twist
That's the spirit
Make your own wish bucket list

Birds fly because they think they can
Ships sink because they lose their wind
Friends unwind and understand
That it takes give and take to win

At times you have to go back
So you can go forward
Sometimes what you lack
Is what will drive you upward

To get on without your doubt

I JUST PASSED MYSELF

Going around that curve at 110
I looked over to see where I'd been
Lo and behold what did I see
That it was myself passing me

Pursuing life in haste
I'd been told and I'd been warned
Don't be a human running in place
Just to be ignored

Looking upward and beyond myself I rationalize
That only the flyer flies
And that one more time and one more mile
Will only hurt for a little while

Sort of like there is no tomorrow
Taking today for what I can beg and borrow
But then the damage sets in
And I start to think of where I've been

Finding out on a scale of one to ten
That I've passed myself again
Alcoholics anonymously repent
Drug addicts find themselves in decent

(continued)

Though I guess I must pay my rent
If I expect to survive till Lent
Slowing down is so hard to do
Coming down from Mountain Dew

Nothing wrong with coming down
To more earthly motives I have found
Time to rest and regroup
So my wings and feathers can recoup

Coming down and roost awhile
It might even give me a human smile
For when I get straightened out from that curve
I didn't weave and I didn't swerve

I went right to the trusty shelf
And dry docked my dreaming self
Yes even this shall pass
But for the sake of being crass

I think I need a good long fast
Passing up my past

CAN YOU LOVE ME

Can you love me without my touch
Can you love me without our time together ... in reverse
Can you love me as a friend and as such
Can you love me for the better ... or worse

It's almost like asking if love is just a thought
And not an act we sought
If love can be our dreams we caught
And not a fact we lack then forgot

I truly think so and believe in our relation
That love is the cement of our imagination
It holds our emotions to our mind
That allows our soul and heart to intertwine

To be physically confined
By the wedding tether
Giving the mortal sign
That we are locked together

(continued)

Like horses with saddles
Boats with saddles
Fools with chattels
Wars with battles

That shroud our relations
When true love without a comma
And complications
Foregoes the drama

By divorcing thoughts of not having you
With commitment and your consent
Foregoing elopement
When our wedding is the event

And a friend's touch is not too much

WHAT THIS COUNTRY MEANS TO ME

Looking across the countryside
I must do so with great pride
America is the spirit applied
And the heart that always tried
For the sake of those alive then died

For all I can see is the work of man
Though there are things I don't understand
I'm amazed at making concrete from the sand
Growing food from the land
Creating technology from the mind and hand

Man's ability to convert seedlings to birth
Of abundance without girth
Granaries stand as shadows in the sky
A salute to man's mortal cry
Of get me work or let me die

This is what this country means to me
It means so much to say I'm free
To stand up each day after I pray
And know that I have a chance
To create reality from circumstance

For there aren't many in this world
With themselves unfurled
Before the Almighty spirit
Embodied in humans that we touch
Before a God we respect so much ... yet fear it

(continued)

Holiness and happiness are the caress
That our country can certainly bless
Individuals creating their individuality
In a land where it is we not just me
So the country is collective in totality

The country is above and beyond passing time
And condoning ordinary crime
Wash away the dirt the grit and grime
It is the here and now divine
For those who are so inclined

It stands there as a symbol of verve
Saluting those who have enough nerve
To sacrifice and serve
To remake themselves out of nonsense
And mark our historical prominence
As a nation of common sense

Yes that's what this country means to me
It means together we are free and
Divided we are alone in our uncertainty
United we become history

That's is our peace and security

IN MY MIND

A newly plowed field looks so clean
A gliding eagle is so serene
But a field of stripped cornstalks
Until the field is clean
Is disheveled and mean

Not so much different is the mind
Unto the planter it shall bind
Until it is free and clear of stalks
Cleansed of the words and talks
Jamming up a mind that balks

Yes clear your mind if you please
If you want to learn with ease
Don't expect miracles and wonders
If all you remember
Are bad tempers and blunders

To be clean it must be cleansed
This takes more than soap and help of friends
It takes a concerted effort to detach
And then divest
Cornstalks planted to hatch
And produce a perennial harvest

(continued)

Bogging down progress
Holding back the wheels of success
Allowing no furrows to be planted
Until the planter is disenchanted
And the season of no other purpose
But to clean that fertile surface

With the good earth now revealed
Giving wings that stalks concealed
As gliding geese is so serene
Hovering over the scene
Until the field is pecked clean

Formerly disheveled and not fit for a bean … stalk

THE CUSTOM

It was the custom in my customized '53 Ford
To tour the square and listen to Bill Haley
To keep from getting bored
Yes, we had slicked back hair
Blue suede shoes
That were brushed daily
So we could dance to Carl Perkins and
The rhythm and blues

In my white sports coat
Still too young to vote

Girls and sports were a big part of the daily routine
Some was by plan and some just by reason
Of being a teen in puberty season
Yes just a part of being sixteen
Elvis was the King
With his moves as well as the beat
The words were too silly to sing
Hound Dog and the Wooly Tree moving your feet

(continued)

To be All Shook Up
You were doing the bop
To Come and Go With Me
We did it and we did it well
King and Queen of the hop
To the tunes of Raunchy the Dell Vikings
Danny and the Juniors we were liking
At the Hop couldn't stop

In my white sports coat
Still too young to vote

So much of dreams were cars, sports and music
We never thought much about next week
Or any goals to seek
It was just who's looking good and feeling good
The way we stoked our stove the way we stood
So girls noticed the car we drove
And how we handled parking and necking
At Fair Acres in the cove

The days sometimes seemed too long
When primarily acne and no girlfriend made things go wrong
Just waiting for the beat of the next Elvis Presley song
Yes this was the '50's
Growing up in a small town
With few aspirations till the '60's
Living by sight and sound

(continued)

Combing the hair
Hoping for a "come-on" stare
And being smart enough to turn down a dare

In my white sports coat
Still too young to vote

Looking back on those low-slung jeans
With T-shirts and youth center scenes
Gives me a yearning to be young again
I feel my soul burning for pat hands to win
Left only to savor the memories
When we go back for the reunions and mortuaries
Do I realize that those Customs predicted our lives

Living and loving never again to feel customized

OUR MAKER

I would rather be a peace maker
Than a war maker
Is peace an option
Is attack the strategy or tactic

Our world is troubled
By religion
By politics
By economics
By social mores

The resolution of such
Does not lie in confrontation
It lies in communication
And compromise

I would rather be a love maker
Than a hate ranker
Is sacrifice an option
Is faith the strategy or rhetoric

Our world is at war with itself
By climate
By outer space
By inner space
By earthly limits

(continued)

The resolution of such
Does not lie in speculation
It lies in problem solving
And accountability

I would rather be a change maker
Than an crisis creator
Our willingness to fail
Enables our world to succeed

Our world is challenged
By hopelessness
By poverty
By fear
By doubt

The resolution of such
Does not lie in doubt
It lies in faith
And effective ideas and leadership

I would prefer to be a job maker
Rather than a law breaker
Is control the rule
Or the confinement of thought

(continued)

Our world is defeated
By dictators
By extremists
By ugly imperialists
By terrorists
By Federalists
While freedom desists

The resolution of such
Does not lie in more enforcement
It lies in peaceful coexistence
And a world of peace

I would rather be a peace maker
Than a war maker
Peace is no option
In God we trust because we must

For God is our Maker and Undertaker

I WANNA BE A TEST PILOT

The daredevil dazzles his audience
The circus performer basks in applause
The rock star is high on chemical science
The test pilot is a little of all these hoorahs

What draws them to the cockpit
Yes it's the danger
The ultimate challenge to their wit
The adulation of the perfect stranger

In defying the risk of altitudes

Do they really think they're going to die
Do they really think it is man's place to fly
Do they think it's a battle cry
To break the speed and clouds on high

Daredevils test pilot sky ranger
Afraid of themselves
And addicts of danger
Intoxicated with power it swells

In defying the risk of magnitudes

Irrational with their feeling that risk deploys
But boys will be boys
Playing with grownup toys
Risking the element that destroys

(continued)

Despite defying the servitudes

The element of gravity of the wind the rain
The pain the driving force of fatigue
Cut and pasted over with visions of intrigue
Yes moving up into the big league

Is the test pilot's goal or his soul

Whether it be the dangerous wing roll
Or to be posthumously inscribed on a scroll
This seems to be the ultimate
The enduring cement
That holds these men to this summit

Challenging themselves up to the limit

A child's play in a man's way
Left to each to inscribe their dismay
"Either fly it climb it or forget it
But don't fear it"
I wanna be a test pilot
The epitaph of the best pilot
And the least violent

For his is the stunt not the hunt

IF YOU WILL

Devil sitting on my shoulder
Getting bolder as I get older
Savior sitting on my head
Saying never or you're dead

With work before me
And my past behind me
Tell me where do I go from here
When fear is only a breath away

But for some reason I can't catch my breath
Since the tide has turned much colder
As I can't make a decision to be the best
With the Devil sitting on my shoulder
And the Savior beating on my chest

Who's to say I even exist
If I've never been
Who's to say there's a moral twist
If there's no mortal sin

So what if my heartbeat wants to hold her
Who's to say love is a heartbeat away
With the Devil sitting on my shoulder
When the Savior is getting in the way

(continued)

*Who's to say I even exist
In a world where even big hitters aren't missed
Maybe I'm the romanticist
Balled up in his own fist*

*With the Devil on my shoulder getting bolder
And the Savior taken aback by my behavior
Trying to tell my mind
It's better in the long run to come from behind*

*If you will
I guess this is the eternal struggle
Be it charging the hill
Or sounding reveille on the bugle*

*It's what you want to make of it
It's what you can live with and call your own
Hello … destiny is calling you on the phone
Saying don't quit*

*For don't expect the Devil to go away
Don't expect the Savior to take your hand on Judgment Day
Unless you can face yourself in the mirror
And feel as if you are less than superior*

(continued)

To those that have fallen
To the Devil on their shoulder
Into hell they've been stolen
With the Savior dead behind their boulder

Rise up they are told
Be brave be bold
With the faith of a soldier
Roll back that boulder

And go marching up that hill
If you will

AS YOU TURN

If you turn I will follow to hear it
If you fall I will pick up your spirit
If you're divided I will pull you together
If you are rough I will smooth each feather
If you wend or detour I will help you back on track
If you tell me that you are afraid I will take your back

If you run away from the mountain
I will lead you to the fountain
If you turn I will turn on a dime
If you stop I will give you the sign
If you slow to the posted limit
I will not pass you or dim it

I will not harass you with bossing
If you wonder why I will help you decide
If you need to have a safe crossing
I will stop cross traffic and turn the tide
If you come upon a dead end
I will secure thee to my compass
I will make you feel alive again
If you get too close to the trespass

(continued)

If you lose your way on the map
I will draw you to me and let you follow
If you turn I will cover each lap
If you speed I will stay with your shadow
I must ride with you through the aftermath
If you comply I will die with your foe
For I am driven along your chosen path

And if you turn don't turn on me
Because being dead right
Is the wrong kind of clarity
Yes if you turn make it into me
Don't turn into infidelity
For in reality
Making a you turn
Towards me
Is God's way of making you learn

To change into yourself ... is my concern

CAUGHT WITH MY HAMMER DOWN

Every six months or so I get caught with my hammer down
Whether it be Effingham or Chicago town
Some people would say it's a bad habit
Some people just say it's needless hurry
The way I act dag nab it
Or is it those Smokey Bears who scurry

They seem to spend their time waiting for me
And I guess I'm just a good customer
Letting most of the real offenders go free
Gotta smile and call them Bears sir
To be truthful I guess I have to take my medicine
I have to swallow regret and say I deserve what I get
Maybe this time I won't let it happen again

Since losing my license is becoming quite a threat
Yes flying high is my trademark I've got to somehow live with
Unless my dog becomes bigger that its bark
And my driving days aren't a myth
Being wheel less is not what I'd call a legend
It's very inefficient to say the least
Even I if I am hedging that my tickets can decrease

Okay officer you caught me with my hammer down
And I guess I'm getting what I asked for
Please don't give me that third impound
Making me a member of the working poor
By the way why are you making that sound
As I close your head in my door

An epitaph to me "hammered to the floor"

BETHROTHED

I am betrothed to a feeling
I am married to a thought
I am embraced by the urge that I've sought

I am betrothed to friendship soft and true
I am married to a soul mate
That's why I'm betrothed to you

I am betrothed to days of brightness
I am betrothed to nights of peace
I am betrothed to happiness

Therefore I must do it my way
I must pay the price
To ride the horse of Desiree

Holding onto the mane of romance
Clutching at the loins of aspiration
And digging my heels into the groin of fate

Yes betrothed to a feeling and a soul mate

Betrothed to a horizon
But divorced from concealing what's on my mind
For its only there that the vines of future can unwind

Betrothed to seek and ye shall find
With your soul entwined with mine

HAND PRINTS

Handprints upon the wall
The wall between you and I
Do or die is our cry
Ground and sky you and I

Handprints on the wall
It's a threat to us all
Not being able to touch each other
Not being able to change one another

Not being able to grip on what is best to do
Me and you
It seems we get so close
So close to that illusive ghost
Called understanding yet we're so far
It's like reaching for a distant star

Saying I want to touch you
I want to need you
I want to get through
Yet all we do is put handprints on the wall

Pushing it back and forth into a stall
Pushing it to and fro
Reacting to where it wants to go
Not knowing what we don't know

(continued)

And I keep asking asking for truth
Why the wall only exists after our youth
Separating us from our desire
When the wall is on fire

Why was our wall built one brick at a time
Without a plan much less design
Some draw a sign of peace
Some beat upon it crying for hate to cease

Others only live with it lean against it
Put handprints upon its girth
Never deciding to rid their minds of its birth
Clasping hands for all they're worth

But for me my hands are getting tired
Tired of pushing tired of holding up the wall
For it serves no purpose we desired
Except to turn our hands into a ball

I'm either going to turn it to cement
Or let it fall without my handprint
We don't seem to get our hands to repent
The love our hearts must consent

To live without a wall at all

A TOUCH OF HONEY

An ounce of honey goes much further
Than pounds of bitterness
A touch of love goes much further
Than pounds of pleasures zest

A touch of you is by far
The pounds of honey you inspire
Of that I never tire
It is our heaven and our fire

A touch of you goes much further

Cast upon a character pauper or prince
Than the embrace of mere satisfaction
Life is nothing but a series of events
And distraction

Laid at the feet of humans one and all
Each person with his or her bouncing ball
Bouncing high or bouncing low
Each individual makes it go

(continued)

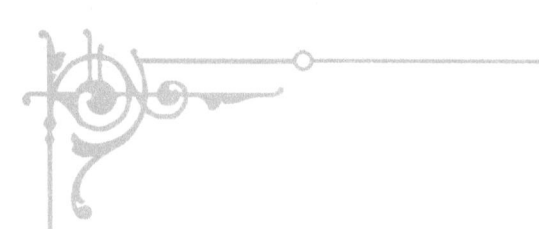

Spins it to
Spins it fro
A touch of gall brings it low
A touch of honey makes it rise
A touch of love is the prize

A touch of honey before it's too late
Is an ounce of love to create
Less pounds of hate
Making happiness our fate

A touch of you goes much further
Then money or honey

AUTUMN LEAVES

The fields are needing to speak
The weather is reaching its peak
Stimulating captivating capitulating
Machines at work cultivating

Cutting those beans close to the ground
Moving stalks into a mound
Grinding up the remains
Into the future grains

The trees are needing to shed
The leaves fall quietly into a bed
Multiple colors hit us in the eye
As summer days fly by

Winter worries us all
The Farmer's Almanac predicts the end of fall
Wanting Indian summer to never end
Until reality brings us the chilling wind

The animals hibernate and wait
For the Spring to emancipate
Though mating and offspring
Reminds us of nature's sting

(continued)

With blowing snow and ice
Bringing the children to entice
Their coats and gloves on the stove
Letting the Autumn glow betroth

The seasons and their mystic rhythm
Evolve into the tune of God's anthem
As the cheek and nose of the ghosts
On Halloween masks and Turkey roasts

Changing our perception of eternity
Are the crops and their intensity
Turning them into bread cereal cloth of clergy
Who call us to the harvest of climate's jury

Its people viewing Autumn as the epitome
"Of loving trees and hating falling leaves"

SHARON MY LOVE

She is the smell of summer
She is the feel of spring
She is the smile of children
She is the strength of a wedding ring

She is the mother of my children
She is the holder of my heart
She is the fend of the wind
She is my end before I start

She is the bottle for my potion
She is the sand in my dreams
She is the earth in motion
She is what forever seems

She is the hand I hold
She is the faith to pursue it
She is the past untold
She is the perfect fit

She is my hope
She is my measuring tape
She is the scope
She is the landscape

(continued)

She is the very truth
She is the memories
She found me in her youth
She is the healer of miseries

She is my love's meaning
She is everything that I need
She is the beginning
She is the ever after decreed

She is this dreamer's font
She is the harvest to my seed
She is wedding of our want
She is married to our need

And 365 reasons we succeed
Love Jerry

INDIVIDUALS COUNT

In America people are independent
Due to a Declaration in 1776
Due to the Constitution in 1774
Due to the Civil Rights Act of 1964
Due to World Wars I and II
Due to the First and Second Amendments

So why do we feel inhibited by Government
Is Enterprise really Free
Since each American is an Enterprise
And most laws are to inhibit this dynamic
With 40,000 laws being passed each year
By lawmakers who vote their own agenda

Not ours any more

What exactly is ours
Is it our work
Is it our ambition
Is it our dreams
Is it our responsibilities
Is it our FREEDOM to vote

(continued)

Then why do we feel helpless
It is not our authority
It is not our preference
It is not our risk that counts
It is not our decision to go to war
It is not our opinion on peace

Not now

Freedom is a right
Freedom is a necessity
Freedom is our only weapon
Against power and poverty
Against enforcement
Against Tyranny

Will Americans let go of freedom
Will Americans go down peacefully
Will Americans lose independence
Ask yourself if you want 40,000 laws per year
Ask yourself if you want lawmakers endlessly making laws
Ask yourself if you have given up or will stand up
For your independence and freedom that won't wait

Your individual answer collectively will determine America's fate

CONTRIDICATIONS

Robert Reich former Secretary of Labor For Bill Clinton
Quoted from an appearance on ABC Sunday morning
"The Government is the purchaser of last resort"

President Obama
Quoted from Congressional presentation on Obama Care
"Health Care Reform will not cost one dime"
"Don't worry you can keep your current insurance policy"

President Bush
Quoted from the aircraft carrier speech
"The war is over"
"There are WMD's in Iraq"

Hillary Clinton, former Secretary of State
Quoted from her testimony before the Senate
"What difference at this point does Bengzi make"

Bill Clinton former President
Quoted from his testimony before the House
"I never had sexual relations with that woman"

Nancy Pelosi, Speaker of the House
Quoted from the House hearings on the bailout of Big banks
"Every month that we do not have an economic recovery package 500 million Americans lose their jobs"

(continued)

Ben Bernanke former Chairman of the Federal Reserve
Quoted from a speech to the media
"The recession is the result of Wall Street's greed"

Who can you believe anymore?
How do you feel when your Senator says
"Now LOOK I am the smart one so let me govern"
"Don't call me unless you want to donate to my campaign"

Who can you trust anymore?
How do you feel when your Congressman
Only wants to discuss issues
Not problems ... is abortion more important than our soldiers dying

Why do we even vote if it doesn't matter?
Since it is the issues between the two parties
To deflect having to solve problems
By making more problems that they don't solve

The solution is obvious ... a contradicting party
That represents solutions not more of the same
The American Enterprise Party
That works for individual freedoms collectively
without thousands of inhibiting laws

Withdrawing the civil rights of enterprising Americans
The ultimate contradiction to our founding sons

CHILDREN

Children – so is today
Adults – so was today
Adolescence – so much for today

No vanity in a child
Know thy ego in adults
Know thy dreams in betweens

Whosoever shall know thyself
Shall ever yet be a child
And no ages shall ever be too old to live

Children – so much for fun
Adults – so much for work
Adolescence – so much for books

No vanity in a child
Like thy ego in adults
Love thy dreams in betweens

Whosoever shall work in fun
Shall ever be a child
And no ages shall ever be too old to play

(continued)

Children – so much for imagination
Adults – so much for technology
Adolescence – so much for impressions

No vanity in a child
Quell thy ego in adults
Dwell thy dreams in betweens

Whosoever shall imagine a scheme
Shall ever be a child
And no ages shall ever be too old to dream

Children are the model for aging
Happy healthy and waging … life for the in between

THE STREAM

The stream is a visual experience depicting movement
But the depiction may not represent the flow beneath the surface
To understand the stream
You must look beneath the surface

You must delve into the current that tows reality
To its circus
For the looks of the stream may be beauty
It makes a pretty picture
It tells an interesting story
It guides an interesting thought

But what does it really mean beneath that stream
To have turbulence misguided thrusts and rocks to tear
The bottom out of life like a knife

Yeah it is true that water is blue
If we see it as blue as you
Some water is not blue
It does not carry that subtle hue
It may be gray or brown or may be green

A mood and personality of the stream
Tis this color that ye need to gaze
Beneath the surface in many ways
By more than visual acuity
The tenure and the texture of its annuity

(continued)

But what does it really mean beneath that stream
To have turbulence misguided thrusts and rocks to tear
The bottom out of life so dear

When you must get below the surface
Get within the view of its substance
Below the hue
That's where its behavior hides
Its intention abides
Its character to change the tides

Because a surface view is not what shall serve you
Its knowing that in a fit to dream
You may be done in by that under towing stream

Then what does it really mean beneath that stream
To have turbulence misguided thrusts and rocks to tear
The heart out of life's affair …

It means dreams are ever like streams
Hiding reality and concealing what life seems

PULL THE TRIGGER

Whose head is on your shoulders
Whose eyes do you see through
Whose life are you living

If the answer is not you or yours
Pull the trigger on metaphors
Do away with talk and level your aim

On life and limb they're just the same
Raise up your eyes within your head
With pride upon your shoulders

And think your thoughts
Pick your own lots
And the days will become forget me nots

For life and limb and all the rest
Demand keeping your shoulders around your chest
So fears you tame can be blessed

With nights less distressed
Taking aim on being the best
By shooting down doubts confessed

Pulling the trigger on metaphors
So your head held high can open all doors
As your mind and heart explores

The opportunities that challenge deplores

THE LATE GREAT FATE

The late great fate was put upon my plate
I was to partake of its mate
That lowly feeling of hate
The spoon handle of too late

The servant of the self
But I did not partake just for the pleasures sake
There was too much at stake
Life liberty and happiness

To name but a few
For the sake of a caress
With no just adieu
Yes the winds of temptation blew across me

Like every mortal beings reason
Looking for a release of passion
Set in fleeting thoughts and a selfish trait
Endangering the reality of the late great fate

The hallowed halls of family and togetherness
Simplicity and peaceful relaxation of at oneness
All culminate in a balance
A balance of mind

A balance of not having to seek to find
A balance of satisfaction with fate right behind
And hate resigned

To its ill wed mind

COURTSHIP

The courtship of Miles Standish
The courtship of Pocahontas
The courtship of King Edward VI
The courtship of Prince Philip
The courtship of John Kennedy
And friends of the courtship

No love can stand the test of time
No courtship can be forever
Without a friendship
Just like no time shall tell the clock
What face to show or where to go

No infatuation can dictate where lovers are to go
For the only way to tie the ends in a forever knot
Is to have a tie of best friends
Before the words are forgot
The I do's and I will's and I love and I give and I want

Hidden deep within the hearts of friends
Fall on shallow ears
In the divorce court taunt

Aiming upon emotion and the fears
Of the ghost of love to haunt

(continued)

Able to relax and talk
Forgiveness and the amends
Which make the strangers balk
Sitting there eye to eye
And sometimes back to back
Setting forth a thoughtful sigh

But knowing what the relationship does lack
Friends of the courtship count the ways and the words
That burst forth
Held within any threat of insecurity
Like a warm wind from the north

Or the singing of birds
About the thoughts and words
Soft touches caresses
Washing away the tears

As even the wildest dream confesses
There is no chance unless the romantic heart
Hears what it thought it heard
Does what it thought it should do
By courting with just three words
LMFT

I love you in marriage forever together

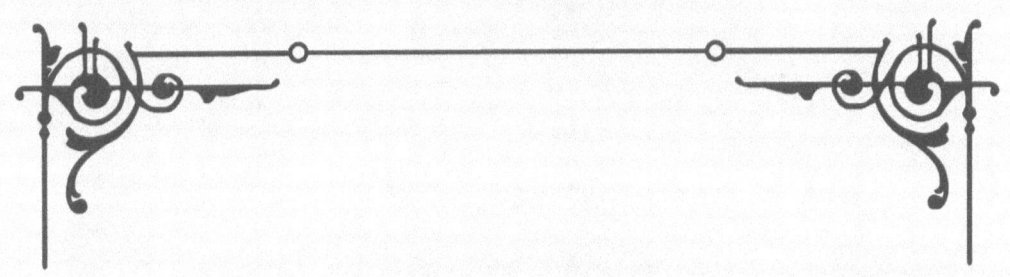

THE SAVIOR

THE SAVIOR

Who shall climb the steepest incline
Who shall reverse the wildest curse
Who shall explore the closed door
Who shall discover the lost lover
Who shall savor that endeavor

Tis the Savior of fitful behavior

The savior of peace and kinship
The savior of love and friendship
The savior of work and courtship
And to whom does the Savior work
To whom does the Savior not shirk … and then guide

To become saved from pride
Tis noble to have been proud
Tis noble to have been well endowed
Tis noble to have been allowed
To leave a fertile field unplowed

Tis noble to have stood in your own shadow
Leaving life fallow

(continued)

Never leaving never conceiving
Never believing nor achieving
Just one in the flock
Spinning time around the clock

And thou shall not be saved
You have misbehaved
If you have been and are forever lost
Be ye shallow and it never was
The desire to be what saved does

As you're in your own cell
For the Savior is not for most
It is for those that decide to dwell
In the realm of the Holy Ghost ... belief is Heaven

And doubt is Hell

Amen

DAMN SNOW STORM

Falling and swirling around
No shelter to be found
Beauty is not its legacy
When driving is its efficacy

Slipping and sliding aground
No warmth can be found
Comfort is not its strength
When humans are on the brink

Breaking our cars and such
While hoping for sun as a crutch
Melting away the ice and the snow
Until the dangerous highways will let go

Remembering the old days
When walking was easier than highways
Now it is the ice covered interstate
That may determine our fate

Whoever would have thought
That being in traffic would be caught

On the heels of a snowplow license plate
Throwing off this awful salt and phosphate

(continued)

All I can think to do is pray
That this snow will dissipate and delay
The blizzard forecast for tomorrow
When I still have a snow thrower to borrow

The only hope in this storm's force
Is the State troopers change of course
Instead of hiding in the bushes
They seek out something with food and wishes

Trending towards my destination
I have lost all fascination
Fighting this endless distraction
While feeling my tires lose traction

Fear sets in as a possibility
As I cannot control the steering or see
Barely ahead of that snow plow
Bringing sweat to my eyebrow

Swallowing hard and squinting
My eyes seek out a reason for venting
Displeasure with weather that chokes us
When sudden hope comes into focus

(continued)

It is my home sweet home
Beautiful in its shades of white foam

And beaconing me to safety
Before this snow gets the best of me

As I swing into my driveway
I lose control and there in the way
Is my classic four-wheel drive jeep
Stuck in the snow ten foot deep

The crunch was loud with the crash
Taking out the front end and the trash
Making me wonder why would I completely ignore
The weather forecast of a blizzard in store

Snowed in again by the way
Thinking it might be on a clear day
Damn that snow storm
Hoping it's not the new norm

Filling out this damn insurance form

POSITIVE LIFE ATTITUDE

A life is but a culmination of thoughts
And these thoughts emanate from a mind
That is kindled by a spirit
That has two roads to your soul

One road most traveled says –
I can't
I shan't
I won't
I don't
I take
I'm number one
I'm the sum
For me we is dumb
And us is for a bum

The less traveled road says –
I can
I will
I shall
I am
I sow
I reap
I seek peace

(continued)

I help
I am humble
I am the good deed
For the he in health
And the we in wealth

One road most traveled is negative
It's self-centered
It's a lonely self
It's an unhappy self
It's unproductive self
It's a cop-out to one's selfish ego

The other road less traveled is a positive life attitude
About the goodness of the positive self
The worthiness of the loving self
The beauty of the giving self

As positive is the inspiration to worthy birth
And more adventurous roads to self-worth
In the Kingdom of heaven on earth

For the joy of I can is in I will
In each epitaph's I am
Worthy of being a positive
Man

PROPOSAL - JUST DO IT

I'm going to do it
Just give me time
Give me room
Don't do it for me

Don't do it before me
I will just do it
So help me I'll do it

Have faith in me
So help me God
Don't do it to be free

Give me time
Give me room
The idea must be mine
Before you can decline

I'm on my way to being the groom
But now is only too soon
Riding in my hot air balloon
Waiting until afternoon

(continued)

Give me time
Give me room
Don't say it your way
Let me replay it my way

Like making love under the moon
Don't do it too soon
For it will maroon
Us from the melody of our Honeymoon

Don't do it for me
I hope I don't blow it

Before we split
Don't you commit that sin
I'm going to do it
Before your doubt can do us in

I will take your hand
As I take a knee
With this ring I command

Will you marry me?

MISSING YOU

Each time I look around you are gone
Each time I reach out you turn away
Each time I say I need help you put me down

Doesn't it matter that I am human
That I'm true and transparent
Just to see through

Each time I miss you

I've thought from time to time
That age would ease my mind
But who can regret a chance never met

Who can believe in themselves
If they can't believe in what they want to get
Because it makes no difference

How I feel or if I miss your reminiscence

So I'd rather kid myself than be true
And my need for something new
Is just that I'm still missing you

(continued)

As my mood turns blue
And my dreams seem to be dreaming me instead of you
I try to sort it all out from being down

I end up feeling like an erotic clown

Who puts on his makeup as a disguise
For to me lost reality is no prize
What is left as we part is a lamenting heart

Romance is overlooked by my failure to start
So missing you may not be real at all
It may just be my dream coming true as I fall apart

Missing you is all I can say
Each time I look you're not around
Each time I reach out you turn away
Each time I need your help you put me down

By saying hold off for another day
Are you're really missing me
And the price I will have to pay
For keeping you is admitting my insecurity

If so say so before I go crazy

LIFE IS AN ECHO

Life is an echo of what you say and know
Life is a friend if what you receive is what you send

Send it with a voice of disdain
And upon your head it shall rain

Send it with a voice of pleasure
And it shall return many a treasure

Send it on the wind of good
Whispering I will for I should

Send it on its way with what you would say
Facing Judgment day

For no matter if it's a boomerang
A chain letter a good deed
Or happy song you sing

That's exactly what life will bring

Sadness or joy
Building or destroy
What your voice has taken as its choice

(continued)

And the echo that resounds
Shall return to make its rounds

Say I love you
And you shall be loved

Say may I help you
And you shall be helped

Say I'm good
And you shall be good

Say I'm a friend
And you shall have friends

Say you will be happy
And you shall be happy

Say you will be healthy
And you will be healthy

Say you will be prosperous
And you will be wealthy

Say it with a voice known to be good
And you will always be understood

As an echo for the misunderstood

STAR DUST

Particles to particles
Dust to Dust

The start of a new beginning
Particles in space looking for a nuclear home
Having been dissipated by time's evolution of energy
To feed the universe with molecules of future mass
Mass to give life to death, to give heat to cold
To give light to dark to give form to chaos
Only to give form then dust

Shining glowing stars in the night
Given the speed of light
Just for our sight

Stars given form to energy
Stars given energy to be
Visible to me

Does the star really persist as we see it
With years gone to dust
When time does not exist

(continued)

Whose energy is of time finite
Telling of the past in flight
Sending a message in the night

Look to the sky to wonder why
Gods of old, gods of now can only try
To foretell this wonder in the sky

Needing to explain the science of why stars die
Only to live again returning once again
To where they've been

Disappearing with the speed of light
Quantum beyond our sight
As energy particles form within the atom
Forming higher levels of mass

Called men

COMMON SENSE

It is said that common sense isn't common

Common sense is like black earth
Supposedly it is everywhere
But as reality is mirth
We look all day and not find it there

Either it's hiding
In the mental processes of man
Or it's not residing
There in a vernacular that a listener can understand

Though many a color is a half tone
And perception may have a hue
The mind of man is not a clone
And common sense must come from you

If the mind positively knows north from south
This infallible logic is going to let the thinker know
That out of your head into your mouth
Productive negativism cannot possibly grow

(continued)

The way to mental magic
Solutions to problems
Glib tongue is a sharp mind
All of these must be developed
Through a disciplined intake so inclined

Assigned their proper place
Whence given a code of common sense
To be recalled from that uncommon space
And enveloped into sets thus assigned
In the mind

To give an opinion or not
Without the subconscious able to deduct
On a spoken word or font
None shall be able to reconstruct
Any notion left to the instant taunt

Deductive in its mental note
Deductive in its approach to thought
Instinctive yet not rote
Very much stimulating if it's taught

(continued)

Yes common sense should be oh so common
For it is the logic and the simplicity that confirms
Reality but oh how uncommon
To think in such common simple terms

Such as, Patrick Henry's
"Give me liberty or give me death"
Was the cry of common sense
Rather than listen to his plea
As the tyrants ignored his defense

To allow this common thought to give
And their solutions thus confirms
That uncommon words for all time will live
In such common sense terms

And though it may have been his bequest
We of stead shall never know
What pitched him with such uncommon breath
Against that fateful foe

"Give me liberty or give me death"

WISH LIST

I wish for more
I wish for happiness
I wish for prosperity

The higher order waits for faith
The success of a vision pursues hope
The life of a dream finds passion

Faith is the silent partner of performance
Hope is the destination's map
Passion is the end zone of results

Will I
Serve Himself
Or myself

More is from effort not need
Happiness is not swallowing the unhappy seed
Prosperity is not money but the lack of greed

Humans are the work of skill
The beginning is not the reason
It is the evolution of the science of will

(continued)

Will I pursue faith with hope
Will I believe in hope to cope
Will I use love's emotion as my potion

Serving one's self sets the values
Understanding one's limits is character
Finding other's passion in one's path is romance

Values character and performance
Are the notion of passion and romance
The route to prosperity from happiness

A list is your prophecy
A wish attained is your legacy
Now known as a bucket list
For a junket not to be missed

Unless you are wishing to far for a falling star

SHE IS

She paints her toenails pink
She wears tight jeans
She smiles at will
She is my means

She has her hair perfect
She keeps her temper below the surface
She is the time in the bomb
She is the paint on her face

She sings along to sad songs
She speaks up for what's right
She holds onto righting wrongs
She is my conscious height

She is the mother of genius
She is my reason and witness
She is the beholder of pride
She is always giving from inside

She is honest to herself
She isn't above being smart

She is the Christmas and my better half
She is all heart

(continued)

She plays games of chance
She can sing and dance
She is always moving
She is so fabulous
And alluring

She is always beautiful
She does not hold on to vanity
She is sincere and never dull
She is the sane in insanity

She reels in my dreams
She feels my thoughts
She feels my scenes
She repeals my ego

She is my first and only choice
She is our family's roots
She is my last rejoice
She will lay me down in my boots

As She paints her finger and toe nails red
To believe she can join me when I'm dead

SAINT
OR
SATAN

SAINT OR SATAN

A wolf in fox's clothing
A carpet bag full of tricks
A clock too slow to be on time
A man too shallow to be true

A love of pleasure
Rather than the love of you
Is it a saint or is it Satan in that pew
That taps me on the shoulder

As I get older

Saying softly in my ear
Never fear venture lead
You have no peer

Is this my ego

Talking louder than the good
Sent to be humble then speak
Is it a sign of being strong or being wrong

Or just plain weak

I guess it can be found all written
There in immortal law
In many forms and many dialects
That says the righteous shall never fall
As the morality is what a soul elects

(continued)

Can this really be

That the Savior is saving me
Or is it this vast body of humanity
That he has taken upon his knee
And chosen yet a few to be ultimately free

For I don't feel this analogy
Shall hold the answer for many
Matter of fact at times I wonder if there are any
Who really believe that they can achieve
Conceive perceive and believe

Because in talking to even the most positive souls
There is skepticism of the true power
Of prayer and goals
They will indicate it sounds good
They will say it's something they should or would
If they had time or understood

That they are diligent souls
They can either paint or read
Looking for a sign that tolls
In a the form of a tangible seed

With words the Bible has decreed

(continued)

Even then the inspiration and perspiration
Don't seem to be there
Maybe it's just not seeing or hearing
Much of a reply from prayer

It's mostly …
I would if I could and knock on wood
Yeah maybe next year
I'll really dedicate myself to a career

So is this situation on target
From which I will get
No sympathy no empathy
Just a maybe and insincerity

But somewhere in my distant deranged mind

We appear to find and assert
That a human being who makes the effort
To be special shall eventually be official
That dedication to an ideal
Is the only way to determine
How it will feel

To be a Saint in spite of Satan's appeal

REVOLUTION

A one man revolution
Is coming its coming
There's no stopping the solution
It's a one man revelation

For tearing down himself is man
Until there's no dignity left
Shattering morals and values
To a dusty dead pan

Taken the Devil is born
Forsaken forlorn
No direction or hope
No will to cope

A one man revolution is coming
Mankind's responsibility is all about
His mental weakness
A revelation of self-doubt

It is the only revolution coming
There's no stopping the solution
To wit we are succumbing
Remember Jesus told us

(continued)

Judgment Day will deal
With man's weaknesses
Not a caress but a staggering blow
Until we all will know

It's a one-man revolution
Society's only solution
Individual responsibility
Within you and me

For it is this slippage
Into the Hell of me
That keeps us from being
Free

Free of self-doubt
Free of fear itself
Free of selfishness and pride
Free of stress

It is Revelations' One-Man Revolution
I am now free of the enemy in me

LIFELINES

Tracing footprints in the sand
Exploring lifelines in your hand
Looking for the clue
That is meaningful to you

From birth to whatever
Doubting the next to never
Without a clue
Of what is really you

From the palm to the thumb
Sounds really dumb
That it would be a clue
To the epitome of true

Seek and ye shall find
For the palm reader to align
Fortune reading what we knew
But changing things very few

Lifelines rescue inhalers
Ordinary fishermen and whalers
Are chosen paths
Not foretelling what heaths

(continued)

Or is it more than that
As is nose scent of the dog and cat
Supernatural beyond belief
Looking for truth and relief

From fear and stress
And all the rest
Just to know
That we are in tow

With the almighty holding the lifelines

Making love with our hand out
Grasping for a mate to tout
Being caught off guard
Is the ultimate reward

A lifeline holding me on board
With my faith restored

IDEALIST

Idealist
The first to fall
The last to give up

He charges the hill
Because he feels on principle
He is right not corrupt

He leaves his flank bare
Because he has faith that
He is in a righteous fight and can't give up

He is astonished
When he is struck down
For the sake of conventional tradition

He gets back up
No wiser but
More determined than ambition

He charges all the harder
Up a steeper hill
That towers ahead of his principles

(continued)

He slips and slides
But falls shorter
Each time less sensible

For I cannot die for unreasonable doubt

As an Incurable Idealist
I'm the first to cry out
Why me ... I exist

And the last to die

THE SENATE

They sit behind
Dappled desks
On seats of power

Surrounded by
The tides of a deep heritage
Of Congress the pursuit of power

With a constitution
And a declaration of independence
Supporting this power

The statues stand
In buildings of stature
And Magnitude

In testimony to
How deep the American
Blood flows to gratitude

Flowing from strong
Dedicated men believing
In sovereign principles

With all others asked to be
As strong
But can they be sensible

(continued)

Can they believe
As deeply
As America's blood flows

Are they more than
Themselves
Or just a picture of their ego

The phantoms of the Senate
Behind dappled desks
That stature bestows

Lining the marbled halls
The seats of power
Revered by shallow men

Distained by the weakling
Loved by idealists
Born from a belief in good fortune

A vein of gold
Inlaid upon a fallow land
Signifying the American heritage

A vein of obscurity
A vein of red white and blue blood
Flowing from the hearts of millions

(continued)

Holding their leaders up to the light
To see if their ideals
Their principles with humility prevail

Tossing away those that are
Transparent and too flexible
To be the levy and the strength

To be our next heritage
The ides of a deep bondage
From the words at Gettysburg

To the dark shadow of Hiroshima
And the conquest of inner space
Far deeper than outer space

Senator Senator hearken
Hear this message or
Perish from the seat of power

(continued)

You are not sacred
You are not above principle
You are only a human flower

Rooted in responsibility
To pledge allegiance
To our heritage that we empower

To you our Republic
For which it stands
One nation indivisible under God

With liberty and justice for all
So do not let the
Great American Enterprise fall

Don't do as the Romans did ... do recall

FOR EGO

Why did you say that to me
Was it for me to do or you to see

For I'm sensitive to what you say
The reasons why and the games we play

For it's not a whimsical mind you blow
Must it be for the inflation of your super ego

For even though your id had hid
Your inner person has fled your head

For thought would say to do my best
To hold your hand and get you undressed

For this is certainly no contest
To defend what you just confessed

For motives and any reasons true
Haven't kept pace with the inner you

For I think what you've chosen to do
Is more for your ego then it's for you

ROMANCE

ROMANCE

Dance old man dance
There's no age to romance
Life has given you your last chance
So dance ole man dance

Some mortals trot and some prance
Others shoot arrows and others throw a lance
But I'm telling you to advance
There's no age to romance

When romance has been unkind
It can seem like yesterday
That you seek and find
That you've not been loved today

Letting me see before I go blind
Age and love are not aligned
So be sure you tell your lover
About those things that years won't uncover

When you discover there's no age
To be a lover
As I stood by the altar of
Time's best friend

(continued)

Romance and love as a timeless blend
And age said, "I do" to a heavy wind
Marking the progress towards the end
Of just being a friend

Allowing me to take my frustration down
And set up the abundance
That I had found
With romance as the crown

Since I live and die in an ageless prance
Telling those who see me by chance
That I shall not age as I dance
To that mortal song called romance

It is the love of life that will enhance
As age does advance

CIRCUMSTANCE OR ROMANCE

Life is lived in certain chosen paths
Is it circumstance or romance
That dictates our past

Or is it a thought and a plan
Dreaming of more than
Shifting sand

Circumstance certainly means
That no matter what it seems
We are not a product of our dreams

While on the other hand
Isn't life at our command
Subject to what we know and understand

Each person must decide
To either jump on the slide
Or stand back because of pride

Caution to better comprehend
Letting the wounds mend
Hoping that the time will transcend

(continued)

While others throw caution to the wind
Letting brothers fight and defend
The rights of others and a friend

When it comes to picking a mate
Is it better to pick and wait
Or move head long into a date

Since fate is at stake
Many are asleep at the plate
Missing each swing to populate

Letting circumstance dictate
Their chance at love or hate
While romance is the thrill to navigate

Taking that chance
Forgetting circumstance
As a happenstance

And risking all for romance

MY LOVE AFFAIR

She's all mine
She has a beautiful body
Her eyes are on high beam
Her hair is racy

Her bumpers are firm
Her rear end is rounded
Her face is perfection
Her grill is white

Her completion is smooth
Her voice is soft
Her mind is sound
Her name is sunshine

Her mind is a computer
Her skin is dazzling
Her wheels are always moving
Her engine never moans

Her throat never groans
Her waist is small
Her strength is of horses
Her power is of mares

(continued)

Her smile is broad
Her styling is classic
Her age is unlimited
Her mileage is real

Her brakes are on
Her weight is in pounds
Her color is blue
Her style is new

A model of few
I love her
I covet her
I make her purr

She is mine all mine
A '64 Mustang divine

SIGNS OF SRENGTH

Death is not man's
Last sign of weakness
His landmark
His track record
His page in the history book
Are his marks
Legends are made by
Overcoming weaknesses

The weakness that shall trail us
To the very end of our time
Or raise us above our recognition
That overcomes for the sublime
Death is the finale on failure

Failure is haunting as the ghosts
Of times gone by
Hanging like barnacles
Upon the reasons we live and die
To those who helter skelter
Misuse and abuse
Life and its many wonders

(continued)

Shall die of weakness
Shall live eternally with failure
And those who follow
Shall have the same choice
To pass this way with weakness and failure

While the strong shall pass
And preserve with effort
The principles dear as an epitaph
Of their path and voice

That they will ever forever rejoice
In the choir of angels the origin
And the embrace of the host
Our virgin

The holy ghost

TWO SHADES OF GRAY

Gray skies were forming
Along the road I rode
The driving rain weighted
Down my heavy load

As the lightening thundered
The Grey fog set in
And I wondered
If this long trip would ever end

The raindrops beat upon my head
Taking my mind from now
To a dry and friendly bed
If only I had it and knew how

To see the road as a lonely place
Lonely as outer space
Lonely for you see no face
And its white and black has no grace

Eerie in the night pitched low
The storm beating welts upon my soul

(continued)

The beams of light come and go
Into a night time black as coal

Grey skies applies
To off color experiences
While pure Gray dies
In a grave of no consequences

Two Shades of Gray (e)
And if I had the urge to pray
These are the words I would apply
If the time ever comes to die
I want it to happen under a blue sky

With my boots tied to my feet
Because gray days can repeat

BETWEEN LOVE AND HATE

You asked me about love hate and fate
I don't know how to explain that
Other than to say
Love is today's sunlight
Hate is tomorrow's fears
And fate is the acting out our
Need to love and hate

The act of love is very quiet
It's more felt than said
It's more belief than grief
It's there when we wed
Yet it borders on the urge to deceive
If our pretenses are to conceive

Hate on the other hand
Is the downwind side
Of sensual pride
Rejection and being denied
Fostered by apprehension and doubt
And the failure to act feelings out

(continued)

But to be able to love
The other side of that emotion is hate
And take a risk with tomorrow
And still deal with fate
And it's sorrow
For fate can be the track
Upon which you elect
Your belief in the love you get

Knowing that we're all to be loved
And that hate is yet a false expression
Of our concern for our selfish pride
Then love and hate are two sides of fate

A matter of fact
A stack of chips
Already stacked

Being played on our table or plate
Lo but many never play this hand
For they never take time to understand
They're too busy for living
Too busy for loving
And only hate can be sensitive
If they do nothing about fate

Caught between love and hate

IF ANDS AND BUTS

If if were but a fact
And a fact was what it seems then
If would be the answer to my dreams

If and if and if
But for excuse and because
All an excuse to pause
And catch my breath
For another conditional cause

If but and if were real
I'd be more than I feel
If I were
And but I wish
Just won't occur
For words just swish

If in realty
My diary
Is written about
What I'm meant to be

(continued)

But if if is true
If in fact that's me
Then why am I asking you
What if if is me

If if were but a fact
And a fact was what it seems then
If would be the answer to my dreams

Telling me what I'm meant to be
Life is a puzzle of ifs ands and buts
If you don't yourself take responsibility

That a butt is no more than an ass to me
(if you can understand this you need to be the poet)

WEDDING DRESS

Silk and lace
Every pleat in place
Flowers on the mantel
Crowd is silently still

Preacher starts to speak
And my knees go weak
For my daughter a young mistress
Is standing there in her wedding dress

To me she's still my little girl
My precious memory of locks and curl
Grown up to be a woman
Grown up to take her man

With silk and lace
Every pleat in place
A beautiful young miss
In her wedding dress

I thought it would never be
But here I am giving her in matrimony
Standing next to her beauty
Giving her hand as my last duty

(continued)

In her wedding dress
Everything is best
More or less

By: the Father of the Bride

Post script:

40 years later has been
Twelve grown grandchildren
Two grandsons as married men
With four great grandsons to begin

By: the Father, Grandfather and Great Grandfather
With these blessings of the sanctity of Marriage
And to my Wife of 60 years
I celebrate with you the loves of our life

CHARADES ... IT'S NOT WHAT YOU SAY

What you say opens your book
What you do lets people look
Charades take for an instance
Visions of time and circumstance

You give some BS
You drag the line
What will be the mess
What will it refine … impressions don't define

The amazing part of human being's fear
For you may think you're hiding it
It'll let people get inside of your inner ear
In spite of your jokes and wit

And their ability to see without saying
To hear without hearing
To know without having any other people know
What I'm seeing and it may not be clear

If you don't have to have an ear to hear
You don't have to have eyes to see
And you don't have to have talk to tell lies
For the real story is told deep within your eyes

(continued)

By the slant of your head
And how you put your shoulders to bed
How you sit and cross your legs
Just another part of the silent language
That your body begs

So don't try to fool your brother
Don't try to jive each other
For the others will know
And so will your druthers

Know about what is fiction
And what is true
By merely watching the bodies motion
Play out what's in your baby blue

The words of silence
The picture of the physical role
The echo of a smile per chance
Communicates the very vernacular of the soul

Nature will not allow you to hide it
So make sure you endow
That your body language exposes your skit
For it's not what you say that counts somehow

It counts more if you're displaying it

THE EIGHTH WONDER OF THE WORLD

Discovered thoughts
Misused words that rhyme
Misspent moments in time
What a crime
The mind is left spinning
From behind

What is this thing of you speak
Is it about today
Or is it next week
Prophet tell me its answers I seek

What is this wonder
You ponder
Well, it's a planet alright
Carried with you day and night
Many have found it
And are using it right
To be perceptive
And somewhat bright

(continued)

The tenth planet
The eighth wonder
Is owned by every man and woman
They've had it since
They could walk and plunder
Left to their willingness
At hand to accept and understand

A nearby diamond
At ready command
Unspoken words
Misused ideas
Broken dreams

All a sign
Of the undiscovered planet
Called the mind

THE EIGHTH WONDER
OF THE WORLD WHERE
MIND OVER MATTER DOES MATTER

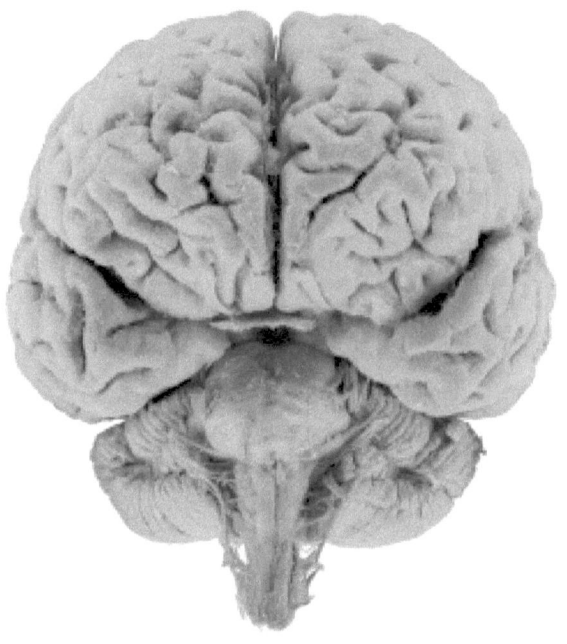

The brain is physical, the mind is metaphysical connecting us to the wonder of our Universe called God.

THE END IS THE BEGINNING

Towards the end of Judgment day
What does God say
For he only speaks
To he who seeks

He pronounces with a natural reason
That beauty is in the closing decision
For tomorrow how fortunate we are
To live among angels…amidst our own star

Closing into darkness the spirit finds its way
As Goodness speaks to the heart's decay
Cutting through space to another time
A continuum is what we will find
Marked in the sky as searching afar
Quiet but alive is the soul of our rising star

Believe it will happen once more

Behind the curtain of now
Gone forever are moments of wow
And questions of how

(continued)

Only to covet the path of the metaphor
The cycle is what it treks as bodies decay
Moving into another continuum's door
Seeking the horizons of peace in the milky-way

Alas the end is the beginning
In the Heaven of ever …. more

Heaven on earth is what is in store
For the winner and reformed sinner

Spinning our own DNA web
As the sign of that mental state
Linking us to the spiritual ebb
Of our immortal fate

For all of mankind
To find the undiscovered planet
Called the mind
Connecting us all to the other nine
A mental Solar system divine

Truly the Eighth Wonder of our mortal confine

An Invitation
Now that you have ventured
This far off your planet into the world of my mind
Are we more nurtured
And attached by the wonder of rhyme

If so
email me
jerry.l.rhoads@gmail.com
for the sequels

www.ingramcontent.com/pod-product-compliance
Lightning Source LLC
LaVergne TN
LVHW041736060526
838201LV00046B/823